WAR & POLITICS IN THE DESERT

SAUL KELLY

SILPHIUM
PRESS

Sally Kuisel

In Memoriam
(1947–2008)

WAR & POLITICS IN THE DESERT

BRITAIN AND LIBYA DURING THE SECOND WORLD WAR

SAUL KELLY
READER IN INTERNATIONAL HISTORY
KING'S COLLEGE, LONDON

SILPHIUM PRESS
2010

Produced by Silphium Press, an imprint of
The Society for Libyan Studies
c/o The Institute of Archaeology
31–34 Gordon Square, London
WC1H OPY
www.britac.ac.uk/institutes/libya

Copyright © 2010 The Society for Libyan Studies

All rights reserved. No part of this publication may be reproduced or stored or transmitted by any means or in any form, electronic or mechanical, including photocopying, recording, or any information storage and retrieval system, without prior written permission from the publisher.

ISBN 978-1-900971-09-6

Cover and interior design by Chris Bell
Edited by Michael Leitch
Maps by David Hopkins
Index by Chris Bell

Printed by Imprint Digital, India

contents

List of maps 7
List of acronyms 8
Acknowledgments 9
Preface 10
Notes to pages 10–12 13

PROLOGUE **Italy, Britain and Libya, 1911 to 1940** 17
Notes to pages 17–27 28

THE FIRST YEAR: 1940–1 **PRELUDE TO THE DECLARATION ON THE SANUSIS** 29
Overview 33
CHAPTER 1: 'Beating the Air': June to October 1940 37
CHAPTER 2: 'Good Days in Africa': November 1940 to April 1941 59
Summary 83
Notes to pages 29–85 86

THE SECOND YEAR: 1941–2 **THE DECLARATION ON THE SANUSIS** 97
Overview 101
CHAPTER 3: 'Ambiguous Promise': May 1941 to January 1942 105
CHAPTER 4: 'A Native State': January to June 1942 123
Summary 137
Notes to pages 97–138 139

THE THIRD YEAR: 1942–3 **THE CONQUEST OF LIBYA** 147
Overview 151
CHAPTER 5: 'Use them justly and graciously with sufficient guard nevertheless': Cyrenaica, July 1942 to December 1943 155
CHAPTER 6: 'Tripolitania is not on all fours with Cyrenaica': November 1942 to February 1943 169
CHAPTER 7: 'Ce Fruit Savoureux du Désert': The Fezzan, September 1942 to June 1943 185
Summary 201
Notes to pages 147–204 205

EPILOGUE **Britain, Libya and the start of the Cold War, 1943 to 1954** 215
Notes to pages 215–236 237

Bibliography 241
Index 249
Silphium Press publications list 253

LIST OF MAPS

Italian Libya 14–15
Libya: Year one 30–1
Libya: Year two 98–9
Libya: Year three 148–9
Libya under British and French military administration 198–9

LIST OF ACRONYMS

BMA	British Military Administration
DCPO	Deputy Chief Political Officer
FO	Foreign Office
FRUS	Foreign Relations of the United States
GHQME	General Headquarters, Middle East
GOCBTE	General Officer Commanding British Troops Egypt
GOCME	General Officer Commanding Middle East
HMG	His Majesty's Government
HQBTE	Headquarters British Troops Egypt
JCS	Joint Chiefs of Staff (US)
JPS	Joint Planning Staff
LAF	Libyan Arab Force
LRDG	Long Range Desert Group
MEDC	Middle East Defence Committee
MEIC	Middle East Intelligence Centre
MEWC	Middle East War Council
NEA	Near Eastern Affairs (US)
OETA	Occupied Enemy Territories Administrations
OTA	Occupied Territories Administrations
SIME	Security Intelligence Middle East
VCIGS	Vice-Chief Imperial General Staff
WO	War Office
WPIS	Weekly Political Intelligence Summaries

ACKNOWLEDGMENTS

Although this book is the result of my own work, it could not have been completed without the help of a number of people and institutions. I would like to acknowledge the assistance of the staffs of The National Archives, London; The British Library, London; The London Library; the libraries of The University of Cambridge, The University of London Senate House Library, The London School of Economics and Political Science, The School of Oriental and African Studies; The National Archives, Washington, DC, and The Library of Congress.

I would like to thank the late Professor J B Kelly and Professor D Cameron Watt for having cast an eye over an earlier version of this book. Professor Claudio Vita Finzi, Paul Bennett and Dr John Wright, my fellow 'Silphs' and members of The Society of Libyan Studies, encouraged me to submit this book for publication by the Society's new imprint, Silphium Press. The new Chairman of the Society, Professor Andrew Wilson, and the editor of Silphium Press, Victoria Leitch, have been generous in their assistance in bringing this book to press. Lyn Reynolds has given me sterling administrative support.

I would like to thank Mohamed Ben Madani, the editor of *The Maghreb Review*, for permission to republish extracts from my two articles with the journal, namely 'Ce Fruit Savoureux de Desert': *Britain, France and the Fezzan, 1941–56*, Vol. 26, No. 1, 2001, p. 2–21 (©*The Maghreb Review*, 2001); and 'Britain, Libya, and the Start of the Cold War', Vol. 31, Acknowledgments 2 Nos 1–2, 2006, p. 42–61 (©*The Maghreb Review*, 2006).

Lastly, I would like to mention the late and much missed Sally Kuisel, who in her cheerful way facilitated my research over a number of years in the Diplomatic Records of the US National Archives in Washington, DC. This book is dedicated to her in memory of the many happy lunches we had together in the courtyard of the National Portrait Gallery.

Saul Kelly
Shrivenham, Wiltshire

preface

IN RECENT YEARS there has been a renewed interest in the 'War in the Desert', that epic struggle of the Second World War between Axis (Italian and German) and Allied (principally British Commonwealth) forces for control of North Africa, from 1940 to 1943. The sixtieth anniversary of the El Alamein battles, fought on the narrow Egyptian coastal strip midway between Mersa Matruh and Alexandria in 1942, brought forth a spate of books.[1] These have added to our understanding of the experience of war in the desert, its nature and above all its importance, as one of the key turning points in the Second World War.

Such contributions to our collective memory of the war have also spurred old comrades, their relatives and a new generation of the curious to make a pilgrimage to the scene of the fighting, to walk the ground (insofar as that is possible in the mine-strewn battlefields) and to pay their respects to the fallen of all nationalities. This has occurred not only in Egypt, where each year the British Embassy in Cairo holds a remembrance ceremony at El Alamein, but in Libya too. The opening up of Libya, after thirty years of international isolation, has made it possible for visitors to that country to make the journey to Benghazi, Tobruk and the battlefields to the south. For the older generation, names like Tobruk, Gazala, 'Knightsbridge', Bir Hakaim and El Agheila are engraved on their memories as, night after night in 1941 and 1942, they heard on the radio of the desperate struggles of Allied and Axis forces for those strong-points, the capture of which would determine the outcome of the desert war. For younger generations, a tour of these battlefields will give a vivid impression of just how difficult it was to fight and win in the desert, and to marvel at what each side managed to achieve. It will provide them with a much-needed corrective to some of the accounts by armchair warriors of what should, or should not, have been done.

There is a marked tendency in much writing about the war in the desert to concentrate on the fighting, the battles fought by the military, to the exclusion of everything else. This is, no doubt, due to the fact that most of the books published on the desert war have been written by military historians or retired generals.[2] As the latter would be the first to admit from their own experience, war cannot be separated from politics. In particular the German generals knew their Clausewitz. As this Prussian military strategist pointed out, war, being an activity carried out by military forces raised by states, is thus, a 'continuation of State policy by other means'.[3] The British generals, though they might have been loath to admit it, were equally aware that the context and the ends for which they fought were ultimately political ones. This was the case, as elsewhere, with the war in the desert. Italy, backed by her Axis partner Germany, was intent on expanding from her powerbases in the colonies of Libya and Italian East Africa into the British-controlled territories of Egypt, the Sudan and the Middle East. It was for this reason that, Germany having overrun and defeated the Low Countries and France in June 1940, Italy decided to seize the moment and declare war on Britain and France on 10 June.

Italy's subsequent military campaigns were intended to conquer territories and to establish a new Roman Empire in the Mediterranean basin. The British, for their part, were determined to resist Italian aggrandisement at their expense, and that of the people whom they protected. In order to achieve this, they had to eradicate the threat posed by the Axis forces to their position in the Middle East. They did so in a series of hard-fought campaigns in the deserts and mountains of North and East Africa between 1940 and 1943. While doing so, however, they had to give some thought to what they were going to do with the Italian colonies, and their Italian settler and indigenous populations, once they had captured them. There have been a number of adequate studies of what happened in East Africa, but none with regard to Libya.[4] This book seeks to remedy the deficiency by chronicling and analysing the debates over the future of the Italian colony of Libya within the British government in London and between the government and their military and political representatives in Egypt.

At that time Libya was far from being a country, let alone a nation-state, as we know it today. The contacts between the British and Libyans, or rather the tribes, sects, factions and their leaders dwelling in Cyrenaica, Tripolitania and the Fezzan between 1939 and 1943, can be seen with hindsight as an important stage in the development of Libya towards independence in 1951. In the war years, however, there were simply too many imponderables in the situation, not least who was going to win the war, to predict this eventuality. This is what has made the twists and turns of the politics of the war in the desert so fascinating not only to the participants at the time but to the historian and the reader of a later age, knowing as they do how the story panned out.

There were three key political events which occurred during the war in the desert that were of fundamental importance for the future of Libya. The first was the British decision in the summer of 1940 to accept the offer by the exiled leader of the Sanusi tribes of Cyrenaica to raise a tribal force to fight against the Italians. The second was the British declaration in January 1942, which had been under active consideration since the summer of 1941, that, in return for helping the Allied cause, the Sanusis of Cyrenaica would be freed from Italian rule after the war. The third was the de facto achievement of this promise with the final British conquest of Italian Libya in 1943.

These three important political events have determined the shape and structure of this book. It is divided into three parts, with each part consisting of a number of short chapters dealing with the successive political phases of the war in the desert. Since each part covers, approximately, a year of the war, I have decided to entitle them accordingly, with a descriptive sub-title. On reflection, it seems an appropriate counter-point given that the Italian Fascists were in the habit, like the French revolutionaries of 1789, of dating events from the start of the regime in 1922 (Anno I, etc.). Before turning to the politics of the war in the desert, however, it is necessary, by way of a prologue, to set the scene with regard to Libya, to describe the period under Italian rule and how Britain was eventually forced to address the question of the future of Italy's so-called 'Fourth Shore' in the Mediterranean.[5]

NOTES

1   A representative selection would include Niall Barr, *Pendulum of War*, London 2004; Stephen Bungay, *Alamein*, London 2003; James Holland, *Together We Stand*, London 2005, and Jon Latimer, *Alamein*, London 2002.

2   Among the military historians, the following stand out: Corelli Barnett, *The Desert Generals*, London 1960; C E Lucas Phillips, *Alamein*, London 1962; Ronald Lewin, with his books on Rommel (1968), Montgomery (1971) and the Afrika Korps (1977); Barrie Pitt's *Crucible of War* trilogy, 1986; Ralph Bennett, *Ultra and Mediterranean Strategy*, London 1989, and the official histories by I S O Playfair on *The Mediterranean and the Middle East*, vols I–IV, London 1954–66, and F H Hinsley on *British Intelligence in the Second World War*, vols I–II, London 1979 and 1984. For the generals see Francis De Guingand, *Operation Victory*, London 1947; Bernard Montgomery, *El Alamein to the River Sangro*, London 1948, and *Memoirs*, London 1958; B H Liddell Hart, *The Rommel Papers*, London 1953; Michael Carver, *Tobruk*, London 1962, *El Alamein*, London 1962, and *Dilemmas of the Desert War*, London 1986.

3   Roger Ashley Leonard, ed., *A Short Guide to Clausewitz on War*, New York 1967, p.13.

4   For Italian East Africa see G K N Trevaskis, *Eritrea. A Colony in Transition, 1941–52*, London 1960; I M Lewis, *A Modern History of Somalia. Nation and State in the Horn of Africa*, Harlow 1980; H G Marcus, *Ethiopia, Great Britain and the United States, 1941–74*, London, 1983; J Markakis, *National and Class Conflict in the Horn of Africa*, Cambridge 1987; W Bowring, 'Great Britain, the United States and the Disposition of Italian East Africa', *The Journal of Imperial and Commonwealth History*, 20, 1992.

5   Contemporary Arab names, whether of people or places, are given in the spelling which readers are most likely to encounter in English-language books, newspapers and maps. The name of any given person or place is spelt in the same way throughout the book, but the same Arab original, in the case of two people or places of the same name, may appear in more than one form, e.g. Sanusi(s) or Senoussi(s). This is due to the influence of the European language predominant in the country concerned or, sometimes, in the case of personal names, simply to the preference of the owner or user of the name. Where a generally accepted English form exists, this has been preferred, e.g. Jaghbub, not the Arabic al-Jagbub, or the Italian Giarabub. Arabic personal names which have passed into history are transliterated on a uniform system.

ITALIAN LIBYA

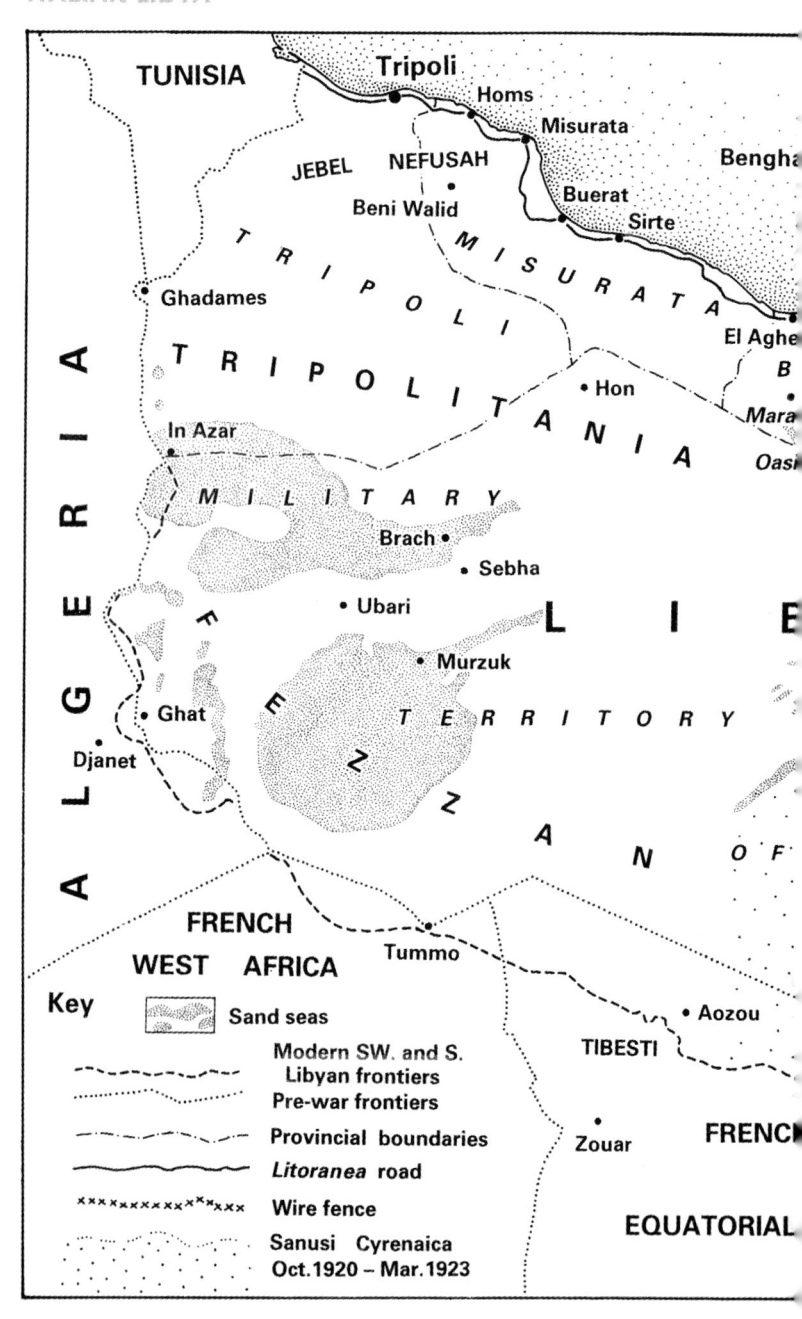

TUNISIA

Tripoli
Homs
Misurata
JEBEL NEFUSAH
Beni Walid
Buerat
Sirte
Benghazi

T R I P O L I
M I S U R A T A

Ghadames

T R I P O L I T A N I A

El Aghe
B
Mara
Oasi

In Azar
• Hon

M I L I T A R Y

Brach
• Sebha
• Ubari

F

L I E

• Murzuk

Ghat

T E R R I T O R Y

Djanet

F E Z Z A N

A N O F

FRENCH WEST AFRICA
Tummo

Key

▨	Sand seas
– – – – –	Modern SW. and S. Libyan frontiers
··········	Pre-war frontiers
–··–··–	Provincial boundaries
————	*Litoranea* road
××××××××	Wire fence
░░░	Sanusi Cyrenaica Oct. 1920 – Mar. 1923

• Aozou
TIBESTI
• Zouar

FRENCH
EQUATORIAL

Map

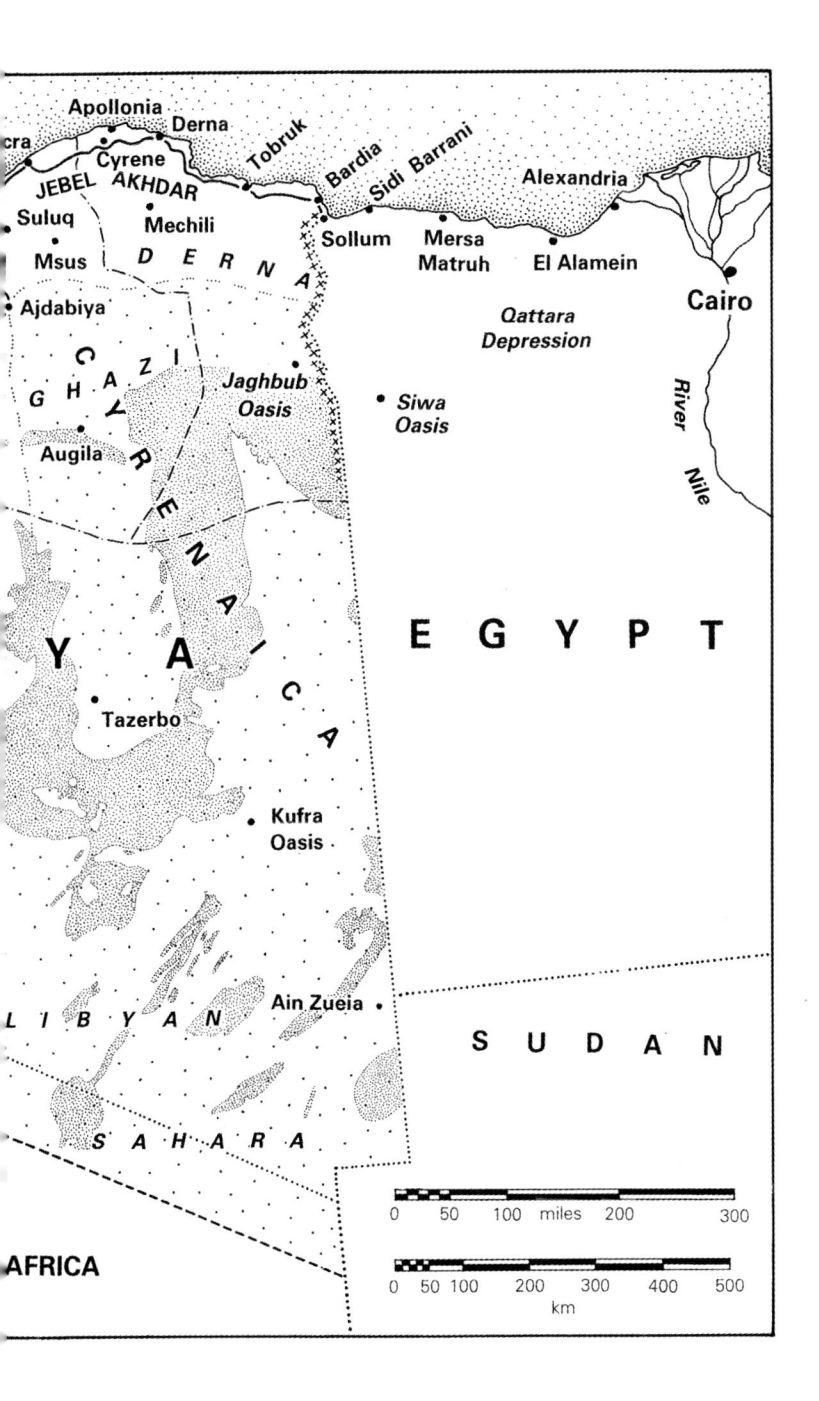

- Apollonia
- Derna
- Cyrene
- JEBEL AKHDAR
- Tobruk
- Bardia
- Sidi Barrani
- Alexandria
- Suluq
- Mechili
- Sollum
- Mersa Matruh
- El Alamein
- Msus
- DERNA
- Cairo
- Ajdabiya
- Qattara Depression
- Jaghbub Oasis
- Siwa Oasis
- Augila
- GHAZI
- CYRENAICA
- River Nile
- LIBYA
- EGYPT
- Tazerbo
- Kufra Oasis
- LIBYAN
- Ain Zueia
- SUDAN
- SAHARA
- AFRICA

0 50 100 miles 200 300

0 50 100 200 300 400 500
km

prologue
ITALY, BRITAIN AND LIBYA
1911 TO 1940

THE ITALIAN CONQUEST OF LIBYA

THE ITALIANS were 'the sturdy beggars' of Europe, according to the Third Marquess of Salisbury, British Foreign Secretary and Prime Minister at the end of the 19th century. They were assiduous in their pursuit of the territorial crumbs which fell from the top table of the greater powers, France, Britain and Germany, during the scramble for African colonies. Since the French occupation of Tunisia in 1881 and the establishment of the British protectorate in Egypt in 1882, the Italians had looked upon the areas of Tripolitania and Cyrenaica, which remained the only provinces of the Ottoman Empire on the Mediterranean African coast not occupied by the Great Powers, as their just reward in North Africa. (They soon rechristened the territory 'Libya', in imitation of the nomenclature of ancient Rome.)

Their reasons were those which had been given before the declaration of the French protectorate to justify Italy's claim to Tunisia, namely the nearness of the country to the homeland and the large Italian community. As in Tunisia, Italian settlement and investment had been encouraged in order to carry out the 'peaceful penetration' of the economic and social life of the territory. Italians had acquired land and set up businesses with the aid of the Banco di Roma.

However, as the French had found in Morocco, occupation depended upon international approval. This had been obtained, after some thirty years of diplomatic wrangling, from Britain, France and Russia on the one hand, and Germany and Austria-Hungary on the other. By 1910 Italian economic penetration of Libya was interrupted by German attempts to take concessions away from Italy and by Turkish harassment of Italian citizens and interference with Italian ships. Domestic considerations and foreign policy concerns impelled Italy to seize Libya. In late September 1911, after the resolution of the Second Moroccan Crisis, Italy declared war on the Ottoman Empire and, in October, invaded Libya.[1]

Contrary to expectations, the Italian army met with stiff resistance. Turkish rule, backed by the Turkish army, was regarded in the coastal cities as the lawful government and, in particular, as the best defence against encroachment from Christian Europe. In the hinterland, Turkish rule had undermined the authority of the tribal chiefs, and created the conditions for the expansion of Turkish influence.

By the late nineteenth century, particularly in Tripolitania, a native political elite had been formed in the tribal population, organised on a local family basis, but educated sometimes in Egypt or Europe and participating in the politics as well as in the administration of the Ottoman Empire. In 1908, Libyan followers of the Committee of Union and Progress (the Young Turks) had become representatives in the Ottoman parliament. Although the rivals whom they defeated in the race for advancement welcomed the Italians as allies they were outnumbered by the supporters of the Ottoman government, who with the help of the Turkish army mobilised the population for war.

In Cyrenaica, less advanced and more remote than Tripolitania, the Turks received aid from the powerful Sanusi order, who regarded the Italians as a greater threat than the Europeanising policies of the Young Turks. As a result, after the initial occupation of Tripoli, Benghazi, Derna and Tobruk, the Italians could not break out of the coastal strip. This only occurred when the Turks, faced with a war in the Balkans, diplomatic pressure from Britain, Germany and Austria-Hungary and the threat from Italy to attack Smyrna, agreed to withdraw from Libya under the Treaty of Lausanne, signed on 18 October 1912. The Turks agreed to grant independence to Libya and to recognise Italian sovereignty, although the Sultan retained his authority as the spiritual leader of the Muslim population. This ambiguous arrangement allowed the Libyan leaders to claim a formal legitimacy in their efforts to continue the war with the help of Turkish officers who remained behind to assist in the organisation of their resistance.

The Turks found a staunch ally in the Sanusi leader, Ahmad al-Sharif. He was above all a holy man. The Sanusis were a Sufi brotherhood who followed the *tariqa* or path of its founder, Sayyid Muhammad Ali al-Sanusi, an Algerian whose studies had been in North Africa and the Hijaz and who had settled in Cyrenaica in the 1840s. His sons and followers were *ikhwan*, missionaries, intent like the Wahabis of Arabia in propagating the true faith. In Cyrenaica they were at the same time *marabouts* in the North African tradition of holy men within a tribal society. Like other *marabouts*, the Sanusis received land and other gifts from the *beduin* in return for their blessing and their arbitration in tribal disputes. The organisation, wealth and prestige of the Sanusis gave them predominance over the pastoral and agricultural tribes of the Jabal Akhdar and the desert.

By the late nineteenth century, the *zawaya* or settlements of the order projected southwards from its headquarters in the oasis of Jaghbub, with its large library and school, to Wadai and Darfur in the Sudan. These settlements were located at tribal centres or at watering places on the pilgrim and trade routes across the Sahara which the Sanusis had developed, and from which the brotherhood drew their wealth. These routes had allowed the order to penetrate Central Sudan. But growing Sanusi influence inevitably aroused the suspicion of the French who, as they advanced rapidly eastwards in the years immediately preceding the Italian invasion, drove the Sanusis from Central Sudan. While the French abolished the order in the lands they had conquered, Ahmad al-Sharif returned northwards to the oases of Kufra and Jaghbub to fight the new enemy, Italy.[3]

The doctrinal hostility of the Sanusis to European influence brought them into armed conflict with European imperialism. When in late 1912 Ahmad al-Sharif claimed to be the rightful amir of Libya in succession to the Turks, he graduated from being simply a man of God into being a man of power, a ruler. But he was regarded as an outsider in Tripolitania and in the coastal cities. The four leading tribal chiefs in Tripolitania, particularly Sulaiman al-Baruni in the Jabal Nafusa, resisted his advances. But they could not themselves agree and co-operate, and after the Treaty of Lausanne, put out peace-feelers to the Italians. In 1913 the Italians broke out of their confinement in the five ports and occupied the entire coastal strip, with the exception of the barren stretch around the Gulf of Sirte.[4]

During the First World War, Italy was not able to devote much attention to Libya, and the Italian position deteriorated accordingly. As an ally of Germany and Austria-Hungary, Turkey had sent officers and agents to Libya to encourage the Arabs to join in the holy war against the enemies of the Ottoman Sultan. Since the Turks regarded Britain as a more important enemy than Italy in Cyrenaica, they persuaded Ahmad al-Sharif to invade Egypt in November 1915, at a time when British forces were heavily engaged against the Turks in the Sinai. Although they achieved some early successes, the Sanusis were eventually driven back into Cyrenaica. Facing defeat and famine, Ahmad al-Sharif abdicated the order and his position in Cyrenaica to his young cousin Muhammad Idris.

Idris had always disapproved of the campaign against the British, having advocated Sanusi neutrality in the war between Britain and Turkey. Following a visit to Egypt, in which he formed friendly relations with the British, Idris gained the tacit support of Britain as a leader and peacemaker, the British being anxious to reconcile the Sanusis with the Italians for the sake of the war in Europe. Such was the start of a friendship between Idris and the British which was to last over fifty years. With the approval of Ahmad al-Sharif, Idris, who preferred his religious duties to his military and political authority, opened negotiations with the British and the Italians in July 1916.

Discussions proceeded slowly but, with the British acting as mediators between Idris and the Italians, a peace agreement was reached at Akrama in the spring of 1917. Under the peace terms the Sanusis were allowed to stay in the Egyptian oasis of Jaghbub and to trade through the Egyptian port of Sallum, while their authority was recognised in Cyrenaica outside the Italian-controlled towns along the coast. The Italians agreed that the sharia law should be applied to their Muslim subjects, and that the Sanusis should be exempt from paying taxes. Although the Sanusis agreed in return to disarm, the Italians supplied them with more arms in order that they might enforce the peace. Thus the Sanusis and the Italians were left facing each other in Cyrenaica in a state of armed truce, and the British were relieved of the Sanusi threat to Egypt. Rather than surrender to the British, Ahmad al-Sharif went into exile in Turkey.[5]

After a brief occupaton of the Fezzan the Italians were driven out in 1914 and, following a serious defeat near Sirte in April 1915, they were once again besieged in four coastal towns in Tripolitania. The power vacuum in the interior left by the Italian withdrawal was filled by the tribal leadership who were supplied with arms by the Central Powers through the port of Misurata. Although they controlled their respective territories, the Tripolitanian leaders squabbled among themselves and with the Sanusis, whose invasion of Tripolitania in 1916 they repulsed. This failure of the Tripolitanians and the Sanusis of Cyrenaica to co-operate, which was to recur in later years, was to prove a fatal flaw in the Libyan resistance to Italian occupation, and a generation later it was to threaten the prospects of the early independence of Libya.

At the end of the First World War, Italy, wracked by serious internal crises, lacked the will to use military force to restore the situation in Libya and attempted to reach political compromises with the Sanusis in Cyrenaica and the Tripolitanian Republic. The latter had been proclaimed in Misurata in 1918 by the four main chiefs, al-Baruni, al-Suwayhili, al-Murayyid and Ibn al-Khaya, with the assistance of the Egyptian nationalist, Azzam Bey. In accordance with the Wilsonian spirit of self-government prevailing at the time, the Italians promulgated the Fundamental Law for Tripolitania in June 1919, followed by the Fundamental Law for Cyrenaica in October 1919, whereby each province was to have its own elected assembly and governing and local councils through which the Italian governors would exercise a nominal control. However, since there was no agreement, either with the Italians on the ultimate fate of the province, or among the Tripolitanian leaders themselves, it was impossible to coerce Italy into introducing the new constitution. This led Azzam, the would-be kingmaker of Libyan politics, to revive a pre-war idea of a Tripolitania under Sanusi leadership, which he hoped would enjoy British support.[6]

As the unchallenged leader of the Cyrenaicans following Ahmad al-Sharif's departure into exile, Idris was in a good position to negotiate with Italy. Moreover, the Italian governor, the liberal Di Martino, trusted Idris and believed that Italy could govern Cyrenaica indirectly through Idris's influence. For his part, Idris was genuinely convinced of the need for a friendly and permanent settlement with the Italians. He accepted the Fundamental Law for Cyrenaica, and in the Agreement of al-Rajma in October 1920 he was given the hereditary title of 'Amir' and recognised as the governor of the autonomous regime of the interior of Cyrenaica, comprising the oases of Jaghbub, Awjila, Jalo and Kufra, with headquarters at Ajdabiya. In return for receiving the honours due to his rank and generous subsidies for himself, his family, his officials and the tribal shaikhs, Idris agreed to limit his army to one thousand men and to suppress within eight months the armed camps and posts and other Sanusi organisations of a political, administrative or military character.

It was intended that the province should be ruled through the Cyrenaican parliament, which first met in April 1921 under the presidency of Idris's cousin, Safi al-Din al-Sanusi. The agreement, which might have created a working arrangement between the Sanusi followers and Italy, broke down over the refusal of the Cyrenaican tribesmen to lay down their arms. After further discussion, Idris and Di Martino agreed a further compromise, under the Bu Maryam Agreement of November 1921, whereby the *adwar* (Sanusi bands) were to be under joint Italian and Sanusi control as a first step towards their disbandment. The agreement failed when shortly afterwards Di Martino died and was replaced by a much less liberal governor, who turned against what he regarded as the appeasement of the Sanusis.[7]

While conditions in Cyrenaica were worsening, it was events in Tripolitania that contributed most to the breakdown of Idris's relations with the Italians. The Tripolitanian leaders, meeting at Gharyan at the instigation of the returned exile Bashir al-Sadawi after their failure to obtain a reply from Italy to their request for implementation of the Fundamental Law for Tripolitania, offered the amirate of Tripolitania to Idris in the hope that he would negotiate with Italy on their behalf. Idris was put in a difficult dilemma by the Tripolitanian offer, which in the face of uncompromising Italian opposition, it was impossible for him to accept. It would have meant breaking off relations with the Italians and leading a revolt which he was, by character, unable to do. He felt also that he could not rely on the Tripolitanians' loyalty and their willingness to fight the Italians. Realising that his position had become impossible Idris, after discussion with his advisers and Azzam Bey, left Cyrenaica in December 1922 and withdrew into exile in Egypt.[8]

The continuing disagreements between the Tripolitanian leaders prevented any effective opposition to the Italian offensive in 1923. The tribesmen were dispersed by bombing. Bashir al-Sadawi left Tripolitania in 1924, while Safi al-Din (Idris's cousin and deputy in Tripolitania) returned to Jaghbub. In Cyrenaica the Italians dissolved the jointly held army and launched surprise attacks on the Sanusi armed camps in March 1923, taking prisoner half the *adwar*. Idris's official capital, Ajdabiya, was seized and the newly-appointed governor, Bongiovanni, denounced all agreements between Italy and Idris. The return from Egypt of the elderly Sanusi shaikh and warrior, Umar al-Mukhtar, to lead the resistance movement against Italy, was the start of a long guerilla war in the desert and the Jabal Akhdar (Green Mountain), in which for ten years the Italians ruled by day and the Sanusis by night.

Cyrenaica was only conquered from 1930 onwards when Colonel Rodolfo Graziani adopted more aggressive military tactics and took drastic steps to control the non-combatants, the revolt's main source of recruits and supplies. The tribal population of northern Cyrenaica were forcibly removed to large concentration camps in the lowlands. The rebel supply routes from Egypt were cut by a 300 km-long barbed-wire fence built along the Egyptian frontier and patrolled by armoured cars and aircraft. The Sanusi brotherhood were treated harshly and Kufra, their last stronghold in Libya, was occupied by the Italians in January

1931. The final blow to the guerilla movement came in September 1931, when Umar al-Mukhtar himself was captured and publicly hanged at Suluq. In January 1932 Marshal Badoglio, the governor of Tripolitania and Cyrenaica (which had been united for the better co-ordination of military operations), proclaimed the end of the Cyrenaican war and the pacification of Libya.[9]

ITALY, BRITAIN AND THE LIBYAN EXILES

Fascist imperialism was identified not only by the renewed Italian determination to conquer but also to colonise. The attempt of the Fascist regime in the mid-1920s to install a large Italian population on the land in Libya, on the pattern developed by the French in Algeria and Tunisia, was energetically renewed in the late 1930s. Despite the enthusiasm of the 1920s, agricultural settlement had proceeded slowly either through private enterprise or by means of companies like the Azienda Tabacchi Italiani. By 1933, although the state and the banks had lent 75 per cent of the necessary capital, there were still no more than 7,000 settlers in Tripolitania. Following the end of the guerilla war in Cyrenaica, the best pasture land in the country was confiscated from the tribes and made available for Italian settlement. The first 150 families were installed in 1934.

The Litoranea, the great coastal road stretching from the Tunisian frontier to the Egyptian frontier, a distance of 1,835 km (1,140 miles), was completed in 1937, providing a vital communications link and a potential invasion route into French North Africa or Egypt. But it was only after the Italian state assumed direct control of settlement and applied far greater sums of money that spectacular results were achieved. It was under the direction of Marshal Italo Balbo (who had become governor of the united colony of Libya in 1934) that Italian labour was imported to help prepare family farms in Tripolitania and Cyrenaica in readiness for the simultaneous settlement of 20,000 selected and state-aided settlers in 1938 and a further 12,000 in 1939. By 1940 the Italian population had risen from 55,000 to over 110,000 (70,000 in Tripolitania).

The previous year the four coastal provinces had been officially integrated into metropolitan Italy. Although there was little prospect that the Fascist policy of 'demographic colonisation' would provide a suitable remedy to the endemic problem of over-population in Italy, it had a considerable effect upon Libya. In 1940 Italy's plans for creating a 'fourth shore' in Libya came closest to realisation. The area under cultivation by the settlers had reached about 225,000 hectares, extensively

Mussolini in Tripoli during a visit to Libya, March 1937, brandishing the 'Sword of Islam' which was presented to him by an Arab delegation. From 'Tobruk', a Ministry of Information film, 1943. By permission of The Imperial War Museum MOI Film 1322.

irrigated by wells and pumps. The appearance of the coastal region, in particular the Jaffara plain in Tripolitania and the slopes of the Jabal Akhdar in Cyrenaica, were transformed by the planting of seven million vines and eight million new trees.[10]

Although Libya was home to about three-quarters of a million Muslims, they were treated as inferior citizens, a fact which could not be disguised by the granting of a 'special citizenship' (*cittadinanza italiana speciale*) to a number of minor officials and merchants from 1939 onwards. The Italians regarded the Libyans as providing a reserve of manpower for the development of the colony and the conquest of Ethiopia. Large numbers of them forsook their traditional pastimes and became wage-earners in the cash economy.

By 1940 no clear programme for the Libyans' future had emerged. The Fascist regime was aware of growing nationalist pressures elsewhere in the Arab world (and did much to encourage them), but expected to counter them in Libya by the reality of the overwhelming presence of Italian settlers. In the face of continuing Arab and Libyan hostility towards Italy, for her record during the conquest of Libya, Mussolini assumed the role of 'Protector of Islam' at a ceremony in Tripoli in 1937. It was a move which was judged at the time to be 'no empty theatrical gesture, but a serious bid for the prestige of the Muslim world'. On the eve of the Second World War, Fascist colonial policy seemed to be aiming at the establishment of the Muslim population of Libya as a peasantry complementary to the Italian settlers.[11]

Opposition to the Italians was centred on Egypt, where there were estimated to be some 14,000 Libyan exiles in 1939, eking out a penurious existence as drivers or labourers. The British had been prepared to use these Libyan exiles to help foment revolt in Libya if Italy had entered the war in September 1939. After securing the co-operation of Sayyid Idris, through the good offices of Muhammad Ali (the Egyptian Crown Prince and uncle of King Farouk), the General Officer Commanding British Troops Egypt (GOCBTE), Henry Maitland Wilson, had drawn up by mid-August 1939 a plan known as the 'G Expansion Scheme'. On the outbreak of war with Italy, five thousand Sanusi tribesmen would be recruited through their tribal leaders into the Frontier Brigade of the Egyptian and Arab Legion, which served in the Western Desert.

These new recruits were to be given equipment and transport and trained in the methods of guerilla warfare, the intention being to use this force in conjunction with an offensive by British forces against the Italians. Its task would be to cut the enemy's communications, carry out sabotage against enemy rear installations and act as the focus of a revolt of dissatisfied tribal elements in Libya. Among possible objectives considered was the capture and use of Jaghbub as a base for the activities of this force. The British were to co-ordinate these activities with a similar French plan which involved recruiting a five thousand-strong tribal force and raising a revolt in the Fezzan and at Kufra (Anglo-French forces operating from Chad and the Sudan were to seize the Kufra oases). This was to occur in conjunction with a major Allied offensive by French forces from Tunisia into Libya.

Italy's decision to remain malevolently neutral towards the Allied nations of Britain, France and Poland after the outbreak of war between them and Germany in September 1939, and the undesirability for the Allies of forcing Italy to choose sides in the war, meant that they were extremely reluctant to carry out any action which might be construed as hostile by the Italians. In the climate of Mediterranean appeasement from September 1939 to May 1940, Allied schemes for raising tribal revolt in Libya languished. Preparations were limited to establishing contact with and paying subsidies to heads of Libyan families in exile in Egypt, Chad and Tunisia; drawing up lists of likely recruits with the help of tribal leaders, stockpiling arms near Libya's frontiers, and planning for the eventual military offensive in Libya at the earliest practical moment after the outbreak of hostilities.

The attempt by the British military authorities in Egypt to have Sanusi tribal chiefs recruited in peacetime into the Egyptian Arab Legion, which was undergoing training in guerilla warfare techniques, fell foul of Egypt's non-belligerent status in the war with Germany. At first, in the summer of 1939 when war with Italy seemed imminent and the Egyptian government expected that Egypt would have to fight, the Egyptians had been willing to grant Egyptian nationality to Libyan refugees and to recruit a number of them into the Arab Legion. Soon after the outbreak of war, however, this had stopped, due partly no doubt to the reluctance of the Egyptian government to offend the Italians. It seems also to have been the result of a disagreement between Sayyid Idris and the Egyptians over the terms of service of the Sanusi tribesmen in the Egyptian Army. This affair had important consequences in that it appears to have convinced Sayyid Idris that the salvation of himself and his people lay in the hands of the British rather than the Egyptians, who were drifting in a neutral direction after September 1939.[12]

In mid-October 1939, Cyrenaican and Tripolitanian emigré leaders had met at Sayyid Idris's house in Alexandria to discuss the opportunity offered by the war for their recovery of Libya. After discussing how best to compose their political differences for the sake of the common struggle against Italy, they elected Sayyid Idris as their leader, provided he appointed a joint committee comprising both Tripolitanian and Cyrenaican leaders to advise him on all future action to be taken for the liberation of Libya. This proviso, to which Sayyid Idris agreed, was later to prove an important bone of contention between the Cyrenaicans and the Tripolitanians.[13]

Following the Alexandria meeting, Sayyid Idris approached General Wilson in November 1939 and requested that the British government give protected status to Libyan exiles in Egypt. He was met with a categorical refusal from Wilson. By the beginning of November, the European situation had stabilised sufficiently for the British to assume that no overt hostile act by Italy was likely in the near future (and the 7th Armoured Division at Mersa Matruh was stood down). In these circumstances the British were not going to jeopardise the fragile peace in the Mediterranean by assuming legal responsibility for rebellious Italian colonial subjects.[14]

In February 1940, after a tour of the Red Sea, the Commander-in-Chief, Middle East, General Archibald Wavell, suggested to the Foreign Office and the Chiefs of Staff in London that he take more active measures, in co-operation with the French, in preparation for war with Italy in Africa. He warned that the longer Britain continued to follow an inactive policy the smaller would be the prospects of causing embarrassment to the Italians through tribal action (as the Italians were suppressing tribal discontent, especially in Italian East Africa). Wavell recommended that the British undertake a propaganda campaign which would counter Italian attempts to undermine British prestige in Egypt, the Sudan and East Africa, attempts which had been partially successful. Wavell wanted guidance as to whether the Sanusi and Ethiopian tribal leaders were to be used, and whether any reference was to be made in British propaganda to the future of Libya and Italian East Africa.

The Foreign Office and the Chiefs of Staff displayed no anxiety, however, at Italian activities in Egypt, the Sudan and East Africa. Above all they were concerned not to arouse Italian enmity by undertaking the measures proposed by Wavell, some of which the Egyptian Department thought 'exceedingly dangerous if they were acted upon'. It was held to be impossible to envisage what policies Britain would adopt or what action she would take in Italian East Africa or Libya if Italy entered the war. Revolts were not to be stirred up except in conjunction with British military pressure on the Italians, and it was felt that propaganda by itself would not have much effect. The British attitude only started to change after Italy declared war on Britain and France on 10 June 1940.[15]

NOTES

1   R J B Bosworth, *Italy, the Least of the Great Powers. Italian Foreign Policy before the First World War*, Cambridge 1979, pp. 136–43, 153, 156–60, 162; M Kraiem, 'La Question de l'annexation italienne de la Libye', *Revue d'histoire Magrebine*, July 1976, no. 6, pp. 157–79; Timothy W Childs, *Italo-Turkish Diplomacy over the War in Libya, 1911–12* (Leiden 1990), pp. 1–11, 30–70; J L Miege, *L'Impérialisme Colonial Italien de 1870 à nos Jours*, Paris 1968, pp. 63, 78.

2   Bosworth, *op. cit.*, pp. 78–89; Kraiem, *op. cit.*; Childs, *op. cit.*, pp. 225–35; E E Evans-Pritchard, *The Sanusi of Cyrenaica*, Oxford 1948, pp. 107–17; E G H Joffe and K McLachlan, ed., *Social and Economic Development of Libya*, Wisbech 1982, pp. 44–6.

3   Evans-Pritchard, *op. cit.*, pp. 1–28.

4   *ibid.*, pp. 114–21; Joffe, *op. cit.*, pp. 46–7; Kraiem, *op. cit.*

5   Evans-Pritchard, *op. cit.*, pp. 121–45; S M Cole, 'Secret Diplomacy and the Cyrenaican Settlement of 1917', *Journal of Italian History*, 1979, vol. II, No. 2, pp. 258–80.

6   Joffe, *op. cit.*, pp. 47–57, 60.

7   Evans-Pritchard, *op. cit.*, pp. 145–53.

8   Research by E A V De Candole in *The Life and Times of King Idris of Libya*, London 1988, pp. 38–9, casts doubt on Evans-Pritchard's assertion in *Sanusi*, pp. 153–5, that Idris decided to accept the offer of the amirate over Tripolitania before leaving for Egypt.

9   Joffe, *op. cit.*, pp. 60–2; K Holmboe, tr. H Holbek, *Desert Encounter. An Adventurous Journey through Italian Africa*, London 1936, p. 203; Evans-Pritchard, *op. cit.*, pp. 156–90; R Rainero, 'La Capture. L'exécution d'Omar El Muktar et la fin de la guérrila libyenne', *Cahiers de Tunisie*, 1980, vol. XXXVIII, nos 111–12, pp. 59–74.

10   M Moore, *The Fourth Shore: Italy's mass colonisation of Libya*, London 1940, pp. 216–17, 221; C C Segre, *Fourth Shore; the Italian colonisation of Libya*, Chicago and London 1974, pp. 161–6.

11   H H Macartney and P Cremona, *Italy's Foreign and Colonial Policy, 1914–37*, London 1938, p. 187; John Wright, *Libya. A Modern History*, London and Canberra, 1981, pp. 40–1; Segre, *op. cit.*, pp. 144–57.

12   Lord Wilson of Libya, *Eight Years Overseas, 1939–47*, London, 1950, pp. 31–2; WO 201/336, Wavell to Beaumont-Nesbitt, 27.iv.40; FO 371/24644/J 1830/281/66, Lampson to Halifax, 23.viii.40.

13   Majid Khadduri, *Modern Libya. A Study in Political Development*, Baltimore 1963, pp. 28–9.

14   Wilson, *op. cit.*, pp. 27–8; FO 371/24644/J1830/281/66, Lampson to Halifax, 23.viii.40.

15   FO 371/24638/J 482/482/1 JIC (40)7, 9.ii.40 and minutes.

THE FIRST YEAR 1940–1941

PRELUDE TO THE DECLARATION ON THE SANUSIS

LIBYA: YEAR ONE

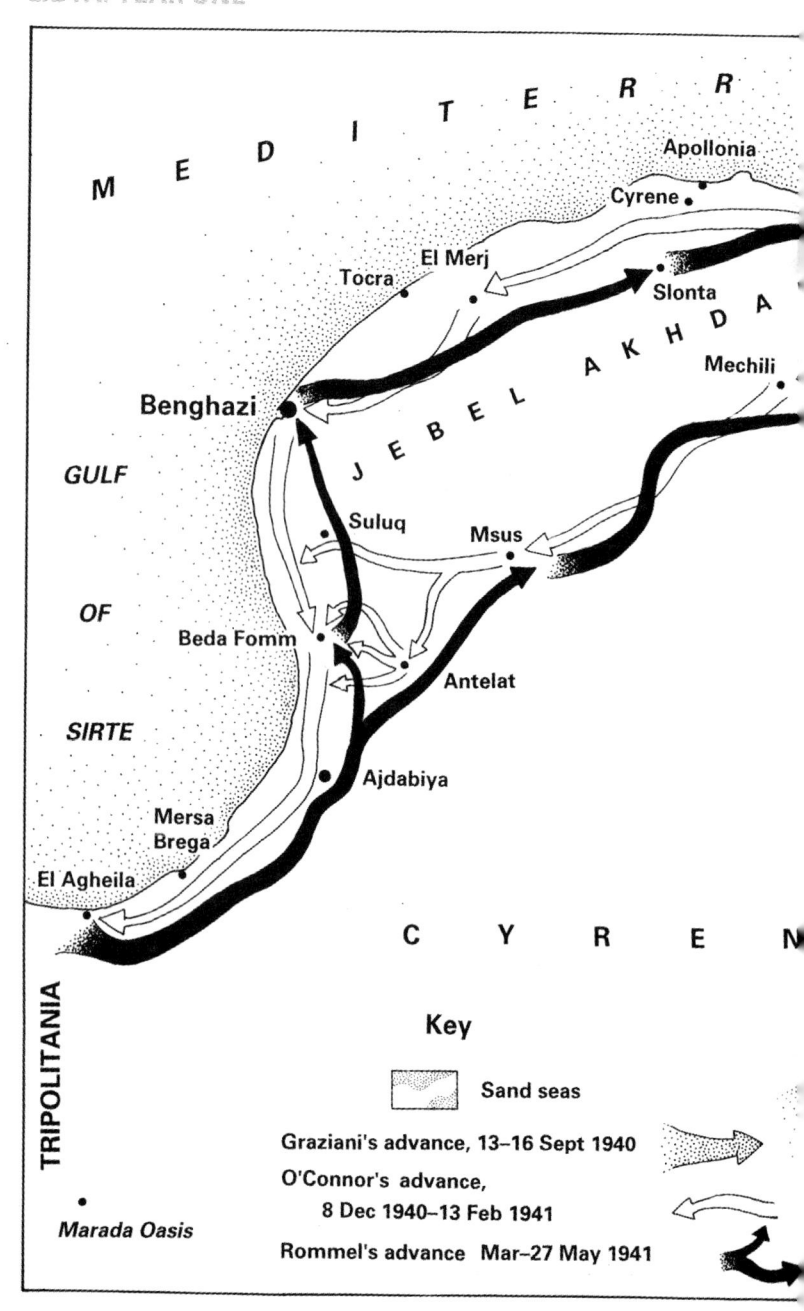

Key

Sand seas

Graziani's advance, 13–16 Sept 1940

O'Connor's advance, 8 Dec 1940–13 Feb 1941

Rommel's advance Mar–27 May 1941

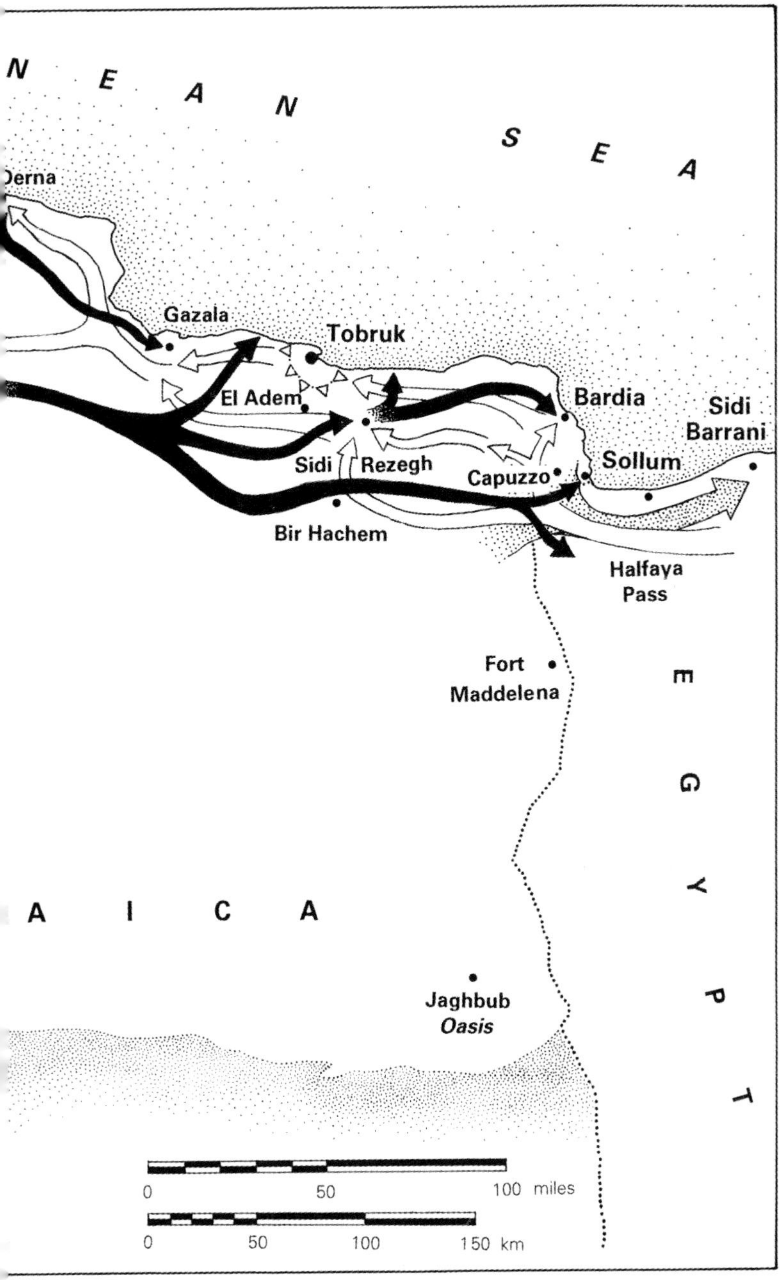
N E A N
S E A
Derna
Gazala
Tobruk
El Adem
Sidi
Rezegh
Bir Hachem
Capuzzo
Bardia
Sidi
Barrani
Sollum
Halfaya
Pass
Fort
Maddelena
E G Y P T
A I C A
Jaghbub
Oasis
0
50
100 miles
0
50
100
150 km

overview

It is usual in any discussion of the immediate origins of Libyan independence to begin with an account of Anthony Eden's statement in Parliament on 8 January 1942, in which he declared that the British government was 'determined that at the end of the war the Sanusis in Cyrenaica will in no circumstances again fall under Italian domination'.[1] In fact, however, British politicians, diplomats and soldiers had shown a sustained interest in the Sanusis, Cyrenaica, and Libya as a whole, since the outbreak of war between Britain and Italy in June 1940. Moreover, the British government had been actively considering making such a declaration since the summer of 1941, in the wake of the military and political crisis in the Eastern Mediterranean occasioned by Germany's intervention in the region.

The period from Italy's entry into the war until the start of the German offensive in the Eastern Mediterranean in the spring of 1941 should be regarded as the prelude to Eden's declaration on the Sanusis of Cyrenaica. Within this period it is necessary to distinguish between the months of British military weakness in the Middle East, which the Italians inadequately exploited, and the time when the British felt strong enough to pass over to the offensive, the eventual outcome of which was the overrunning of much of the Italian colonial empire in Africa.

In the earlier phase, from June to early December 1940, there was an air of unreality about the discussions in Britain and Italy of the plans and demands being put forward from various quarters concerning the division of the spoils of empire. While the British debated whether or not to make a declaration concerning the future of a country, Libya, which they had not yet conquered, the Italians dreamed that, following the capture of Egypt, they would create a great empire stretching from Tunisia to the Persian Gulf and from Palestine to Kenya.

Italy's bid for empire ended in disaster in the mountains of Albania and Ethiopia, and the desert wastes of North Africa in the winter and spring of 1940–41. The shock sustained by Italy encouraged many in the British government to believe that discontent among the Italian civilian population and the armed forces might lead to the overthrow of the Fascist regime, and to Italy making a separate peace with Britain. This possibility, combined with the British occupation of Cyrenaica, gave a greater urgency and also a more solid basis to the discussion of Libya's future which took place within British political, diplomatic and military circles from mid-December 1940 to early April 1941.

THE DIPLOMATIC BALANCE

The fact that the British government did not undertake any definite commitments on the future of Libya during the period from June 1940 to April 1941 was due largely to the reluctance of the British Ambassador to Egypt, Sir Miles Lampson, and the Commander in Chief in the Middle East, General Sir Archibald Wavell, to do anything which might conceivably worsen Britain's already strained relations with the quasi-independent countries of the Middle East, in particular Egypt. They were supported in this by the Foreign Office which was generally inclined against making political commitments at such an early stage of the war, and without consulting Britain's allies.

Despite their caution, however, in the excitement and turmoil engendered by the Italian threat to Egypt in the summer of 1940 statements were made which were later interpreted as commitments. In particular, the General Officer Commanding British Troops in Egypt (GOCBTE), Henry Maitland Wilson, was to give a vaguely worded pledge that the Sanusis would be liberated from Italian rule. This was intended as part of a recruiting drive to encourage the Sanusis of Cyrenaica to co-operate with the British

General Henry Maitland 'Jumbo' Wilson, GOC British Troops Egypt in 1940. (He later became Field Marshal Lord Wilson of Libya and Stowenlangtoft.)
By permission of The Imperial War Museum
TA 12864.

in fighting the Italians. It came to assume a significance which had not been originally envisaged.

The British military and diplomatic authorities in Cairo and the Foreign Office in London also had to contend with the far-reaching schemes for Libya's future of influential individuals within the British government. These included the Prime Minister, Winston Churchill, the Secretary of State for the Colonies, Lord Lloyd, and the eminent archaeologist, Sir Leonard Woolley (on secondment to the War Office), who had the qualified backing of the Secretary of State for War, Anthony Eden.

The evolution of Eden's thinking on the future of Libya began during this period and certain important clues to his subsequent decisions can be found during the latter part of his tenure at the War Office and the opening months of his long reign at the Foreign Office. The bureaucratic stalemate which had ensued on this question by late March 1941 was broken only by Rommel's counter-offensive in Cyrenaica in April which heralded the limited German offensive against Britain's position in the Eastern Mediterranean. The subsequent political crisis which faced Britain in the Middle East changed the whole nature of the debate on the future of Libya.

Lastly, it should be stressed that British policy towards Libya was not created in a vacuum. British actions were determined not only by local considerations but by developments in Italy, French North Africa, the Balkans, Egypt and the Arab world. In particular, the debate over Libya was inextricably linked from the beginning with the consideration of Egyptian nationalist demands and general Arab aspirations concerning independence, unity and the future of Palestine.

chapter 1
'BEATING THE AIR'
JUNE–OCTOBER 1940

> As I have often suggested, "intense diplomatic activity" is beating the air unless backed by military prowess.
>
> Sir Alexander Cadogan, minute of 20 October 1940[2]

EGYPTIAN AND SAUDI PLANS FOR LIBYA

AFTER THE outbreak of war in September 1939, many Middle Eastern potentates and politicians were quick to realise that the preoccupation of Britain and France with events in Europe offered them a splendid opportunity to extract concessions from the Allies on such issues as treaty rights, Arab unity and Palestine. Thus the Palace government of Ali Mahir in Egypt demanded as the price of an Egyptian declaration of war on Germany that Britain should commit herself to a complete evacuation of her forces from Egypt at the end of the war, that Britain should declare her acceptance of Egypt's claims in the Sudan, and that Britain should declare her 'support of the aspirations of the Egyptian people for Arab unity'. Since the British refused to make such concessions Egypt withheld its declaration of war.[3]

From the autumn of 1939 onwards the Egyptian, Iraqi and Saudi governments, with King Abd al-Aziz al-Saud to the fore, exerted pressure on Britain over Palestine. They wished the British government to declare a general amnesty for those involved in the recent Arab Revolt, to reach agreement with the Higher Arab Committee, and to establish a Palestinian Arab government. Britain was not prepared to go any further, as she made clear in February 1940, than to allow the deported Palestinian leaders to return to their country.

The pressure on Britain to meet Arab demands increased in the spring and summer of 1940 as the result of the German military victories in Europe, the collapse of France, the entry of Italy into the war, and the effects of anti-British and anti-Jewish propaganda in the

Middle East. A British defeat appeared to be imminent and Middle Eastern leaders indulged in a positive orgy of competition to see who could extract the greatest concessions from a battered Britain, and at the same time reinsure themselves with Germany and Italy who seemed to be the coming powers in the Middle East.

On 25 May 1940, while the Battle for France was raging and Italy was preparing herself to declare war on the Allies, the Foreign Minister of Iraq, Nuri al-Said, in an endeavour to bolster his own sagging position within the Iraqi government and the Arab world, proposed to the British Ambassador, Sir Basil Newton, that Britain and, if possible, France should make 'a clear and unambiguous pronouncement guaranteeing immediately or at least at the end of the war, the execution of the promises already given for the organisation of self-government in Palestine and Syria'. In other words, the British government was required to implement the constitutional provisions of the 1939 White Paper on Palestine whereas the French government, if it was still able to, was asked to implement the 1936 treaty with Syria which it had not yet ratified. In return Iraq would participate in the fight against the German propaganda offensive in the Middle East.[4]

The Saudi Minister to Britain, Hafiz Wahba, made a similar proposal on Palestine and Syria in conversation with Lacy Baggallay (head of the Eastern Department in the Foreign Office) on 7 June 1940. He suggested also, on his own initiative, that if war broke out between Italy and the Allies the latter should make a declaration that after the war Libya would be free and that they would protect the Muslims of Ethiopia against their Amhara rulers. Hafiz Wahba was sure that this would do the Allied cause much good in the Muslim world and especially in the Arab countries as there was considerable interest among the latter in the fate of their co-religionists in Libya and Ethiopia. Hafiz Wahba revealed his true colours as an old Egyptian nationalist, however, when he pointed out that as Libya was too weak to stand alone as a state then she should be included in some form of federation with Egypt, although with safeguards for her autonomy.

Initially the Foreign Office was negative in its response to these Arab initiatives. Baggallay felt a certain repugnance, which he expressed to Hafiz Wahba, at the idea of Britain making declarations with regard to Libya and Ethiopia which might come to mean more in the future than was intended at the time. The British would not help themselves by publicly reiterating their adherence to the 1939 White Paper policy on Palestine, since this might offend the Americans at a critical moment and would not satisfy Arab aspirations for an independent Arab Palestine. Only Allied military victories would restore the waning prestige of Britain and France in the Middle East.[5]

The Foreign Office revised its opinion, however, as a result of Italy's declaration of war on Britain and France on 10 June 1940, the collapse of French resistance and the onset of simultaneous crises in Anglo-Egyptian and Anglo-Iraqi relations. The governments of Ali Mahir in Egypt and Rashid Ali al-Gaylani in Iraq proved reluctant to co-operate with Britain, and rushed to reinsure themselves with the Axis. The Foreign Office and the Colonial Office realised that British options were severely limited, with Britain now standing alone against the Axis and a new front being opened up in the Middle East. They therefore favoured placating Pan-Arab opinion by taking a more conciliatory line in Palestine, i.e. by declaring, as desired by Nuri al-Said, that Britain would implement the 1939 White Paper policy after the war. They were thwarted in this by a War Cabinet dominated by opponents of the 1939 White Paper who wanted to avoid a public statement specifically re-endorsing it, in order to avoid any dangerous repercussions on opinion in the United States.

By early July 1940 the Foreign Office and the Colonial Office were prepared to accept a compromise by which Nuri al-Said would simply be told that the British government saw no reason to change the 1939 White Paper policy on Palestine during the war and that it remained unchanged. If pressed, British diplomatic representatives in the Middle East were to state that they hoped and expected that conditions in Palestine after the war would permit the implementation of the provisions of the 1939 White Paper. This non-committal reply seemed more appropriate at a time when the Iraqi government still refused to break diplomatic ties with Italy.[6]

The Colonial Office and the Foreign Office were divided, however, over making a declaration on the future of Libya. Following the entry of Italy into the war Hafiz Wahba's suggestion, that Libya become an autonomous province of Egypt, was taken up by Sir Leonard Woolley, who worked for a branch of Military Intelligence (MI7b) in the War Office, and Lord Lloyd, the Colonial Secretary. Woolley and Lloyd were survivors from what T E Lawrence described as that 'band of wildmen ... all claws and teeth' who had served in Cairo in the Arab Bureau, and on intelligence missions and guerilla raids in the Middle East during the First World War.[7]

Upon the outbreak of war with Italy they lost no time in addressing themselves to the question of raising revolt among the tribes of Libya and Ethiopia. Both men held strongly pro-Arab views and had long experience of Egypt. They were concerned to counter what they perceived as the deleterious effects on British prestige in the Middle East of the Allied defeats and Axis propaganda, by exploiting the general Arab dislike and fear of Italy to the advantage of Britain. They thought this could be best done by appealing to the rising tide of Pan-Arabism in Egypt and the Fertile Crescent.

In swift succession (they would seem to have consulted on this beforehand) Woolley on 12 June and Lloyd on 14 June 1940 put their ideas on the future of Libya to the Foreign Office. Their argument was straightforward and appealing in its logic. It was presumed that Britain and France would not want to annexe or assume mandatory responsibility for Libya after the war, as they would be accused of territorial aggrandisement which would be opposed by the United States and the Arab world. It would be difficult to return Libya to Italy both because of Italian misrule, of which British propaganda had made much, and because of Arab reactions to that misrule. As the country could not become independent (the implication being that it could not support itself) then Britain should announce at once that 'the natural and historical condition of Libya was that it should be an autonomous province of the Kingdom of Egypt'.

Woolley and Lloyd held that a declaration on the above lines would be immediately welcomed by Egypt, i.e. by King Faruk and by Egyptian politicians who would jump at the chance of government posts. It would put the Sudan Question in abeyance; it would absolve Britain of any taint of selfish motives, and it would gain 'the approval and support of Pan-Arab nationalists everywhere, completely nullifying German propaganda addressed to the Pan-Arabs'.[8]

At a time when the Palace government of Ali Mahir refused to declare war on Italy (even after Egyptian forces and installations in the Western Desert had been bombed by the Italian Air Force) and prevaricated over taking the security measures requested by the British, the proposal to declare that Libya should become an autonomous province of Egypt after the war should probably be seen as a bribe to entice Egypt to enter the war against the Axis. The necessary precondition of territorial gain as a result of war is usually either participation or at least benevolent neutrality in that war.

In the circumstances of the day, when France was collapsing and the Egyptian crisis was reaching its climax (on 17 June France began armistice negotiations with Germany and Sir Miles Lampson presented his ultimatum to King Faruk to dismiss Ali Mahir as Prime Minister or risk being dethroned), the idea that one of Britain's peace aims should be that Libya become an autonomous province of Egypt had some attraction for the Foreign Office. However, the possibility of winning over Egyptian and Pan-Arab opinion to Britain's side seems to have been outweighed in the collective mind of the Foreign Office (the views of the Egyptian and Southern Departments, not the Eastern Department, prevailed) by the fact that the Italian Empire was still in existence and that it was too early to start talking about its future, especially as Britain would first have to consult all its Allies, and in particular France, over the fate of Tripolitania.[9]

Furthermore it was felt that it would be a mistake to threaten Italy with the loss of such a major part of her overseas possessions as this would unite opinion in Italy against Britain. It was in Britain's interest to maintain a divided Italy in the hope that this might provoke the Italians into a quarrel with Germany. The Foreign Secretary, Lord Halifax, therefore made it clear to Lord Lloyd on 20 June 1940 that it would be best for Britain simply to say that, because of Italy's unprovoked entry into the war, the British government reserved full liberty of action in respect of any engagements entered into with regard to the Mediterranean, North and East Africa and the Middle East. This would not preclude Britain from stirring up trouble for Italy in Libya.[10]

The capitulation of France had a dramatic effect on the naval and military balance in the Mediterranean and the Middle East. Together the French and British Mediterranean fleets had dominated the inland sea, and their armies in Algeria, Tunisia and Egypt had contained the Italian forces in Libya. Without France, Britain faced a serious Italian naval challenge in the Mediterranean and a major military threat to Egypt and the Sudan from Libya and Italian East Africa.

During those months of uncertainty in the summer of 1940 British political and military leaders were prepared to consider and occasionally sanction demands and schemes which previously they had rejected as undesirable or impracticable. Thus in late June and throughout July the Foreign Office, with the approval of the Colonial Office, attempted to follow up a suggestion that Hafiz Wahba had made more than once that Ibn Saud might be able to help the British in stirring up disaffection in Italian-controlled territory, especially Libya. Hafiz's idea was that Ibn Saud should influence some of the Libyan refugees in Saudi Arabia and neighbouring countries (presumably Ibn Saud intended to accomplish this through the medium of his two Tripolitanian advisers, Bashir al-Sadawi and Khalil al-Hud). Libyan refugees were scattered throughout the Middle East, from Tunisia and Chad to Syria and Iraq, in the interior of Oman and in the Yemen, but most were to be found in Egypt and the Sudan.

The permanent officials of the Foreign Office and the Colonial Office realised that Ibn Saud might demand a fee for rendering such a service. Sir John Shuckburgh, Deputy Under Secretary of State for the Colonies, worried that Ibn Saud might ask, for instance, for assurances on Palestine which might prove very embarrassing for the British. The last thing they wanted was 'to be manoeuvred into a new set of McMahon pledges' (a reference to the controversial written statements on the future of the Arab world made during the First World War by the British High Commissioner in Egypt, Sir Henry McMahon, to Shari Hussein of the Hejaz, to incite the revolt against the Turks).

C J Norton, head of the Egyptian Department in the Foreign Office, thought that the most the British could then offer in the way of encouragement to dissident Libyans, the Egyptians and Ibn Saud was 'that we think Libya should be freed from the domination of Italy ...'. The Foreign Office was aware, however, that General Headquarters, Middle East (GHQME) had their own plans for stirring up trouble for the Italians in Libya. When the Commander in Chief in the Middle East, General Wavell, curtly dismissed Hafiz Wahba's proposal at the end of July 1940, the Foreign Office dropped the matter.[11]

In fact the British military authorities in Egypt were aware already of the military potential of Libyan refugees, and were ready to exploit it. No doubt this was the main reason why Wavell rejected the idea of Ibn Saud's help as far as Libya was concerned, although Wavell suggested that if Ibn Saud's offer were genuine the latter could carry out his plan in the Yemen, where the situation was unsatisfactory for Britain. Despite the Imam's oppressive rule, the Foreign Office preferred the existing situation there to disorder which might lead to Italian intervention. A contributory factor might have been the divided state of Libyan exile politics and the decision of GHQME, for reasons of military expediency (as will be seen shortly), to side with the Cyrenaicans against the Tripolitanians. A number of Ibn Saud's closest advisers were Egyptians and Tripolitanians.

GENERAL WILSON, SAYYID IDRIS AND THE SANUSI ARAB FORCE

As fate would have it, the British military authorities in Egypt were soon to find themselves without the opportunity or the means for causing internal disturbances in Libya, and thereby hampering Italian military operations. The collapse of France meant that there would be no early offensive by French forces from Tunisia into Libya (although Free

French control of Chad was to offer opportunities for offensive action in the future). Once the bulk of Marshal Graziani's Italian army had been switched to the Egyptian front to face Britain's heavily outnumbered Western Desert Force, the prospects of an early British offensive into Libya appeared dim.

This severely affected the plans drawn up in 1939 for raising a tribal revolt in Libya (see Prologue), it having been been a cardinal rule of the Allies that they would not encourage a revolt except in conjunction with a military offensive into Libya. Otherwise it was feared that the Italians would be able to suppress the discontent, which would prejudice any tribal rising in the future. In addition, the decision of the Egyptian government not to declare war on Italy and Germany, in other words to maintain its policy of non-belligerency, effectively wrecked British plans for using the Frontier Brigade of the Egyptian Arab Legion as the nucleus around which a general tribal rising in Libya would be developed (known as the 'G Expansion Scheme').

Although at first GHQME had sought authorisation from the War Office (which they received on 19 June) to go ahead with the 'G Expansion Scheme' in the expectation that Egypt would enter the war against Italy, this scheme was quietly scrapped when the Egyptian position became clear.[12] The continuing desire to stir up trouble for the Italians in Libya, and the shortage of manpower in the Middle East in the summer of 1940, led the British military authorities in Egypt to accept with alacrity an offer made in late June by Sayyid Muhammad Idris al-Sanusi to help raise battalions of Sanusi tribesmen for service with the British forces against the Italians in Libya. The impressive speed with which both Sayyid Idris and the British military acted to establish the Sanusi Arab Force was due not only to the exigency of war, but also to the divided state of Libyan politics.

The joint advisory committee of Tripolitanian and Cyrenaican (Sanusi) emigré leaders, which had been set up in October 1939 to ensure a common approach to the war, never functioned properly. Strong personal differences between the leaders, dating back to the First World War, continued to sour relations between them. The Tripolitanian notables had always rebelled against the idea of Sanusi overlordship. Their repeated failure, however, to elect one of their own as overall leader (e.g. during the short-lived Tripolitanian Republic after the First World War and in 1939) and their overwhelming desire for independence drove them to accept, albeit reluctantly, the leadership of Sayyid Idris (as they had done before in July 1922 and October 1939). His authority as head of the Sanusi Order and his proven ability to secure political concessions from the Great Powers (e.g. the agreements with Britain and Italy during and after the First World War) had given him an unrivalled prominence in Libyan politics, which he had retained in exile.

After the outbreak of war between Britain and Italy, however, the fragile accord between Libyan leaders broke down completely as they failed to agree on a policy of co-operation with Britain. The Tripolitanian leaders believed, as did many others in the Middle East at the time, that the Axis powers were likely to win the war and that Britain could not survive. They were unwilling, therefore, to incur the wrath of Italy by siding with Britain in case this led to reprisals by the Italians at a later date. The Tripolitanians had not suffered to the same extent as the Sanusis of Cyrenaica under Italian rule. The former were more ambivalent than the latter in their attitude to the European invaders. Apart from the wholesale expropriation of land by the Italians, which had affected Tripolitania less than it had Cyrenaica, where there was a shortage of cultivable land, the Tripolitanian rebellion of 1922–23 was but a faint memory for Tripolitanians compared to the long and bitter guerilla war in Cyrenaica, which lasted from 1923 to 1932 and had such a traumatic effect on the Sanusi tribes.

Sayyid Idris, Lt. Colonel Bromilow (Assistant Military Secretary to General Wilson and later CO Sanusi Arab Force) and Shaikh en Nasr. By permission of Faraj Najem Collection.

Sayyid Idris, in contrast, had no compunction at all in the latter half of June 1940 in ignoring Tripolitanian objections, and volunteering to co-operate with the British. The opportunity to strike a blow against the Italians, which might lead to the liberation of Libya, dictated his decision and overrode all other considerations.[13] But Sayyid Idris had to move quickly to outpace his enemies and, with British assistance, to achieve his aims. In a secret meeting on 1 July 1940 with General Wilson and Lt. Col. Bromilow (Assistant Military Secretary to GOCBTE and later CO Sanusi Arab Force), Sayyid Idris explained that he would be prepared to support any plan which the British might have for raising battalions of Sanusis to fight the Italians, if the British observed his conditions. They must undertake the organisation and control of this force (the implication being that the Egyptians should not be involved). Certain prisoners should be released (this could be a reference to the camps of Sanusi refugees in Egypt and the Sudan), and the whole project should go ahead immediately.

The hard-pressed British military leaders, in Cairo and in London, eagerly complied with these conditions. On 5 July 1940 the War Office granted permission to General Wilson's request to raise up to ten battalions of Sanusi tribesmen from among the refugees in Egypt, subject to the approval of the Egyptian government. There were to be five hundred men per battalion, with British and Arab officers. Two battalions were to be raised at once. The Egyptians gave their grudging approval to the scheme on 9 July on the condition, which the British accepted, that they did not have to render any assistance and thereby prejudice their relations with Italy.[14]

Sayyid Idris took the first public step towards the recruitment of a Sanusi military force when he invited Cyrenaican and Tripolitanian leaders to a meeting in Cairo (in the Garden City) on 8 August 1940 to discuss the assistance to be rendered to the British. Aware of Tripolitanian opposition to co-operation with Britain, Sayyid Idris presented them with a fait accompli when he convened the meeting a day early, on 7 August, and made an opening address in which he appealed to his countrymen to take part in the military operations for the liberation of Libya. The assembled leaders, who were mostly Sanusis from Cyrenaica, overwhelmingly endorsed the course of action proposed by Sayyid Idris.

On 9 August 1940 General Wilson told the emigré leaders the terms of their service and requested that both the British and the Libyans should co-operate to carry out this project 'with sincerity and loyalty, so that the Arabs may be enabled to regain their freedom and take

Cyrenaican shaikhs meeting with Sayyid Muhammad Idris al-Sanusi, Garden City, Cairo, 7 August 1940. By permission of Faraj Najem Collection.

back their lands from the Italian oppressors and to restore their independence'. The Libyan leaders signalled their agreement by passing a series of resolutions which called for participation in the war alongside the British forces, and under the banner of the Sanusi amirate.[15] They reiterated their desire for a Sanusi amirate of Cyrenaica and Tripolitania under the Amir Idris (the latter was recognised as such by his own people, if not by the Great Powers).

There was to be another joint advisory council to the Amir. A provisional Sanusi government and an official recruiting board were to be set up. Britain was to finance the Sanusi war effort and administration. Lastly, the Amir was given the authority to make political, financial and military agreements or treaties with the British in order to further the cause of Libya's independence. The document embodying these resolutions was signed by 21 of the 25 Libyan emigré leaders at the meeting, and presented as a petition to General Wilson. It was subsequently endorsed by Libyan emigrés in Syria, the Sudan and Tunisia.

Two of the most important Tripolitanian shaikhs, Ahmad al-Murayyid and Ahmad al-Suwayhili (or Shutaywi), arrived too late in the day, after Wilson's speech on 9 August, to sway the assembled Libyan leaders against co-operation with the British. They registered their disagreement by refusing to endorse the resolutions and, with several other Tripolitanian leaders, withdrew from the proceedings. In order to disguise their reluctance to affront Italy by siding with Britain at a time when an Axis victory appeared likely, al-Suwayhili and al-Murayyid were later to employ specious reasoning to justify their action. They claimed that they were opposed to Libyan participation in the fighting until they had extracted from the British government a promise that after the war Libya would become independent.[16] They criticised Sayyid Idris for not obtaining such a pledge from the British, for not consulting the joint advisory committee before deciding to collaborate with the British, and for labelling all those who desired to fight as Sanusis without first consulting them.

The Tripolitanian shaikhs' final objection hinted at a more fundamental reason, apart from not wanting to fight Italy, for the refusal of al-Murayyid and al-Suwayhili to co-operate in the raising of the

Sayyid Idris with British officers and NCOs, and Libyan NCOs, of the Sanusi/Libyan Arab Force. By permission of Faraj Najem Collection.

Monument to the raising of the Sanusi/Libyan Arab Force, located in Giza, Cairo, on the road to Alexandria.
By permission of Russell McGuirk Collection.

Sanusi Arab Force. They did not acknowledge Sanusi overlordship, which participation in the Sanusi Arab Force would imply. This would seem to be confirmed by the fact that al-Murayyid and al-Suwayhili, with other Tripolitanian shaikhs, later established a Tripolitanian Committee and requested that they be allowed to form a separate Tripolitanian army. They offered even to co-operate with the British on the same terms as those accepted by Sayyid Idris, but without acknowledging his leadership.

The British would not recognise the Tripolitanian Committee (which would give the Tripolitanians a platform from which to put forward separate political demands) and continued to urge reconciliation on Tripolitanians and Cyrenaicans, though without much success. Through their own intransigence these Tripolitanian leaders had excluded themselves at an early stage from the counsels of the British authorities in Egypt, and thereby left the way clear for Sayyid Idris to become the sole spokesman for Libyan (or rather Sanusi) aspirations.[17]

Sayyid Idris was not slow in utilising his renewed authority as Amir to try and negotiate agreements with the British government which would help bring about Libyan independence. Following up the petition (embodying the resolutions of the Cairo meeting of 9 August) to General Wilson earlier in the month, Sayyid Idris on 27 August 1940 requested the British to accede to the petition. He also called on the British to announce, as soon as possible, that after Libya had been conquered Britain would assume a protectorate over the country. It was claimed that a declaration along these lines would have an extremely favourable effect not only on Libyans, but on other 'oppressed' peoples under Italian rule and throughout the Muslim world.

It was admitted by Sayyid Idris that an independent Libya would be too weak to stand alone in the modern world. It would need a strong power not only to protect it from external enemies but also to help develop the country with financial, economic and military aid. Sayyid Idris would only trust Britain to undertake this responsibility because 'Great Britain is the only Power which can help countries to advance and build nations up, and which preserves the rights of the weak' (Egypt, Iraq and Palestine were cited as examples).

He rejected the idea of a League of Nations protectorate over Libya because he did not think the League capable of preserving the independence of its own members, let alone that of other countries.

Sayyid Idris was making a shrewd bid for British support for his aim of a Sanusi amirate of Libya, under a Muslim Amir (i.e. himself) acceptable both to the Libyans and the British; this would be self-governing and dependent upon external aid and protection.[18] In exchange for this help the obvious implication was that the British would gain another ally in the Middle East, one who would be prepared to co-operate politically and militarily with Britain in the future. Sayyid Idris sought a reassurance from the British, however, that in the event of the war ending before they had conquered Libya, they would try to persuade the Egyptian government to grant the Sanusis land in Egypt. If this proved impossible then the Sanusis should be allowed to settle in another friendly Arab country.[19]

RENEWING THE DEBATE ON THE FUTURE OF LIBYA

Sayyid Idris's initiative led to a renewal of the debate within the British government over the desirability of a declaration on the future of Libya, an issue which had been dormant since June 1940. The renewed debate took place against the background of Italian military advances in Africa and the Balkans in the late summer and autumn of 1940. The British suffered the loss of Kassala and other Sudanese and Kenyan frontier posts, and incursions into northern Kenya in July; the fall of British Somaliland in mid-August; the invasion of Egypt in mid-September, and the invasion of Greece at the end of October 1940.

These setbacks had a significant influence on the discussions over Libya. In early September Sir Miles Lampson relayed to the Foreign Office the demand by Sayyid Idris for a declaration by Britain of a protectorate over Libya. At the same time, in answer to an earlier inquiry from the Foreign Office, Lampson gave a brief report on the preparations for raising a tribal revolt in Libya. He said that the British military authorities in Egypt had refrained from action within Libya, except for establishing contact with the tribes, and would continue to do so until the British forces launched an offensive into Libya in order not to prejudice the chances of a revolt in the future. Lampson confirmed also the raising of the Sanusi Arab Force.[20]

Lampson seems to have had an ambivalent attitude to the idea of a British protectorate over Libya. He did not rule out the idea altogether, but he did not appear to favour giving pledges in advance of events (i.e. the British conquest of Libya). He outlined to the Foreign Office some of the difficulties involved in meeting Sayyid Idris's demands. He pointed out that Sanusi influence was much stronger in Cyrenaica than in Tripolitania, which was illustrated by Tripolitanian opposition to the Sanusis over British recruitment of Libyans. If the British decided to offer independence to the Libyans, then the former would have to work out the details with the rival factions of the latter in Egypt. The British would also have to take into account possible Egyptian aspirations concerning Libya in the event of Egypt entering the war against the Axis. These considerations led Lampson to suggest that all that was necessary at this stage was for the British to contemplate what political inducements they might offer to the Libyans regarding their future.[21]

The Foreign Office began to be aware of the dilemma facing them. The head of the Egyptian Department, C J Norton, admitted that there was much in what Lampson said about not giving pledges in advance of events. In addition it had yet to be decided what Britain should do with Libya if she occupied that country. Britain would have to consider whether it would be politic to deprive Italy of all her African possessions, or simply to demilitarise them. If Italy were to lose her colonies then the question would arise whether Libya should become a British protectorate or mandated territory, or a condominium with Egypt. Alternatively, should the whole country, or just part of it, be annexed by Egypt? There were also strategic and economic factors which had to be taken into account. Norton did not think it was yet possible to reach a definite conclusion on this matter.

Set against these problems was the stark fact that if the British wanted the Sanusis to fight alongside them against Italy, 'then presumably it could only be on the understanding that Cyrenaica was to be liberated from Italian colonisation'. Norton proposed to resolve this dilemma by instructing Lampson that the British were not yet prepared to enter into discussions with the Sanusi leaders on the future of Libya, but that the British must encourage the Sanusis to believe that once Britain had conquered Libya, 'they will have a say in the future of their country'. The superintending Under Secretary of State

'BEATING THE AIR': JUNE–OCTOBER 1940

Marshal Graziani, Commander of the Italian Army in Libya, photographed at Fifth Army headquarters after his capture, 30 April 1945. Marshal Graziani conducted the early Italian campaign in 1940. By permission of The Imperial War Museum NA 24746.

for Eastern, Egyptian and Far Eastern Departments, Sir Horace Seymour, agreed with Norton that this was the line they should pursue. Seymour identified another dimension of this problem, which was that any suggestion of an Egyptian protectorate of Libya would discourage the Sanusis, who were likely to be more useful to the British than the Egyptians when it came to fighting the Italians.[22] The question of whether, in Norton's words, 'a sort of Limehouse campaign of promises to the Libyans would powerfully assist our military defensive in the Western Desert', assumed a far greater urgency following the Italian invasion of Egypt on 13 September 1940 and the advance of Marshal Graziani's forces to Sidi Barrani by 16 September. (Norton was here employing a synonym for the denunciation of one's political opponents, after David Lloyd George's vociferous defence of his budget in the Limehouse parish of the East End of London in 1909.)

For the next two and a half months the Italians were to encamp in Egyptian territory facing much smaller British forces. In these circumstances it seemed vital for Britain to ensure the continued co-operation of both the Egyptian government and Sayyid Idris and the Sanusis in the defence of Egypt. There was a division of opinion, however, between the 'men-on-the- spot' in Egypt (Wavell and Lampson) backed by the Foreign Office, and the 'men-in-committee' in Whitehall (Lloyd and Eden on the Ministerial Committee on Military Policy in the Middle East), over how best to achieve this object.

Sayyid Idris took advantage of the new military situation in the Western Desert. On 17 September 1940, he renewed his pressure on the British to make a declaration stating their intention of establishing a protectorate over an autonomous Sanusi amirate of Libya after the war. Sayyid Idris claimed that this was necessary in order to persuade Libyans to join the Sanusi Arab Force, which was under recruitment, and to counter Italian attempts to win over leading members of the Sanusi family still residing in Libya. Although Lampson was aware of the need to continue to encourage Sayyid Idris and the Sanusis, there were other considerations which had to be allowed for. One of these was the French interest in western Libya (Tripolitania). Another and, in Lampson's mind, far more important factor was the possibility of Egyptian aspirations in Libya.

In late September and early October 1940, Lampson reported to the Foreign Office that, following the Italian invasion of Egypt, there was a greater prospect of Egypt entering the war. If this occurred, then Lampson felt that Britain would have to discuss with the Egyptian government the questions of Libyan co-operation and the future of Libya. Lampson's advice, therefore, was that it was probably best to delay any decision on meeting the wishes of Sayyid Idris until it was clear whether or not Egypt would declare war on the Axis powers. Meanwhile, the British could only tell Sayyid Idris that the matter was receiving due consideration and continue to encourage him by holding out the prospect of the Sanusis recovering their lands in Libya.[23]

While the Foreign Office accepted Lampson's advice, they were impeded in implementing it by the desire of the Colonial Office and the War Office for more immediate measures to counter the Italian threat. In late September and early October 1940, by virtue of their respective responsibilities in the Middle East, Lloyd and Eden urged different courses of action on Halifax with regard to the future of Libya.[24]

Lloyd had become almost a 'supplementary Foreign Secretary' with his advocacy of various schemes for rallying the sympathies of the Muslim world. In his opinion there was a grave danger that the Muslims might succumb to Axis propaganda if some positive steps were not taken to re-establish the British position in the Middle East. Lloyd favoured British concessions on Palestine and supported in principle some form of Arab unity. (He thought that the Palestine problem could be solved only through some form of federation with the neighbouring states of Transjordan and Syria.)[25]

Unlike Lampson and the Foreign Office, Lloyd favoured Britain making the immediate declaration desired by Sayyid Idris, even though this might add to Egyptian hesitations about entering the war. A note of bitterness had crept into Lloyd's attitude towards Egypt since June 1940, when he had advocated that Libya should become an autonomous province of Egypt. By late September 1940, Lloyd was remarking that as Britain was doing all the fighting the Egyptians 'could hardly ask the British for more than to protect the integrity of their own land'. He was worried that if the British delayed a decision on the declaration demanded by Sayyid Idris until Egypt entered the war, then the British would have to discuss the future of Libya with Egypt and would be obliged to concede the Egyptian claim to control Libya. If this occurred, then Lloyd feared that Sayyid Idris would turn against the British.

Lampson and the Foreign Office did not share Lloyd's concern at the possibility that Sayyid Idris might defect to the Italians. Lampson pointed out on 10 October 1940 that Sayyid Idris could never be sure of striking a bargain with the Italians. Moreover, Sayyid Idris would prefer Egyptian suzerainty over Libya to Italian domination, provided the Egyptian government confirmed the promise made to him already about the restoration of Sanusi lands in Libya. Lampson said that he was doing all he could to encourage Sayyid Idris in order to prevent him from 'cooling off'–'short of committing ourselves to promises regarding [the] disposal of Libya which we may be unable or unwilling to implement at a later stage of the war'.[26]

Lampson and Wavell still thought that the British should delay a decision on this matter until the issue of Egypt's entry into the war became clearer, and in the meantime to encourage Sayyid Idris. The 'men-on-the-spot' were supported in their belief by the Foreign Office. The latter was not convinced by Lloyd's argument that Britain would be obliged to give Libya to Egypt in the event of the Egyptians declaring war on Italy.[27]

Lloyd was prevented in the summer and autumn of 1940 from pursuing the policies he advocated on Palestine, Arab unity and Libya by the opposition of the Foreign Office, and in the case of the first two issues by the bulk of the War Cabinet. Lloyd also believed that when the war ended and Britain emerged victorious, she would be in a position to dictate a peace settlement for the Middle East. His ideas on Arab Federation and Libya were precursors of that settlement, with its serious implications for France's position in the Levant and Italy's presence in North Africa.[28]

The views of the Foreign Office on this question were to be modified only slightly by the intervention in early October 1940 of the War Office. As in June 1940, the pro-Arab Lloyd and his friend Sir Leonard Woolley would seem to have co-operated in the autumn of 1940 to try and impose their views on the Foreign Office. Whereas Lloyd had switched his support from an Egyptian to a Sanusi solution for Libya by late September, Woolley continued to favour a scheme whereby Libya should become an autonomous province of Egypt. They were both convinced, however, that the British government should make an immediate declaration. This would appear to have been their main concern, rather than the exact terms of the declaration.

Lloyd and Woolley were strong advocates of a British propaganda crusade in the Middle East, pending British military victories, as a means of countering the harmful effects which Axis military triumphs and propaganda were having on Britain's standing with the Arabs. They thought that British propaganda could only succeed if it gave proof of Britain's complete confidence in her ultimate victory, and if this also embodied a policy of which the Arabs could approve. Hence the emphasis by Lloyd and Woolley on Britain making declarations on such issues as Palestine, Arab unity and Libya, which would contain concessions to the Arabs.

Woolley pressed his views about Libya on the Foreign Office through the medium of his Secretary of State at the War Office, Eden, and through Churchill's personal assistant, Major Desmond Morton. In the aftermath of the Italian conquest of British Somaliland in mid-August 1940, which had come as a shock to British public opinion, Woolley had drawn up a memorandum in which he argued that this latest British reverse would damage Britain's position in the Middle East unless swiftly countered. (This document was not forwarded to the Foreign Secretary until early October 1940.)

Halifax seems to have agreed with Woolley's prediction that the Italian triumph would encourage the anti-British elements in Egypt and

Iraq, would accentuate the difficulties in the Yemen, and would undermine even further Saudi confidence in Britain. Woolley thought that this would be 'the right psychological moment for Britain to depart from its usual policy of saying nothing about post-war aims and make a clear declaration that in view of the nature of Italian rule in Libya, which was emphasised in British propaganda, it was morally impossible for Britain to leave Libya in Italian possession and that Britain had no desire or intention of territorial aggrandisement and that Britain proposed, and would further by all means, the establishment of Libya as an autonomous province of the Kingdom of Egypt.'

Woolley pointed out that the question of Libya's future would have to be faced eventually by Britain and that it would be less embarrassing to make a voluntary declaration immediately, rather than being forced into making one later. Woolley claimed that the Sanusis would welcome such a solution as it would give them freedom under a Muslim government and encourage them to take an active part in the war. As for the Egyptians, Woolley held that it would appeal 'to the vanity of King Farouk and to the cupidity of Wafdist office-seekers, and should go far towards solving the Egyptian question. Incidentally, it might relegate to the background the claims of Egypt to the Sudan.'

Woolley was also convinced that it would be welcomed by Pan-Arab circles in Egypt, Arabia and Iraq as a practical step towards Arab unity. (As evidence of this he cited the Saudi proposal on these lines, made by Hafiz Wahba in June 1940.) It would also successfully counter Axis propaganda among the Pan-Arabs. Finally, Woolley thought such a declaration would largely offset the damage to British prestige which had been sustained as a result of the fall of British Somaliland to the Italians. It would confirm to the Arabs that their interests were bound up with those of Britain, and it would win the active support of the Muslim world for the British cause.

Initially, the political and permanent heads of the Foreign Office, Halifax and Cadogan, were favourably inclined towards Woolley's proposal. The Permanent Under-Secretary remarked on 5 October 1940 that they should consider what would have the greatest propaganda effect, first in Egypt, and second in the rest of the Muslim world. The Sanusis, who were small in number, would have to accept the suzerainty of the King of Egypt. However, the permanent officials of the Egyptian and Eastern Departments, under the wary eye of Sir Horace Seymour, managed to convince Halifax and Cadogan that this was not a suitable moment for Britain to make a statement of 'peace aims' on Libya. Apart from the fact that the Italians were 'well-entrenched on

Egyptian soil', the Foreign Office seemed now to believe that Britain faced a real dilemma as to whether it would help her cause in Egypt by promising Libya to the Libyans (and it was pointed out that the Sanusis did not represent all Libyans), or among Libyans by promising that Libya would become a province, even autonomous, of Egypt. Halifax was prepared, however, to suspend final judgment on this question until Eden had returned from his visit to the Middle East (which lasted from 11 October to 8 November 1940).[29]

The enforced delay in reaching a decision on this question only fed the doubts of the Foreign Office about the wisdom of making an immediate declaration on the future of Libya. A V Coverley-Price (Eastern Department) thought that, if possible, Britain should avoid making a declaration which would commit her to a line of action which she might not be able to follow later, and he referred to the controversial pledges given by Britain to Jews and Arabs during the First World War, and the difficulties these had caused. He warned that if Britain made a promise about Libya then she would find it hard to avoid making similar promises on Palestine, Syria or other controversial areas. He added, 'It often paid to keep people guessing as to one's intentions. A promise or declaration could be twisted or misinterpreted and if nothing worse happens, someone is nearly always disappointed.'

Coverley-Price was worried that the Axis powers might make political capital out of any British declaration, saying that it was just another empty promise. He questioned also whether the incorporation of Libya within Egypt would appeal to Pan-Arab circles in Iraq. Nuri al-Said's idea of Arab Federation did not seem to include Egypt. There were geographical reasons for this, apart from Iraq's desire for leadership, and the aggrandisement of Egypt might seem to offer the possibility of a larger federation in which Egypt, not Iraq, would predominate. Coverley-Price was against Britain following the example of German propaganda which appealed 'to the baser instincts of the human race by playing on the vanity and cupidity of Egyptian office seekers'.[30] He recommended that if Britain had to follow the Nazi example at all it should be, if possible, to seek a cheap victory somewhere. 'A success, however small, was more likely to inspire confidence in the future than any promises, appeals or declarations.' In this concluding remark Coverley-Price had identified the crux of the matter, which was recognised both by the Foreign Office and by Eden during his tour of the Middle East. As Cadogan pointed out, until Britain had a success or at least halted 'our tale of failure' then Britain's promises would not have much effect. 'If we could show success, we could put a good price on any promise. As I have often suggested, "intense diplomatic activity" is beating the air unless backed by military prowess.'[31]

Within a week of his arrival in the Middle East, Eden had reached the same conclusion as the Foreign Office. As he informed Churchill on 16 October 1940, 'Politically [the] whole situation here would be immeasurably improved if we were able to gain some military success.' At first Eden was under the impression that action against Italian East Africa offered the most likely prospect of success in the near future. By early November, however, Eden learnt that Wavell had approved General Sir Richard O'Connor's plan for a 'five days raid' on the Italian positions around Sidi Barani. As the month of November progressed, the attention of the British was to become increasingly focused on the coming military operations in the Western Desert. The issue of an immediate declaration on the future of Libya was to recede into the background, as it became clear that all would depend on the success or failure of O'Connor's small force.[32]

In fact there was to be very little speculation on the future of Libya from late October 1940 to early January 1941, as the British were preoccupied with the military crisis in the Eastern Mediterranean. In these circumstances 'the men-on-the-spot' (Lampson and Wavell) and the Foreign Office became confirmed in their belief that it was good policy to refrain for the present from making any declarations as to the future of Libya. The only encouragement they were prepared to give to Sayyid Idris was to express the vague hope that 'the Arabs may regain their freedom and take back their lands from the Italian oppressor and restore their independence once more'.[33] Doubt was expressed over whether it was in the interests of either Sayyid Idris or Libya for him to try to establish a political sovereignty over the whole of Libya, which would be based solely on his religious influence, in the form of a Sanusi amirate.[34] It was recognised, however, that Cyrenaicans and Tripolitanians might be opposed to Egyptian rule.[35] Yet there was an understandable reluctance to see Britain assume a protectorate over Libya.[36]

The steadfast opposition of the Foreign Office to pressure from Arab leaders, and their sympathisers within the British government, to meet their different aspirations, whether on Arab unity, Palestine or Libya, did not last long. Signs of a weakening in its stance can be detected soon after Eden was appointed Foreign Secretary in December 1940. Halifax had never been enthusiastic about a policy of support for Pan-Arabism. In contrast Eden had shown a proclivity for treating individual problems in the Middle East not on their own, but in a general regional context (e.g. his approach to Palestine in 1936–37).

Already, before succeeding Halifax, Eden had begun to develop his thinking on the future of Libya. In putting Woolley's proposal to Halifax on 7 October 1940, Eden had expressed a reservation that perhaps some Libyans did not want to become a province, even an autonomous one, of Egypt. On 18 October, in conversation with a local commissioner in Haifa who hinted that if the Arabs had a cause to fight for they might participate in the war, Eden 'asked whether a declaration that we intended to free Libya from Italian rule without further defining the future, would help at all.' The local commissioner replied, 'Yes, definitely.'[37]

chapter 2
'GOOD DAYS IN AFRICA'
NOVEMBER 1940–APRIL 1941

> We all feel that we are having our good days in Africa but that there is much rough weather ahead in [the] Central Mediterranean and Balkans.
>
> Eden diary entry for 29/1/41[38]

THE FIRST BRITISH OCCUPATION OF CYRENAICA

EDEN'S RETURN to the Foreign Office on 23 December 1940 coincided with a significant improvement in Britain's military fortunes in the Mediterranean, and a corresponding decline in those of Italy. These developments were to have important political repercussions in the Middle East and in Italy, influencing the debate within the British government on the future of Libya when it was revived in early 1941.

The Greek success in repulsing an Italian invasion; the devastating blow which the British struck Italian naval power at Taranto on the night of 11–12 November 1940 (which eliminated even the local predominance of the Italian navy in the Central Mediterranean); the turning of a 'five days raid' against the Italian positions around Sidi Barani into a major British victory in mid-December 1940, ending the Italian threat to Egypt and opening the way to the British invasion of Cyrenaica in early 1941 – all changed the military balance in the Mediterranean and demonstrated the ability of Britain and her allies to defend her vital interests in the region.

This had a salutary effect throughout the Middle East. In Egypt the situation stabilised, although there was still much disagreement within the Egyptian ruling circle as to the degree of co-operation to be given to Britain (there was an abortive army officers' conspiracy to stage an anti-British uprising). The steady build-up of British forces in Egypt, however, ensured continued security for Britain's vital interests in the country. British victories in the Mediterranean, and later in the Red Sea, helped prevent the Saudis from abandoning their watchful, waiting attitude towards the war. In Palestine the situation remained calm, at least on the surface. In Syria the Vichy regime patiently awaited developments. It was only in Iraq that the British continued to face serious difficulties. By the autumn of 1940 the British government had become convinced that the Prime Minister of Iraq, Rashid Ali al-Gaylani, backed by the ex-Mufti of Jerusalem and the Iraqi army, was intent on aligning Iraq with the Axis.

This constituted a serious threat to Britain's position in the Middle East, given the importance of Iraq for imperial communications and as a source of oil. Consequently the British made a determined effort to oust Rashid Ali from power and replace him with a more pro-British leader such as Nuri al-Said.

In order to help bolster the position of the Regent, Prince Abd al-Illah, the Foreign Minister, Nuri al-Said, and other pro-British politicians in Iraq, vis-à-vis Rashid Ali and the pro-Axis faction, the Foreign Office early in 1941 considered making a significant concession to the Pan-Arabs. The new head of the Eastern Department, C W Baxter (probably with the support of Eden and Cadogan) informed the Colonial Office on 20 January 1941 that the Foreign Office had been 'giving some thought to the desirability of making some declaration on policy covering the Middle East'. Its main purpose would be 'not to win over the anti-British extremists, but to show our friends in the Middle East exactly what our views and intentions are towards the Arab world.'

Baxter thought that any such declaration would have to go further than a vague statement of British sympathy for Arab aspirations for independence and unity. Britain would have to declare and show, as a matter of policy, her active support for Pan-Arabism. For the moment, however, the Foreign Office was reluctant to alter its traditionally reserved attitude towards Pan-Arabism, and Eden had to wait until the early summer of 1941, when the military situation had undergone a radical change, to follow a more pro-Arab line in the Middle East. This was the background against which, in early 1941, the Foreign Office considered various demands for concessions to the Arabs over the future of Libya.[39]

Mussolini's bid for supremacy in the Mediterranean in his 'parallel war' against Britain had resulted in military disaster at Taranto, in the Albanian mountains and in the Western Desert. Italy's quest for great-power status had been effectively ended. The Fascist regime had suffered the most damaging blow to its prestige since the rout of the Italian 'volunteer' divisions at Guadalajara in 1937. It had received the greatest shock to its internal stability since the Matteotti crisis of 1924.

The possibility that Italy might seek an early peace became a subject of general speculation in late 1940 and early 1941, and resulted in a struggle between Britain and Germany for the allegiance of Italy, reminiscent of the period of non-belligerence. Hitler was to triumph in the short term, averting an Italian defection from the Axis by his swift commitment of the Luftwaffe and Rommel's Afrika Korps to the Mediterranean, and the direction of the Italian war effort in that theatre. It was not until the spring of 1941, however, that the Germans managed to stabilise the military situation in the Mediterranean through their successes in the Balkans and North Africa, and to check the dissolution of Mussolini's power which had begun during the winter.

In the interim, the internal crisis in Italy had led many in the Italian army and navy to consider the idea of a coup, and had created the disaffection within the Fascist party which was to lead eventually to Mussolini's dismissal in July 1943 and the downfall of the regime. It was this discontent within the establishment, and disillusionment among large sections of the public with the progress of the war, that the British sought to exploit in the winter of 1940–41.[40]

In mid-December 1940, following the victory at Sidi Barani and the expulsion of the Italian forces from Egypt, the British Chiefs of Staff defined their strategy with regard to Italy. It was too early to tell how the situation in Italy would develop, but Britain's aim was to persuade Italy to defect from the Axis before Germany could intervene to prevent an Italian betrayal and entrench herself in Italy. If Britain failed in this then she must bring about a complete Italian military collapse and the overthrow of Mussolini's government.

Britain's immediate objective was 'to eliminate Italy from the war as soon as possible. To achieve this, we must intensify to the maximum our military and economic pressure, at the same time endeavouring by every stratagem of propaganda and subversive activity to detach the Italian people, armed forces and colonies from Germany and to bring about an overthrow of the present fascist government and rally as many anti-German forces as possible under some such figure as the Prince of Piedmont or the Duke of Aosta.' In other words, Britain would press Italy as hard as possible on the military front but at the same would try to seduce her with propaganda, the main thrust of which would be that Britain would not impose harsh terms on Italy if the latter renounced the German alliance and overthrew the Fascist government.[41]

An important element of British strategy towards Italy would seem to have been the encouragement of a Free French-type solution for the Italian colonies in Africa. This is borne out by the proposals in early

1941 for a British guarantee of Italy's future in Eritrea and Somalia, and a Free Italian colony in Cyrenaica or Eritrea. The idea, however, of a 'peaceful Italy' retaining these colonies appears to have begun to gestate in British minds in mid-December 1940 when the Foreign Office, in considering the policy towards Italy outlined by the Chiefs of Staff, contemplated the possible armistice terms which Britain might offer Italy in the event of the latter seeking a peace.

Sir Alexander Cadogan and Sir Orme Sargent did not think that this was yet a practical possibility, but in identifying Britain's central requirements in any armistice with Italy they neglected to refer to Libya, Eritrea and Somalia.[42] Italy would be obliged to evacuate Ethiopia, Albania and the Dodecanese only. This seemed to imply that Italian forces and administrators would be allowed to remain in Libya, Eritrea and Somalia. This is comprehensible if it is remembered that in mid-December 1940 the British were not yet in possession of these territories, and intended only to carry out limited operations against the Italians in Africa in the winter of 1940–41. Cadogan and Sargent had more faith, however, in the efficacy of military measures than in propaganda in forcing the Italians to the peace-table, and preferred to 'wait-and-see' what happened on the military front before deliberating further on the terms to be offered to Italy.[43]

There were, therefore, two major influences competing with each other to determine British policy towards Libya in early 1941. One was the question of the desirability of placating Arab opinion by favouring an Arab solution for Libya. The other consideration was the possibility of securing Italy's exit from the war by, among other things, guaranteeing her continued presence in Libya. As General O'Connor's 13th Corps advanced into Cyrenaica in January 1941 in pursuit of the remnants of the Italian 10th Army, the British government was forced to face the problems raised by the disintegration of Italian rule in eastern Libya.

There was no disagreement in British military and political circles in London and Cairo about the immediate practical needs of the situation. The swift conclusion of the campaign in Cyrenaica confronted the British in early February 1941 with the task of administering the newly occupied enemy territory. General Wavell had given prior consideration to this question and proposed to the War Office on 25 January 1941, in concert with his Chief Political Officer, Sir Philip Mitchell, that a military government be set up in Cyrenaica (and in any other Italian colonies occupied by the British). This would follow the forms used in the Middle East during and towards the end of the First World War.

Wavell's previous experience under General Allenby in Palestine and Syria had impressed on him the importance of ensuring that policy did not conflict with military exigencies. This meant that the final decision on all matters of policy and form of government had to be taken by the Commander in Chief himself. Wavell proposed to appoint a military governor to Cyrenaica, 'the occupation following the general principles laid down by chapter 14 of the Manual of Military Law (based on the Hague Convention of 1907), with the necessary modifications on account of colonial conditions'.[44] Wavell intended to delegate the actual organisation and operation of the administration to Sir Philip Mitchell, in accordance with the policy that he, Wavell, had laid down (Mitchell would appoint a Deputy Chief Political Officer, DCPO, to assist the Military Governor).[45]

Wavell's proposed arrangements were approved in London by 20 February 1941, and it was decided that the War Office should be the department with overall responsibility for the administration of the occupied territories. As the Lord Privy Seal, C R Attlee, explained to the War Cabinet, 'The Foreign Office is not suitably organised to direct an administration, and if the Colonial Office were put in charge of any of the enemy territories, we should be suspected of seeking to incorporate them in our Empire.' The latter object was far from British minds in early 1941 (although Sir Miles Lampson entertained thoughts along these lines) but the establishment of military government in Cyrenaica brought with it political problems.[46]

The first British Military Administration (BMA) in Cyrenaica was in operation for too short a time (from 1 February to 31 March 1941) to accomplish anything more than the most elementary work of establishing an administration. It was soon made aware, however, of the main problem which would face the British in the future, that of reconciling their priorities with those of the Sanusis. The BMA, as a temporary administration, was concerned above all with restoring law and order and the local economy in Cyrenaica. The Sanusis were intent on reclaiming their lands and establishing their own government under their Amir, Idris.

The Military Governor of Cyrenaica, General Wilson, and the DCPO, Brigadier Longrigg, found Cyrenaica in considerable disorder. There had been substantial damage to communications, and about half the resident Italian population of 30,000 (including many senior fascist officials) had fled to Tripolitania in the wake of the Italian defeats in the Western Desert. Many Italians still remained, however, especially in the recently established agricultural settlements in the Jabal Akhdar.

The British administrators decided to follow the Italian Graziani's advice and to keep the Italian farms going in order to maintain a constant supply of food (in addition to that supplied by the British Army) to the population of Cyrenaica. This raised the problem of ensuring the security of the farms in case the Sanusi tribesmen decided to reclaim their land. There was a certain irony in the fact that it was the Sanusi refugee battalions, which had been raised in the summer of 1940 in order to help liberate Cyrenaica, that should be given the task of protecting the Italian settlers.[47]

British propaganda had also to change its tune, from previously inciting the local native population against the Italians to reconciling the Sanusi tribesmen to the presence of the surviving Italian settlers, in order to avoid reprisals and violence. Fortunately, Cyrenaica remained generally peaceful during the first British occupation. The Sanusis were well behaved and reasonable towards the Italians. Longrigg was unsure, however, how long the goodwill of the Arab population of Cyrenaica would last once it became clear that the British supported the continued Italian occupancy of the best agricultural land, and would punish anyone who tried to dispute it. Similarly, he was concerned at the local Arab reaction when the BMA proclaimed that it was a temporary regime which was more interested in economic order than in setting up an Arab amirate. The British fear of creating 'a second Palestine' in Cyrenaica proved unjustified. It was nipped in the bud by Rommel's recapture of the territory in the spring of 1941.[48]

SANUSI AND EGYPTIAN CLAIMS TO CYRENAICA

The Cyrenaican leadership in exile was disappointed that a Sanusi government was not established at once following Wavell's occupation of Cyrenaica. In mid-January 1941, Sayyid Idris had pressed for the Libyan Arab Force (as the Sanusi Arab Force had been renamed) to take a more active part in military operations in Cyrenaica in order to justify his repeated attempts to persuade the British to give an undertaking regarding a national government of Libya, of which he would become head.[49]

The British military and diplomatic authorities in Egypt were prepared to meet Sayyid Idris's demands for the expansion of the Libyan Arab Force (LAF), increased subsidies to the Sanusi shaikhs and discriminatory treatment for his enemies.[50] They refused, however, and were supported in this by the Foreign Office in London, to make any political commitment to Sayyid Idris on the future of Libya. General

Wilson replied on 22 January 1941 that he was prevented by the King's Commission from taking the mutual oath of loyalty (in the carrying out of their respective aims) proposed by Sayyid Idris. Wilson said that international law required the British military to act as trustees for the inhabitants of Libya until their future was decided by the peace treaty.

The new head of the Egyptian Department in the Foreign Office, C H Bateman, categorically dismissed Sayyid Idris's ambitions, and the part played by the Sanusis in the war, in a derisory fashion. He commented, 'All this vague talk of Senussi "National aspirations" is bunkum!' Bateman suspected that Sayyid Idris was probably trying to create the idea of a Sanusi nation because he wanted to become Amir of all Libya under British protection. If so he was 'opening his mouth too wide'. Bateman reiterated the opinion first expressed by Lampson in October 1940 (which the Egyptian Department had found 'new and interesting' at the time even though it was of doubtful provenance) that a political sovereignty based on the religious influence of Sayyid Idris was in 'no-one's interest'.

Libyan shaikhs attend the ceremony when Sayyid Idris visits a Libyan battalion, March 1941. By permission of the Australian War Memorial: Negative 006186.

Officers of the Libyan Arab Force battalions saluting Sayyid Idris, March 1941.
By permission of the Australian War Memorial: Negative 006180.

Bateman said that the Sanusis were only a puritan sect of Islam, and he cited as an authority Hassanein Bey's *Lost Oases* (1923). The Sanusis, Bateman argued, bore 'more or less the same relation to Islam as say, the Wesleyans bear to the Church of England. No-one would dream of setting up a Wesleyan autonomy (except in religious matters) and it is equally absurd to talk of setting up a temporal Senussi emirate.' The head of the Egyptian Department contrasted Sayyid Idris with Ibn Saud who had managed, according to Bateman, to establish his rule in Arabia because he was far from Europe and had no aggressive neighbours. Moreover, the Sanusi shrines of Kufra and Jaghbub could not be compared in importance to Mecca as a holy place. Bateman thought that the best the British could do for Sayyid Idris was to ensure him peace and religious domination in his own domain, southern Cyrenaica.[51]

There was concern also that if a Sanusi government headed by Sayyid Idris were to be established in Cyrenaica it would soon become a rival authority to the BMA, with whom it would be unlikely to co-operate. Longrigg thought that it would be a serious error to allow Sayyid Idris to return to Cyrenaica, although he admitted that initially it would be a great success. Longrigg feared, however, that Sayyid Idris would fall under strong anti-Italian influences, presumably from the tribal shaikhs. This would embarrass the British and might prejudice the future of Libya. Longrigg preferred to hold back 'this potentially useful card' and to play it later when Sayyid Idris could return to Cyrenaica on the basis of an agreed policy, which would be one of moderation and restraint.[52]

In addition, the British had to bear in mind Egyptian and Italian claims to Cyrenaica which (as will be seen later) were preoccupying British attention in early 1941. All these considerations ensured that when Sayyid Idris met Eden in Cairo, on or about 7 March 1941, he failed to obtain a more definite political declaration on Libya's future from the British. He was told that there could be no Sanusi participation in the administration, and that the British were not prepared to make any statement about the future of Cyrenaica (or, by implication, Libya) which would have to remain under the BMA until the peace conference dealt with the issue. When Sayyid Idris requested the next day that the Sanusis be represented at the peace conference Eden was non-committal, simply replying that Britain would 'take note' of his wishes. If Sayyid Idris had pressed the British on this point, however, they would have refused his request. Nevertheless, Sayyid Idris and the Sanusis remained pro-British, or rather anti-Italian and therefore wholeheartedly on the side of Britain in her war against Italy.[53]

It would appear that the most the British military authorities in Egypt were prepared to concede to Sayyid Idris was to allow the latter to appoint a representative to act as liaison and adviser to the British political officer at Jaghbub, following its capture by elements of 6th Australian Division on 21 March 1941. But Sayyid Idris's request to visit the Sanusi shrine seems to have been rejected by the CPO, Sir Philip Mitchell, who had become responsible for Sanusi affairs at this time.[54]

The Egyptian government was just as eager as Sayyid Idris to capitalise on British successes in the Western Desert in the winter of 1940–41. On 3 January 1941, as O'Connor's forces laid siege to Bardia, the Egyptian Prime Minister, Husain Sirri, informed Sir Miles Lampson that whatever views Britain might have about the future of Libya, Egypt had a special claim, both strategic and religious, to Jaghbub. On the eve of the fall of Tobruk on 21 January 1941, Husain Sirri had submitted a note to Lampson (drawn up by his Foreign Minister, Badawi Pasha), which stated that the Egyptian government, while reserving its position on the future status of Libya, put forward a claim to the immediate transfer to Egypt of all Libyan territory east of the Kitchener Line A of 1912. This included Jaghbub and Bardia within Egypt, although the Egyptian note made no specific reference to Bardia. Such a transfer would include within Egypt the inhabitants of the frontier region (mainly Sanusis) who had claimed Egyptian nationality between the wars in order to escape Italian persecution.

There were different reactions among British officials to the Egyptian claim to a restoration of the pre-1925 frontier with Libya, with the annexation of Bardia as well. After reporting to the Foreign Office the contents of the Egyptian note, Lampson commented that the Kitchener Line A was a more natural strategic frontier than the present border. The British had forced Egypt in 1925 to cede Jaghbub to Italy, in accordance with the Milner-Scialoja Agreement of 1920, while Egypt had been granted a slight extension of the frontier at Sallum, on the coast, to include a well. Lampson thought that whereas Egypt had a strong claim to Jaghbub, her 'moral claim' to Bardia was non-existent. He questioned also whether the Sanusi tribesmen of the frontier region, if now liberated from the Italians, would want to be under an Egyptian government.

The crux of the matter for Lampson, however, was that Egypt had done little so far in the war to justify such a gain in territory. The Kitchener Line A had, after all, been secured for Egypt as a result of British efforts on her behalf in negotiations with Turkey and Italy before the First World War. While Lampson was prepared to concede that the Egyptian government had fulfilled the letter of the Anglo-Egyptian Treaty of 1936 by carrying out their obligations since the outbreak of war with Germany, 'it can hardly be said,' he reminded the Foreign Office, 'that they have been enthusiastically loyal. Indeed, it may be said that King Farouk and Aly Maher have on occasion been definitely disloyal; and successive governments since the outbreak of the war have done little to stem the tide of defeatism.' Although the British victories had won over the wavering elements in Egypt, Lampson thought the Egyptian claim for immediate possession of the frontier lands 'is not without its impudent side in view of the refusal of the Egyptian Government (when pressed earlier – now it does not suit us) to declare war on Italy or to allow Egyptian troops to participate in the campaign even when Italian troops had invaded Egypt.'[55]

Italian soldiers captured by Australian forces at Bardia, January 1941.
By permission of The Imperial War Museum E 1579.

Lampson and Wavell favoured a non-committal British reply which would merely state that in accordance with international law enemy territory occupied by British forces would be governed by British military authorities for the duration of the war, and that the future status of such territory would be considered by the peace conference. Lampson concluded that Britain's final attitude towards Egyptian claims would depend on British 'political and strategic policy in the Mediterranean' after the war, which could not yet be determined.[56]

Opinion within the Foreign Office was sharply divided over how to respond to the Egyptian demand. Bateman thought that the claim by Egypt to Jaghbub was fully justified (and by implication that to Bardia also since this was to the east of Kitchener Line A), and that it was a question of 'righting a frontier wrong done to Egypt, through the agency of HMG when the latter was pursuing the mirage of Mussolini's goodwill.' He thought that if Britain wanted to keep Egypt 'sweet' (and the British were spending twenty-five million pounds a year to achieve this) then the least the British could do was to recognise the Egyptian claim 'to the lot of sand and drop of water called Jaghbub', which would cost Britain nothing.

Bateman proposed that Lampson should not only make his suggested reply to the Egyptian government, but also he should tell the Egyptian Prime Minister that Britain considered that the Egyptian claim

Sayyid Idris visiting captured Italian colonial (Libyan) troops, winter 1940–1.
By permission of Faraj Najem Collection.

was well-founded, even though no actual transfer of territory would take place until the peace conference. This would keep the Egyptians quiet until the end of the war, which was what Wavell desired.[57]

Lampson objected to Bateman's idea on the grounds that Sayyid Idris might object to the cession of Jaghbub to Egypt (although Lampson thought that this would probably not be a sufficient reason for not giving Jaghbub to Egypt) and that admitting the Egyptian claim to Jaghbub might lead to a further dispute with the Egyptians over Bardia. Bateman rightly suspected that Lampson was creating unnecessary difficulties (Lampson had his own ideas on Libya, as we shall see). The head of the Egyptian Department reiterated his conviction that Sayyid Idris had no claim to 'temporal leadership' in Libya and if he put this forward the British should 'stamp on this idea at once'. Bateman pointed out, in addition, that the Egyptians had not yet put forward a claim to Bardia.

However, he was overruled by Sir Horace Seymour who, having been ambivalent in mid-February towards the Egyptian claim, eventually sided with Lampson by mid-March 1941. Seymour in turn was supported by Cadogan and the Parliamentary Under-Secretary of State, R A Butler. The British did not want to get involved at this stage of the war in a wrangle with the Egyptians over the extent of frontier rectifications. There was thought to be a danger of this occurring because Bardia was within the territory claimed by Egypt. Accordingly, Lampson told the Egyptian Prime Minister on 21 March 1941, the day the British seized Jaghbub, that captured Libyan territory was to be put under

British military administration until the peace conference, when its fate would be decided.[58]

Concurrent with its discussion of Egyptian frontier claims the Foreign Office had been considering Egypt's claim to Cyrenaica as a whole. Egypt's most powerful advocate in Whitehall was Sir Leonard Woolley, who had returned to the attack on 6 February 1941 with a plan which embodied his personal views (not those of the War Office) on the future of Cyrenaica which he had prepared at the request of Sir Horace Seymour. Woolley had reiterated the argument that he had used following Italy's entry into the war in June 1940, and again after the fall of British Somaliland in mid-August. He adapted it, however, to fit the situation in February 1941. Instead of proposing, as before, that all Libya should become an autonomous province of Egypt, Woolley thought now that only Cyrenaica should be incorporated in Egypt, but that its cultural autonomy and Sayyid Idris's position as the 'Grand Sanusi' would have to be safeguarded. He called it 'a gratuitous act of generosity based on general principles of equity'.

In the circumstances of early 1941, according to Woolley, the offer would strengthen the hand of the then Prime Minister of Egypt, Husain Sirri, with King Faruk (thus countering the influence at court of Ali Mahir) since the offer would not have been made whilst Ali Mahir had been in power. Woolley predicted also that Egypt would become involved in administrative problems in Libya which might distract her attention for a time from the Sudan. The Arabs would welcome it (Ibn Saud, or rather Hafiz Wahba, had suggested it after all) and they would recognise that it was a disinterested act by Britain. The Pan-Arabs would see it as a step towards Arab union and would compare it favourably with the doubtful promises of the Axis powers. British strategic interests could be secured by ensuring that Britain was able to lease one or two air and/or sea bases in Cyrenaica.

Woolley recommended that the British government should make an immediate declaration that Cyrenaica would become an autonomous province of Egypt after the war, although without mentioning the position of Sayyid Idris or the leasing of bases by Britain. Until then the BMA would continue to administer Cyrenaica, and Sayyid Idris might assist in this. Unless the British made such a statement Woolley feared that they would be accused of aggrandisement. The Arabs would presume that, having installed the BMA, the British intended to annex Cyrenaica and this would be exploited by Axis propaganda. Apart from the above advantages, Woolley prophesied that a British declaration along these lines would be a grave blow to

Lieutenant General Sir Henry Maitland Wilson, Commander in Chief Cyrenaica, inspects men of the captured Tripolitanian Camel Corps, Libya, 25 February 1941.
By permission of The Imperial War Museum E 2100.

the Fascist regime in Italy, whose prestige was so bound up with imperial expansion. It would counter the rumour being spread by the Germans in occupied France, which played on the French suspicion that the British coveted France's colonial empire, that once the British had conquered Libya they would advance into French North Africa and would be reluctant to relinquish control of it.

The Foreign Office was impressed by Woolley's argument, especially as it ran counter to a proposal on Cyrenaica put forward less than a week later by the Prime Minister, Winston Churchill (see below). Beyond using Woolley's reasoning to put an effective brake on Prime Ministerial initiative, however, the Foreign Office showed no inclination to follow Woolley's main suggestion for an immediate declaration by Britain that Cyrenaica would become an autonomous province of Egypt after the war. As Geoffrey Thompson (Egyptian Department) pointed out, apart from anything else the war was not over and it was impossible to predict what was going to happen.[59]

Perhaps the most interesting aspect of Woolley's proposal for Cyrenaica's future was that it envisaged the establishment of British air and naval bases in the territory after the war. The successful British campaign in Cyrenaica had removed, albeit temporarily, the threat posed to Egypt and had enabled the British Mediterranean Fleet to dispute Axis control of the Central Mediterranean. For the first time the British were made aware of the vital importance of the airfields and ports of Bardia, Tobruk and Benghazi for Britain's defence of her position in the Middle East. The bolder observers began to think in terms of securing defence facilities in Cyrenaica not only for the present but for the future, although they differed over the best means to accomplish it.

Woolley thought that Egypt would grant Britain permission to lease a base or bases in Cyrenaica. He implied that if Italy regained control of Cyrenaica she would refuse all facilities to Britain, and the British would continue to suffer the disadvantage of having no airbase between Gibraltar and Egypt, with the exception of Malta. In contrast, Churchill seemed to believe that the one did not necessarily exclude the other. He indicated the drift of his thinking in his broadcast to Britain and the Empire on 9 February 1941 (his first for five months). He said that after the victories of Generals Wavell and Wilson, Egypt and the Suez Canal were now safe, and the port, the base and the airfields of Benghazi constituted 'a strategic point of high consequence to the whole of the war in the Eastern Mediterranean'. Two days later he was to broach the idea of setting up a Free Italian colony in Cyrenaica and raising an anti-fascist force to fight Mussolini. Unlike Woolley, Churchill envisaged a continued Italian presence in Cyrenaica which did not preclude British use of strategic facilities in that territory, at least during the war.[60]

CHURCHILL AND A FREE ITALIAN CYRENAICA

The speed with which O'Connor's forces had overrun Cyrenaica came as a surprise to Churchill. He had expected that it would be another three weeks before Benghazi and everything east of it would be in British possession, and occupied as a military and naval base. The capture of Benghazi on 6 February 1941 and O'Connor's annihilation of the Italian 10th Army at Beda Fomm on 6–7 February had opened the road to Tripoli, and with it the prospect of eliminating Italian dominion in North Africa. Neither Graziani nor the four remaining Italian divisions in Tripolitania were likely to stop the 13th Corps. The Italian war effort in North Africa had collapsed.[61]

It is ironic that it was Hitler rather than Churchill who realised the full implications for Britain of the Italian defeat. As the Führer explained to his generals on 3 February 1941, anticipating events, the loss of North Africa was militarily bearable, but the 'strong psychological repercussions' in Italy would be catastrophic. 'England could then put a pistol to Italy's breast and force it to choose between concluding peace and retaining its extra-European possessions, or exposing itself to the harshest air bombardment.'

The elimination of the Italian military presence in North Africa would also enable the British to free considerable forces for use in other theatres. Hitler concluded therefore that the Germans must hold Tripolitania, and he acted accordingly. He ordered the Luftwaffe air corps, then operating from Sicily and southern Italy against the British Mediterranean Fleet, to mount strikes against Benghazi and the British lines of communication in western Cyrenaica to slow O'Connor's advance. He decided to reinforce the Sperrverband (a light blocking force which he had proposed on 20 January 1941 to send to North Africa) with a Panzer division. He appointed General Rommel on 5 February 1941 to command German forces in Africa, and demanded that the Italians place their few mobile forces under German command. The Germans insisted on a forward defence in the Sirte Desert. Rommel arrived at Tripoli on 12 February and elements of the Sperrverband, acting as a blocking force, had been deployed west of El-Agheila by 16 February. The German war in Africa had begun, and the British had lost their fleeting opportunity to seize Tripoli, thereby striking a deadly blow against Italy, with its concomitant effects in French North Africa.[62]

Churchill and the Chiefs of Staff had consciously decided on 10 February 1941 that O'Connor's 13th Corps should not make any serious effort to capture Tripoli, despite the advice of O'Connor and Wavell. Britain's major effort in the Eastern Mediterranean was now to aid Greece and/or Turkey against the growing German threat in the Balkans. In his congratulatory telegram of 11 February 1941 to Wavell, Churchill ordered him to make himself secure in Cyrenaica and concentrate all available forces in the Nile Delta in preparation for their movement to Europe. Almost in passing, Churchill noted that the British could reconsider an advance on Tripoli if they could not reach any practical agreement with the Greeks. By then, of course, it would have been too late as O'Connor's well-honed force would have been disbanded and the Germans ensconced in Tripolitania.

It should be remembered, however, that Churchill had a limited objective in Libya in early 1941. He was concerned only with securing Egypt's 'Desert Flank' in order that the British could concentrate their attention on meeting the German menace to Turkey and Greece, which threatened Britain's position in the Middle East from the north. Churchill would have been content with making a safe flank for Egypt at Tobruk, and he regarded the seizure of Benghazi and the collection of 'other delectable prizes on the Libyan shore' as worthwhile only insofar as it gave added protection to Egypt from the west (and at minimum cost in casualties to 13th Corps). Thereafter Churchill was interested simply in consolidating Britain's military position in Cyrenaica, and in making political capital out of a British victory.[63]

At this time the British were entertaining hopes of a change of regime in Italy and an Italian request for an armistice with Britain. Reports from Italy indicated that morale was low among civilians and in the armed forces following a succession of military defeats, and the growing dependence on Germany which bred fear and resentment. Although there was no sign yet of an open or organised revolt against Mussolini, it was hoped that continued military reverses would see the end of fascism and the setting up of a military dictatorship by Marshal Badoglio and the King or Crown Prince, with whom the British government could negotiate a peace. In their Italian propaganda the British were anxious to stress the betrayal of the armed forces and the people by the Fascist leaders and to exploit the hatred of the Germans, in order to encourage disaffection in Italy. The British held out the bait of a lenient peace to spur Badoglio and the King to overthrow Mussolini.[64]

Churchill was quick to realise the propaganda value accruing from the fall of the first Italian colony in Africa. Since Beda Fomm, the British had been considering the idea of raising a 'Free Italian Force' from Italian POWs in Egypt. Although of neglible military value, such a force would be important 'from the psychological point of view', as it would serve as a rallying point for anti-Mussolini forces.

On 11 February 1941 Churchill was inspired to suggest to the Chiefs of Staff that they consider raising this volunteer Free Italian Force in Cyrenaica rather than Egypt. He waxed enthusiastic about this idea, 'We might even rule Cyrenaica under the Free Italian flag and treat it in the same way as de Gaulle's colonies are being treated subject to our military control. Anyhow, I wish Cyrenaica to be petted and made extremely comfortable and prosperous, more money being spent upon them than they are intrinsically worth. Can we not make this place a base for starting a real split in Italy and the source of anti-Mussolini propaganda? We might make it a model of British rule, hold it in trust for the Italian people and have 4,000 or 5,000 Italian troops sworn to the liberation of Italy from the German and Mussolini yoke. This could be run as world propaganda.[65]

Churchill's initiative had the effect of galvanising the debate on the future of Libya, which had been going on sporadically within the British government since the summer of 1940. The Foreign Office was ordered to investigate an idea which had 'wide political considerations'. While the permanent officials deliberated in committee in London, the Foreign Secretary was to consult the British military and diplomatic authorities in Egypt during his forthcoming visit to the Mediterranean theatre, to deal with the increasingly complicated situation there.[66] It was a matter which required considerable thought, especially as it cut across the respective proposals of Woolley and Bateman – the one for an immediate declaration by Britain that Cyrenaica would become an autonomous province of Egypt after the war, the other for Britain pledging her support for the frontier rectifications with Cyrenaica demanded by Egypt. Although the Foreign Office was interested in the idea of raising a Free Italian Force, it had doubts from the very start about the political wisdom of establishing it in Cyrenaica.

The Sargent Committee was the first to report its findings to the War Cabinet in early March 1941. (In its deliberations it had also taken into account the possibility of dissident elements within the Italian navy being prepared to surrender their ships to the British in the event of an Italian collapse, in order to prevent them from being captured by the Germans.)[67] The Committee concluded that Churchill's scheme, if and when feasible, might encourage the Italian fleet to defect to the British. It would be easier for the ships to make for a Free Italian colony than for an enemy port such as Alexandria. The families of the crews could be settled among their compatriots in Cyrenaica. An Italian admiral might become head of the Free Italian Movement. There was a major drawback, however, in that the ports of Cyrenaica could not take the largest vessels of the Italian fleet. Certainly, the scheme would be very valuable from the point of view of Britain's propaganda to Italy, since the existence of a Free Italian colony would enable Britain to encourage the Italians to hope that the future of Italy was not inextricably intertwined with the fate of Fascism and Germany.

There were difficulties in the way of Churchill's proposal, however, about which the Committee said it needed more information, as well as the views of Wavell and Lampson, before reaching definite conclusions. The Committee did not know whether there was sufficient material among local Italians in Cyrenaica, Italian POWs in Egypt, and the Italian community in Alexandria, to start a Free Italian Movement or Force, and no suitable leader for the movement had yet been found.

The increase of the Italian civil or military population in Cyrenaica would increase the administrative difficulties which would have to be met in supplying the needs of the local Arab population. It was hoped, however, that this would not hold up the scheme if it was thought feasible. The scheme might also be interpreted as a British commitment to hand Cyrenaica to a non-Fascist Italy after the war. Britain might be prepared to do this in certain circumstances, but she did not want to tie her hands at this stage.

Italian misrule in Cyrenaica made it very difficult to justify such a decision, and it would be regarded as a betrayal by the local Arabs who were very anti-Italian. Britain might find herself in a similar situation to that in Palestine, whereby she would have to mediate between local Italians and Arabs in a Free Italian colony. In addition, Arab feeling throughout the Middle East would be hostile to the scheme, and there were already indications that it was hoped that Cyrenaica would be liberated from Italian rule by being put under Egypt, or even Turkey.[68] It would be very difficult to make Cyrenaica 'prosperous and happy' because the territory was not self-supporting. It was very reliant on outside sources of supplies and the present supply situation in the Mediterranean was difficult, although the military authorities were doing what they could to stabilise the situation.

The Foreign Office suggested that it might be possible to circumvent these political difficulties by setting up a Free Italian colony not in Cyrenaica but in Eritrea, where relations between the Italian and native population were not so strained (according to the Committee the inhabitants of Eritrea were less race-conscious than the Arabs). It might be an advantage, so the Foreign Office argued, if and when the Italian fleet left Italy, that it should move out of the Mediterranean altogether and sail down the Red Sea to Eritrea. Cyrenaica might for some time be within range of German bombers, and this might demoralise the Free Italian Movement. There would be no danger of German bombers reaching Eritrea. Admittedly, the Italian fleet could not be accommodated in Eritrean ports, but it could shelter in the large natural anchorage at Annesley Bay, 16 km south-east of Massawa (where Sir Robert Napier landed his expedition to Abyssinia in 1868), even though it had no shore facilities. Again the Committee recommended, and the Cabinet approved in early March 1941, that the Commander in Chief in the Middle East and the British Ambassador to Egypt should be consulted on these questions before the British government gave any further consideration to Churchill's scheme.[69]

The British military and diplomatic authorities in the Middle East had been giving sustained attention to 'a general settlement of Italian Middle East Affairs' since Eden arrived in Cairo on 19 February 1941.[70] Lampson was to prove the most powerful influence on Eden. By late February 1941 Lampson had indicated his preference for entirely British post-war control of Cyrenaica to one man, General Wilson, and he proceeded subtly to implant this idea in the minds of both Eden and the permanent officials of the Foreign Office.[71] In order to accomplish this he had to persuade Eden not to make an immediate declaration on Cyrenaica in favour of either Egypt or Italy, as Eden was being urged to do by the head of the Egyptian Department, C H Bateman, and Sir Leonard Woolley on the one hand, and the Prime Minister on the other. Lampson had to ensure also that no commitment was made to Sayyid Idris.

When Eden returned to Cairo on 6 March 1941 from his trip around the Eastern Mediterranean, Lampson expounded his ideas on the future of Libya for the benefit of the Foreign Secretary. Lampson's thinking helped not only to guide but also to determine the outcome of the discussions in the following week between Eden, Lampson and Wavell on the proposal for establishing a Free Italian colony in Cyrenaica and raising a Free Italian Force there. Lampson stressed to Eden that it was most inadvisable for Britain to make any commitments on the future of Libya until after the war, unless there was an obvious advantage in using it as a bargaining counter (i.e. with Italy). The future of Libya would be determined to a large extent by political expediency and post-war strategic requirements, which could not yet be foreseen. Lampson proceeded to list, however, the possible alternatives in order to help clarify thinking on this question.

To return Libya to a reformed Italy would be a great blow to the Libyans, whom the British had encouraged to hope for liberation from Italy. There would be no adequate guarantees for the native population under Italian rule. This course of action would be very unpopular in the Arab world. The British might give Libya to France in order to coax her into re-entering the war, but Britain could not give her Cyrenaica as this would mean that a first-class European military power would be on the Egyptian frontier. Libya might be given to Greece, but the latter would be able to hold the country only with British support, and this would cause trouble for the British in Egypt and with Arab opinion.

Another possibility was to return Libya to Turkey, although it was not clear whether the latter would want to resume this responsibility. Lampson thought Turkey might be interested because she had offered

Turkish army officers to Britain and Egypt in the summer of 1939 to help stir up disaffection among the Libyan tribes.[72] Turkey in Libya would be less dangerous to Britain than a European power, but she might be encouraged to interfere in the Arab world (e.g. put forward claims to northern Syria and Iraq) and in Egyptian affairs and politics. The Sanusis might not appreciate their subjection to the secular government of modern Turkey, which had shunned the former head of the Sanusis, Sayyid Ahmad, when he had lived there in exile between the wars.

Such a solution might be less unpopular in Tripolitania (although there was no way of knowing this). Libya thought of herself as being part of the Arab world, and the Arab states did not like the idea of one of their number being subject to Turkey. Egypt would object, given her traditional dislike of Turkey (although the few Turco-Egyptians would approve).

The British might give Libya to Egypt but the Egyptians were not competent to run their own government let alone govern another country. Lampson's opinion was that: 'The Egyptians do not understand or like the Arabs or the semi-Arab elements. Moreover, Egypt under the nationalist effendi class and with the growth of a half-educated unemployed, would be a disturbing element in Libya. Egypt, thus swollen by the acquisition of Libya, might be encouraged to play a heavier role in the politics of the Arab world to the disturbance of our acquired positions in it.' Lampson admitted, however, that it might be safer for Britain if Egypt held Libya rather than any European power.

In setting out his objections to any of the above alternatives for Libya's future, Lampson was preparing the ground for the sympathetic consideration of his own choice, viz. for Britain to hold Libya. He clothed the recommendation in an attractive garb by proposing British or international control (civil or military) of Libya for an indefinite period with either a Libyan government (which would be run in the interests of the Libyans rather than the Italian settlers), an Italian-Libyan condominium (if post-war Italy was reformed), or a local government with no connection with Italy (in which both Libyans and Italians would be represented).

The latter two suggestions were intended to secure an equitable compromise between the interests of Libyans and those of the local Italians. Cyrenaica and Tripolitania would be treated as separate territories, but would be linked by a customs union. In a revealing remark, Lampson suggested that if it was necessary for Britain to assume military responsibility in Libya then she should do so in Cyrenaica rather than Tripolitania, as the former was more readily defensible than the latter, given the great natural barrier of the Sirte Desert. Lampson concluded by linking his new proposal for eventual British control of Libya with his initial admonition against making any commitments during the war. This was intended to impress upon Eden the need to oppose any of the proposals which advocated an immediate declaration of support from Britain.[73]

Eden was convinced by Lampson's arguments and Wavell's doubts about the declaration. He decided to oppose Churchill's idea of establishing a Free Italian colony, and raising a Free Italian Force in Cyrenaica. On 14 March 1941 he informed London accordingly, but without referring to Lampson's proposal for British post-war control of Libya. He kept to his War Cabinet brief and concentrated exclusively on the objections to a Free Italian Cyrenaica. Eden pointed out that the Italian settlers in Cyrenaica, who were loyal Fascists, would be doubtful recruits for a strong Free Italian Movement. There was an anti-Fascist movement (largely Jewish) among the Italian expatriate community in Egypt, but it suffered from not having any leaders. It was thought that there might be suitable leaders in France, providing they could escape to Egypt. (A propagandist, Professor Calosso, was in transit from Portugal, but he was not regarded as a potential leader.) Wavell was investigating the possibility of raising a Free Italian Force from Italian POWs, but he thought that it would be dangerous to experiment with a Free Italian Movement in Cyrenaica as long as there was a threat of enemy counter-attack from Tripolitania.[74]

Eden in his report conveyed the collective opinion of the British authorities in Egypt that there would be unfavourable reactions from the Sanusis, Egypt and the Arab world to a Free Italian Cyrenaica. Eden played on the belief within the War Cabinet that military considerations were of paramount concern. 'For the above reasons, and in particular in the light of Wavell's views, arguments against such an experiment in Cyrenaica seem to be decisive for the time being,' he wrote.

As a palliative Eden mentioned Cairo's qualified interest in the idea of a Free Italian Eritrea. He said there were stronger arguments for trying out the scheme in Eritrea, but to make an announcement to this effect at that time might lead to a belief among the exiled Emperor Haile Selassie and the Ethiopian tribesmen fighting the Italians that the British were thinking of striking a bargain with Italy over Ethiopia. This would 'cool patriotic enthusiasm'. Cairo would give further consideration to the Eritrean project, but Eden was against going ahead with it in East Africa before Italian resistance in the region had collapsed.[75]

The objections of the men-on-the-spot in the Middle East were decisive in killing Churchill's idea of establishing a Free Italian Movement and raising a Free Italian Force in Cyrenaica. The Foreign Office seem to have expected this negative response from Cairo. It was realised that Eritrea rather than Cyrenaica appeared to be a more suitable territory for the 'Free Italy experiment' and that it was best to await the British occupation of Eritrea before speculating further on this question. After Keren fell to General Platt's forces on 27 March 1941, the fate of Eritrea was sealed. Asmara surrendered on 1 April and Massawa on 8 April. Addis Ababa had fallen to General Cunningham's forces on 5 April 1941.[76]

In the changed circumstances of spring 1941 in North and East Africa, the British lost interest in the Free Italy idea. The collapse of Italian East Africa confronted the British with a host of political, economic and administrative problems which made it undesirable for Eritrea to become a Free Italian colony. Despite the loss of the East African empire there was a discernible improvement in Italian morale as a result of Rommel's recapture of Cyrenaica in April 1941, and the subsequent British defeats in Greece and Crete. This was not a suitable climate in which to rally disillusioned Italians to the cause of a Free Italian Movement based in Africa. In addition, there were seemingly insurmountable problems involved in organising a Free Italian Force, although it continued to be of sporadic interest to the Foreign Office until October 1941.

Not only was there a lack of a suitable military leader, but by late July 1941 Egypt was regarded as too insecure for British political propaganda to have any effect among Italian POWs there. It was decided to concentrate instead on investigating the possibility of raising a Free Italian Force from Italian POWs in India (in the end this project never came to anything). Likewise, the plot within the Italian navy for surrendering part of the fleet to the British seems to have been discovered by Mussolini in the late spring or early summer of 1941, thus rendering obsolete the British plan for harbouring Italian ships in a Free Italian colony, preferably Eritrea.[77]

In the late summer of 1941 the Foreign Office had lost interest in the Italian internal situation, and the possibility of Italy withdrawing from the war. It was decided that Britain should concentrate on causing a military collapse of Italy, the weak link of the Axis, rather than seeking a political solution in the form of a negotiated peace.[78] In this new atmosphere it seemed neither desirable nor necessary for the British to give an implied guarantee to Italy concerning her colonies, through the Free Italian colony scheme.

The Foreign Office gave no further thought to Churchill's proposal.[79] Speculation on the future of Libya within British military, political and diplomatic circles in London and Cairo tailed off dramatically in April 1941, as attention switched to the military front, following Rommel's first desert offensive which succeeded in recapturing Cyrenaica for the Axis.

Wavell had underestimated Rommel's ability to mount a full-scale attack with the limited forces at his disposal so soon after his arrival in North Africa. Wavell had run risks in Cyrenaica, maintaining a weak garrison there in order to provide maximum support for the British Expeditionary Force to Greece. Once Rommel had seized the inadequately defended El Agheila defile (the 'gateway to Cyrenaica') on 24 March 1941, and broken through to Ajdabiya by 2 April, mauling the green British 2nd Armoured Division in the process, Benghazi and everything to the west of Tobruk was imperilled. Rommel took Benghazi on 4 April, Derna on 7 April, and after by-passing Tobruk on 10 April reached the Egyptian frontier, where by the middle of April he had established defensive positions in the Bardia-Sallum-Sidi Omar area. On 26 April 1941 he recaptured the Halfaya Pass.

Churchill thought that 'the beating in of our Desert Flank while we were full-spread in the Greek adventure ... [was] a disaster of the first magnitude'. The expedition to Greece, which had been mounted with the slender resources available, had to be further reduced. The expedition to seize Rhodes, which was an essential part of British plans in the Aegean, had to be cancelled. In exculpatory fashion Churchill explained later that the securing of the 'Desert Flank in North Africa' had been 'the peg on which all else hung, and there was no idea in any quarter of losing or risking that for the sake of Greece or anything in the Balkans'.

The British had lost Cyrenaica (with the exception of Tobruk, which Churchill regarded as 'an invaluable bridgehead or sally-port', but which Wavell saw as an 'an additional excrescence') and the threat to Egypt had been renewed.[80] This development, followed by the double disaster for Britain in Greece and Crete, the revolt in Iraq and the British invasion of Syria and the Lebanon, ushered in a new situation in the Eastern Mediterranean. This had a radical effect on British thinking on the future of Libya in the summer of 1941.

The projection of German military power into the Eastern Mediterranean also marked the end of Italy's own war in that theatre. A bemused Mussolini had followed in Hitler's wake in the invasion of Yugoslavia and Greece, and the reoccupation of Cyrenaica. Nothing remained now but for Italy to follow where Germany led, until it ended either in a German triumph or in disaster for Mussolini's Fascist regime. As the British became aware of the extent of Italy's dependence upon Germany they began to review their attitude towards Italy's colonial empire in Africa.

summary

FROM THE foregoing account it will be seen that the main features of the Libyan problem emerged during the short period of Italy's 'parallel war' against Britain in the Mediterranean, from June 1940 to April 1941. In considering the future of Libya, the British had to take into account the overriding desire of the Sanusis of Cyrenaica to rid themselves of Italian rule. Yet there were doubts about whether the Sanusis, and their exiled leader Sayyid Idris, were capable of ruling themselves. In addition, Sanusi aspirations to overlordship of Libya were disputed by the Tripolitanian leaders in exile.

There were difficulties in imposing external rule in Libya. If the Italians were to be forced out of their North African territory by British conquest, who was to replace them? The Egyptians appear to have been regarded at this stage as the most likely suzerains of Libya. The British tended to perceive 'the land west of the Nile' in terms of the defence of Egypt, and it made sense, therefore, that they should contemplate the post-war control of Libya by Egypt. The latter could then grant Britain the defence facilities she would require in Cyrenaica to guard Egypt's 'Desert Flank'. This solution had the added benefit, in British eyes, of enmeshing the Egyptians in administrative problems, and thus diverting their attention from the Sudan. There were serious drawbacks, however, to this scheme.

It was doubted whether the Sanusis would be likely to accept even nominal Egyptian rule in Cyrenaica especially if, as expected, it was exercised in a heavy-handed way (the attitude of the Tripolitanians was unclear at this point). Furthermore, the British did not want to encourage Egypt to play a greater role in Arab politics, to the detriment of Britain's position in the Middle East.

The only realistic alternatives to Egyptian rule of Libya seemed to be British or international control. The latter solution did not have any serious proponents at this stage of the war. However, both Sayyid Idris and Sir Miles Lampson had indicated, in different fashions, that they were interested in the idea of a British presence in Libya or at least Cyrenaica after the war.

The declaration of a British protectorate over Cyrenaica would have certain advantages. It would enable the establishment and protection of some form of native state in Libya, thus meeting at least Sanusi aspirations. This would be welcomed by Arab opinion. At the same time it would allow Britain the strategic advantage of denying Libya to an enemy power, thus giving security to Egypt and protection from the west to Britain's position in the Middle East. The objections to a protectorate lay in the international sphere. Britain would have to consult her allies before reaching any decision. France was classified as an ally for this purpose, and British officials gave due consideration to the French interest in Tripolitania. It was anticipated, however, that the United States would object to any aggrandisement by Britain in Libya, even though the Americans had yet to start formulating their views on this question.

The permanent officials of the Foreign Office, as we have seen, were wary of Britain making any commitment at this stage to Libyans, Egyptians or Italians on the future of Libya, being acutely conscious of the problems that the British had caused themselves in the Middle East as a consequence of promises made to Jews and Arabs during the First World War. However, even by the early stages of the Second World War the internal dynamics of the Libyan situation forced the British to retreat somewhat from the rigid stance of opposition to any pledges on the future of Libya.

In order to secure the co-operation of the Sanusis of Cyrenaica in Britain's war against Italy in North Africa, the British military and diplomatic authorities in Egypt had to encourage Sayyid Idris to believe that the Sanusis of Cyrenaica would have some say in their future. This implied at the very least a drastic curtailment of Italian authority in eastern Libya, if not the complete end of Italian rule in the territory. General Wilson had strongly hinted at this on 9 August 1940 in his address to exiled Libyan leaders (mostly Sanusis) in Cairo, when he requested that the British and the Libyans should co-operate in the raising of the Sanusi Arab Force 'with sincerity and loyalty, so that the Arabs may be enabled to regain their freedom and take back their lands from the Italian oppressors, and to restore their independence'.

Although the Foreign Office was slow to realise the importance of Wilson's statement (and then only under the pressure of events in the autumn of 1941) the fact remains that by the summer of 1940, soon after the outbreak of war with Italy, a prominent British authority in Egypt had pledged in effect that the Sanusis of Cyrenaica would never again come under Italian rule. There is evidence that Eden also began thinking along these lines in the autumn of 1940. These developments should be seen as the first steps taken by the British government along the road towards the declaration on the Sanusis of Cyrenaica in January 1942.

NOTES

1 Parl. Debs., 5th ser., H of C, vol. 377, cols. 77–78.
2 J 1830/281/66, FO 371/24644.
3 The Wafd Party made similar demands (these issues were the touchstones of Egyptian politics) in March 1940 in a memorandum presented to the British Ambassador to Egypt, Sir Miles Lampson. Then in opposition, the Wafd wanted to demonstrate its fitness to rule, and to maintain pressure on Ali Mahir's government. That month the latter tried, unsuccessfully, to renew agitation over the revision of treaty rights in the Sudan in favour of Egypt. It met with stiff British opposition. As will be seen, the Sudan question was to affect British consideration of the future of Libya. Yeshoshua Porath, *In Search of Arab Unity 1930–1945*. London 1986, pp. 185–186; C Tripp, 'Ali Mahir Pasha and the Palace in Egyptian Politics 1936–42. Seeking Mass Enthusiasm for Democracy,' PhD thesis, University of London, 1984, pp. 328–32; P J Vatikiotis, *The History of Egypt*, third edition, London, 1985, pp. 343–44.
4 Porath, *op. cit.*, pp.173–4.
5 Baggallay, 'Interest of Saudi Arabia in a War between the Allies and Italy', 8 June 1940, E 2121/2060/25, FO 371/24590; Michael J Cohen, *Palestine: Retreat from the Mandate, The Making of British Policy, 1936–45*, London 1978, p. 91.
6 *ibid.*, pp. 91–2.
7 T E Lawrence, *Seven Pillars of Wisdom*, second edition, eighth reprint, London 1949, p. 56–7; see also H V F Winstone, *The Illicit Adventure*, London 1982, p. 180.
8 Woolley, 'The Libyan Question After the Defeat of Italy', undated, E 2121/2060/25, FO 371/24590; Lloyd to Halifax, 14 June 1940, J 1605/281/66, FO 371/24644.
9 In addition, by 20 June 1940 the Foreign Office had begun to see advantages in Egypt's continued non-belligerency, and Lampson was instructed to inform King Faruk that Britain no longer expected a declaration of war against the Axis. The Foreign Office realised that this might benefit Britain in treaty negotiations after the war with Egypt. Britain would be able to stress, and prove by recent example, how invaluable she was for the defence of Egypt (Tripp, *op. cit.*, p. 338, n. 153, p. 355, n. 217). This consideration obviated any need for a territorial concession to Egypt to entice her into entering the war.
10 In effect, Halifax was simply referring Lloyd to the statement along these lines which had been made by R A Butler in the House of Commons on 19 June 1940. An FO circular telegram of 21 June 1940 to British Representatives overseas made it clear that this statement was intended to free Britain from commitments assumed in the past, particularly under the Anglo-Italian Agreement of 1938, without binding Britain as to the future. See Sir Llewellyn Woodward, British Foreign Policy in the Second World War, vol. 1, London 1970, p. 245; Halifax to Lloyd, 20 June 1940, and minutes on J 1605/281/66; minutes on E 2121/2060/25, FO 371/24590.
11 Baggallay, 'Anglo-Saudi Relations', 6 June 1940, Shuckburgh to Baggallay, 20 June 1940, FO to Lampson (Cairo), tel. 639, 17 July 1940 Lampson to FO, unnumbered tel., 27 July 1940, and minutes on E 2106/2055/25, FO 371/24590.
12 GHQME to WO, tel. 231, 14 June 1940, WO to GHQME, tel. 74429, 19 June 1940, WO 201/336.

13 As Sayyid Idris explained twenty years later (when he had become king of an independent Libya), 'This opportunity was regarded as our chance to shoot the last arrow against our country's enemy. If we succeeded, the country would be recovered; if we failed, nothing would have been lost, since our own country was already in the hands of the enemy.' Majid Khadduri, Modern Libya. A Study in Political Development, Baltimore 1963, p. 29.
14 The War Office also approved on 8 July 1940 a request by HQBTE for the establishment of a military mission (no. 102) to serve with the tribes. WO to GHQME, tels. 75652, 5 July, and 75864, 8 July 1940, WO 201/336.
15 The Libyan leaders called themselves the Tripoli-Barqa (Cyrenaica) Society. Among the Tripolitanians it was the exiled leaders of the Sanusi tribes of eastern Tripolitania who, in the main, supported Sayyid Idris and joined the Sanusi Arab Force.
16 It is possible to detect the hand here of the Egyptian Pan-Arab Abd al-Rahman Azzam, who had demanded that the British make a similar concession to Egypt in September 1939 as the condition of Egypt's entry into the war against Germany (Azzam was Minister for Wafds, religious endowments, in Ali Mahir's government). Azzam was in contact with, and had great influence over, the Tripolitanians. As Secretary of the Reform Committee, which governed the short-lived Tripolitanian Republic after the First World War, he had been the amir-maker of Tripolitanian politics. His first choice as amir of an independent Tripolitania had been Ramadan al-Suwayhili (or Shutaywi), lord of Misurata and the adjacent coasts. Ramadan had prevented the Sanusis from extending their influence into Tripolitania by defeating Sayyid Safi al-Din (cousin and rival of Sayyid Idris) in battle near Beni Ulid in 1916. Sanusi influence was thereafter limited to Cyrenaica, parts of the Fezzan and the Sirte Desert. Ramadan had his own plans for conquering Tripolitania, but these were cut short by his death in battle in August 1920. After Ramadan's death, Azzam took up the cause of the mediocre chairman of the Reform Committee, Ahmad al-Murayyid of Tarhuna. Azzam continued to dabble in Libyan politics. It is interesting to note that his renowned hatred for the Italians did not persuade him to sanction war against Italy by Egypt or the Libyans in the summer of 1940. Azzam was so enraged by the forced resignation of the Ali Mahir government in June 1940, and so convinced that a German victory was imminent in July 1940, that he had tried with other Egyptian malcontents to conspire with Pan-Arabs in the Iraqi government to hold a Pan-Arab conference in Baghdad, with a view to entering into relations with Germany. Azzam was frustrated in his aims, however, by the Iraqi government's preference for dealing with and influencing the new Egyptian Prime Minister, Hasan Sabri. See John Wright, *Libya*, London 1969, pp. 141–2; Porath, *op. cit.*, p. 198; Lampson to Halifax, despatch 838, 23 August 1940, J 1830/281/66, FO 371/24644.
17 Khadduri, *op. cit.*, pp. 29–33; Lampson to Halifax, despatches 838, 23 August, and 951, 14 October 1940, with enclosures, J 1830/281/66, FO 371/24644.
18 In defining the boundaries of the Sanusi amirate of Libya, Sayyid Idris advanced a claim to the Egyptian port of Sallum, upon which the Sanusi tribes of the frontier region were dependent for trade.
19 Sayyid Idris had been even more specific than this. In August 1940 he had asked that, if the Italians succeeded in overrunning Egypt, the British should make a ship available to carry the families of the Libyan leaders in Egypt, numbering about 250 people, to safety in the Hijaz. Lampson to Halifax, despatches

838, 23 August, and 951, 14 October 1940, with enclosures, J 1830/281/66, FO 371/24644.
20 The initial response of the exiled Sanusi tribesmen in Egypt to appeals from their leaders to enrol in the Sanusi Arab Force had been encouraging. The first battalion, of 500 men, had been raised immediately, and another was formed by October 1940.
21 Lampson to FO, tel. 1027, 2 September 1940, J 1830/281/66, FO 371/24644.
22 Minutes by Norton, 6 September, and Seymour, 7 September 1940, J 1830/281/66, FO 371/24644.
23 Lampson seemed to have implied that he wanted to keep open the option of using Libya as a bargaining counter to secure Egyptian participation in the war. Whether Lampson, and the Foreign Office which had followed his advice, genuinely believed that there was still a chance of Egypt entering the war is not clear. There is evidence to the contrary (see Tripp, *op. cit.*, p. 355, n. 217) which suggests that in the latter half of September 1940 the British no longer regarded a declaration of war by Egypt as either necessary or desirable. The determined opposition of the Palace to Egypt declaring war on the Axis was demonstrated when the Egyptian Prime Minister, Hasan Sabri, forced the resignation of the Sa'adist members of his government on 21 September 1940. The Sa'adists had been the only party in Egypt to advocate that Egypt should declare war, and should take an active part in its own defence, if for no other reason than to prevent Britain from arguing after the war that a British military presence was vital to that country's defence. Lampson had noted on 21 September 1940 the irony of the British supporting the Palace against the Sa'adists. This would seem to indicate that the men-on-the-spot in Egypt (Wavell and Lampson), backed by the Foreign Office, had no illusions about Egyptian opposition to entering the war, but did not intend to press the Egyptian government to change its mind. If this was the case, then it would be hard to justify delaying a decision on whether to make a declaration in favour of the Sanusis on the grounds that this might prejudice a declaration of war by Egypt, as was done by the Foreign Office in late September and October 1940. It is possible that the Foreign Office did not want to make any declaration at all on the future of Libya at this stage and sought to block, by every means possible, the attempt of the men-in-committee (Lloyd and Eden) to secure such a declaration. Lampson to FO, tels. 1170, 24 September and 1268, 10 October 1940, J 1830/281/66, FO 371/24644.
24 Since July 1940, Lampson's reports and proposals on Libya had been referred by the Foreign Office to the Secretary of State for the Colonies, Lord Lloyd. Apart from his personal interest in Arab and Egyptian affairs (in the Arab Bureau and during the First World War, and as High Commissioner for Egypt from 1925 to 1929), Lloyd wanted to raise tribal revolts in Libya and Italian East Africa which would tie down the large Italian forces in those territories and prevent the Italians from launching offensives against Egypt and the Sudan. It was hoped that this would gain valuable time for Britain to build up her weak defences in the Middle East. The latter task was the concern of the Secretary of State for War, Anthony Eden, who with Lloyd and L S Amery, the Secretary of State for India, dominated the Ministerial Committee on Military Policy in the Middle East. This committee had been set up by Churchill to keep a close watch on developments in the Middle East, and to assess the needs of British forces in the region at a time when Britain was concerned above all with the defence of the home islands. Eden, Amery and Lloyd appear to have taken to heart Churchill's exhortation to them 'to lift our affairs in the Middle East out of

the catalepsy by which they are smitten'. Their committee was very active in the late summer and early autumn of 1940 in trying to organise an effective defence of the Middle East. This body was not popular in Whitehall, however, as its activities often encroached upon the traditional preserves of the Chiefs of Staff and the Foreign Office. The Foreign Office seems to have resented, in particular, Lord Lloyd's incursions into the field of foreign affairs. The Permanent Under-Secretary, Sir Alexander Cadogan, complained after meeting Lloyd on 9 August 1940 that 'he's becoming a bore – as supplementary Foreign Secretary'. The Whitehall mandarins soon found an effective way of blocking the committee's initiatives. They simply starved it of information. By late October–November 1940 both Lloyd and Amery complained that they were not being kept adequately informed of events in the Middle East. The Committee was wound up by Churchill in early 1941, following Eden's move to the Foreign Office and Lloyd's death. The Earl of Avon, *The Eden Memoirs: The Reckoning*, London 1965, p. 126; Martin Gilbert, *Finest Hour. Winston S Churchill 1939–1941*, London 1983, p. 477; Lord Ismay, *The Memoirs of General Lord Ismay*, London 1960, p. 192; David Dilks, ed., *The Diaries of Sir Alexander Cadogan 1938–1945*, London 1971, p. 320; Ministerial Committee on Military Policy in the Middle East, ME (M) 40–41, CAB 95/2, and CAB 21/1182.

25 Porath, *op. cit.*, pp. 77–9, 114–9, 241–3; ME (M) 40 4th Meeting 25 July, 6th Meeting 12 August, 7th Meeting 23 August 1940, CAB 95/2.

26 Majid Khadduri claims that during this period, 'It was tacitly agreed that Libya, like Transjordan, would be established as an Amirate which would enjoy self-government and be guided by British advisers, although no definite assurance concerning the future of Libya was given by the British government.' Khadduri, *op. cit.*, p. 34. It is likely that Khadduri was given this information by King Idris in an interview held on 31 August 1961. There is no evidence in the British documents to suggest that such a tacit agreement was made by the British with Sayyid Idris in the autumn of 1940. On the contrary, British policy at this time was to avoid such commitments, although encouraging Sayyid Idris with general expressions of sympathy for Sanusi aspirations, in order to secure his continued co-operation with Britain. It is, of course, possible that Sayyid Idris chose to interpret these vague assurances as support for his aim of an autonomous Sanusi amirate in Libya, under a British protectorate.

27 Lloyd to Halifax, 28 September 1940, FO to Lampson, tel. 1039, 2 October 1940, Lampson to FO, tel. 1268, 10 October 1940 and minutes on J 1830/281/66, FO 371/24644.

28 Porath, *op. cit*, pp. 89–91.

29 Morton to Hopkinson, 4 October 1940, enclosing Woolley, 'After Somaliland', 22 August 1940, Eden to Halifax, 7 October 1940, Cadogan minute, 5 October 1940, Halifax to Eden, 10 October 1940, Hopkinson to Morton, 14 October 1940, J 1830/281/66, FO 371/24644.

30 In fact, in order not to offend Italy, which had territorial ambitions in the Near East, Germany was prepared in 1940 only to express general sympathy for Arab aspirations to independence and unity. A joint declaration along these lines was broadcast (in Arabic) by Rome and Berlin radios on 23 October 1940, and published in *Oriente Moderno* and *Völkischer Beobachter* in December. Lukasz Hirszowicz, *The Third Reich and the Arab East*, London 1966, p. 92.

31 Minutes by Norton of 17 October, Coverley-Price of 18 October, Seymour and Cadogan of 20 October 1940, J 1830/281/66, FO 371/24644.

32 Avon, *op. cit.*, pp. 153, 168–75.
33 Beaumont Nesbitt to Norton, 21 November 1940, enclosing Wavell, 'Note for Secretary of State on Propaganda in Italian East Africa', 23 October 1940, Thompson to Beaumont Nesbitt, 17 December 1940, and minutes on J 2211/2211/66, FO 371/24645.
34 In trying to stress the fact that the power of the Sanusis was confined to Cyrenaica, Lampson seems to downplay the political significance of Sayyid Idris's religious authority (which was implicit in Islam). Lampson appeared to have forgotten that Sayyid Idris, recognised as head of the Sanusis and Amir of Cyrenaica by the Sanusis, was also regarded as the de facto ruler of Cyrenaica by both the British and the Italians between 1916 and 1922. He was prevented from becoming Amir of Tripolitania as well in 1922–23 because the Italians decided against continuing their policy of ruling with the consent of the Libyans, and embarked upon a policy of establishing their rule by force. Lampson to Halifax, despatch 951, 14 October 1940, J 1830/281/66, FO 371/24644.
35 The Foreign Office learnt in early November 1940 that Sayyid Idris had said, in a talk with General Wilson in November 1939, that if the British did not take over Cyrenaica and the territory came under Egyptian rule, that any Egyptian viceroy should have a British commissioner by his side. Sayyid Idris was not impressed by the administrative abilities of the Egyptian government of Ali Mahir. The Hon. Evelyn Baring (then serving in the Egyptian Department, on secondment from the Consular Service) commented on 1 December 1940, 'This is scarcely surprising, since the period during which Egypt controlled the Sudan – the only example of her ruling over another people – provided a model of misrule.' Lampson to Halifax, despatch 951, 14 October 1940, Baring minute, 1 November 1940, J 1830/281/66, FO 371/24644.
36 C J Norton (head of the Egyptian Department) put the call by Sayyid Idris for British protection into a broader context, 'So many of these people like the Gallas in SW Abyssinia, & the Druzes (in 1920), pray for British protection partly because they know they can't stand alone & partly because they dislike their immediate neighbours. I hope we shall not take on all these thankless tasks.' Norton minute, 1 November 1940, J 1830/281/66, FO 371/24644.
37 Porath, *op. cit.*, p. 244; Avon, *op. cit.*, p. 156; Eden to Halifax, 7 October 1940, J 1830/281/66, FO 371/24644.
38 Avon, op cit., p. 188.
39 Daniel Silverfarb, *Britain's Informal Empire in the Middle East, A Case Study of Iraq, 1929–1941*, New York 1986, p. 114–22; Porath, *op. cit.*, p. 244.
40 Macgregor Knox, *Mussolini Unleashed 1939–1941. Politics and Strategy in Fascist Italy's Last War*, Cambridge 1982, chapter 6 and Conclusion.
41 Antonio Varsori, 'Italy, Britain and the Problem of a Separate Peace During the Second World War: 1940–1943', *Journal of Italian History*, vol. 1, no. 3, winter 1978, p. 459–60; COS (40) 1037 (final), 'Propaganda Policy in Relation to an Italian Collapse', CAB 80/24; Bowker minute, 31 December 1940, Norton, 'Egypt and the Sudan', 30 November 1940, J 2211/2211/66, FO 371/ 24645.
42 Britain's other main requirements were: a refusal to negotiate with Mussolini, the withdrawal of all Italian claims on France, the surrender of the Italian fleet, British bases in Italy, the expulsion of the Germans from Italy and a commitment from the Italians to resist any German attempt to occupy Italy.
43 Varsori, *op. cit.*, p. 461.

44 Under the Hague Convention a military government was obliged to administer the existing laws of the country. The occupying power could alter or suspend only those laws which it thought infringed human rights, or might have prejudiced the safety of the forces of occupation. Military governments were not intended or organised to administer a country on more than a care and maintenance basis consistent with the needs of the occupying power. Military government was intended as a temporary regime which should be succeeded by a civil administration as soon as military exigencies permitted. This occurred usually as a result of an armistice, peace treaty or annexation. Lord Rennell of Rodd, *British Military Administration of Occupied Territories in Africa During the Years 1941–1947*, London 1948, pp. 20–1.

45 Wavell set up a separate military command in Cyrenaica, directly responsible to GHQME, on 1 February 1941 headed by General Sir Henry Maitland Wilson, who was to act as both Commander-in-Chief and Governor of Cyrenaica. Brigadier S H Longrigg became Wilson's DCPO. Wilson was congratulated on his new appointment by Egyptian friends who, recalling the days of Ottoman rule in Libya before the First World War, told him that his financial fortune was assured. They suggested also that he take the title of his Turkish predecessors, the Wali of Barqa. Neither Wilson nor his successor, General Neame, occupied their posts long enough either to provide for their financial security or satisfy any desires they may have had for reviving the former splendours of the Ottoman *vilayet* of Cyrenaica! Lord Wilson of Libya, *Eight Years Overseas 1939–1947*, London 1950, pp. 58–9.

46 Rennell, *op. cit.*, pp. 23–4; WP(G) (41) 20, 'Administration of Occupied Enemy Territories in Africa', memorandum by the Secretary of State for War, 11 February 1941, WP(G)(41) 21, 'Administration of Occupied Enemy Territories in Africa', report by the Lord Privy Seal, 19 February 1941, CAB 66/14; WM 19(41)11, 20 February 1941, CAB 65/17; minutes on J 234/124/66, FO 371/27555.

47 The Sanusi Arab Force did not see active service during the Cyrenaican campaign in the winter of 1940–41. This was due to the lack of transport, the small size of the force, and the fact that it was poorly equipped. In late 1940 it seems that the Sanusi refugee battalions were reorganised along regular lines. They had been intended, and trained, to conduct guerilla operations in the Jabal Akhdar. The large number of Libyan troops captured at Sidi Barani by the British enabled more battalions to be raised. The Libyan Arab Force (LAF), as it became known, eventually comprised four battalions. Two LAF battalions were converted, however, into a gendarmerie in early 1941 to help maintain law and order in Cyrenaica. Unfortunately they took up their duties just when Rommel attacked and overran Cyrenaica in April 1941, and many were captured. An LAF battalion formed part of the besieged garrison at Tobruk in 1941. The role of the LAF was, in the main, to perform ancillary duties, guarding prisoners, installations and lines of communications.

48 Contrasting accounts of the first British occupation of Cyrenaica are given by official British and Italian sources. Whereas both Rennell and Longrigg give the impression that by and large law and order was maintained by the BMA in Cyrenaica from 1 February to 31 March 1941, Segre has reached the opposite conclusion. As a result of his research in the records of the Instituto Agronomico per l'Oltremare, Firenze, Osservatorio Rurale, he says that: 'The demographic villages in the Gebel were especially hard hit during the first two-month British occupation in the spring of 1941.' Apparently the morale of the Italian colonists was dealt an irrevocable blow by the murders, rapes and robberies committed against them (attributed to both Libyans and Australians by Fascist propagandists), by the return of the Sanusi tribesmen to their lands, and by the widespread demolition of agricultural installations carried out by the retreating British army in April 1941. While the destruction and outrages cannot be denied, it should be remembered that Cyrenaica was a war zone and incidents were bound to occur. It was official British policy to maintain Italian agricultural production in the Jabal Akhdar (which the Sanusis were slow to realise), and if the British had not policed the farms then it is likely that many more outrages would have been committed against Italian colonists. Rennell, *op. cit.*, pp. 34–9; 'First Quarterly Report by the Deputy Chief Political Officer, Cyrenaica, on the Occupied Enemy Territory of Cyrenaica for the period 1 February to 31 March 1941', Section 11, Politics, Longrigg Papers; Claudio G Segre, *Fourth Shore. The Italian Colonization of Libya*, Chicago 1974, p. 167; Bateman minute, 11 March 1941, J 3102/143/66 FO 371/27571.

49 Sayyid Idris had a ready defender in the person of the eminent orientalist and Laudian Professor of Arabic at Oxford, H A R Gibb. At a meeting on 14 January 1941 of the Middle East Committee of the Foreign Press and Research Service (part of the academic war-effort run by Professor Arnold Toynbee, of the Royal Institute of International Affairs, to provide scholarly advice to the Foreign Office), at which R A Butler had been present, the possible political consequences of the liberation of Cyrenaica were discussed. Gibb called for the restoration of 'the former autonomous emirate of the "Grand Senoussi", whose hereditary authority is the only one accepted as of right by the tribesmen, and to administer it by the now well-tried methods of indirect rule'. Gibb thought it would meet with the approval of the Arab world, and it would be a just recompense for the atrocities committed by the Italians against the Sanusis. Gibb was also an ardent supporter of Arab unity. As will be seen later, although the Foreign Office realised the need to safeguard Sanusi rights in any settlement of Cyrenaica's future, they preferred the advice of the men-on-the-spot, Wavell and Lampson, to that of the dons of Balliol. Toynbee to Bateman, 15 January 1941, enclosing Gibb note, undated, and minutes on J 143/143/66; Bateman minute of 11 March 1941, J 3102/143/66, FO 371/27571. For Gibb's Arab unity schemes see Porath, passim.

50 It was agreed that the British would have no dealings with Sayyid Idris's cousin and rival Sayyid Safi al-Din, whom the British had regarded in 1939 as a possible leader of a Libyan revolt. He had been the last Sanusi guerilla chief to cease fighting the Italians in the early 1930s. Anti-British Tripolitanians were also to be interned, if necessary. In early 1941 the Saudis, or at least Hafiz Wahba, seemed to be backing the formation of a separate Tripolitanian force, which would comprise Tripolitanian exiles and POWs. Ibn Saud's Tripolitanian advisers, Khalil al-Hud and Bashir Sa'adawi, were mentioned as possible leaders. The former had acted as Ibn Saud's emissary to Germany before the war. Bashir was a prominent Arab nationalist, involved in Syrian politics, who played an important role in post-war Libya. The Foreign Office displayed no interest in this scheme. Butler, 'Talk with Hafiz Wahba', 22 January 1941, J 157/34/16, Eyre minute, 25 January 1941, J 249/34/16, FO 371/27549.

51 Lampson to Eden, despatch 66, 29 January 1941, with enclosures, Bateman minute, 11 March 1941, J 479/143/66, FO 371/27571.

52 Longrigg, *op. cit.*, Section 11, Politics.
53 Draft MEWC (Middle East War Council), 'The Senussi. Memorandum by the Minister of State', 21 August 1941, J 2841/368/66, FO 371/27573; Lampson to Acting Secretary of State for Foreign Affairs (Churchill), despatch 227, 14 March 1941, with enclosures, Baring minute, 11 April 1941, J 874/368/66, FO 371/27573.
54 Diary (MS) of Sir Philip Mitchell, entries for 19 February, 3, 4, 18, 19, 22 March 1941.
55 King Faruk's uncle, Prince Muhammad Ali, agreed with Lampson's estimation of the Egyptians. He told Lampson that they were 'a thoroughly worthless lot and neither deserved nor should receive any territorial concession in Libya'. Diary (MS) of Lord Killearn, entry for 7 January 1941.
56 *ibid.*, entries for 3 and 29 January 1941; Lampson to FO, unnumbered tel., 23 January 1941, J 153/153/16, FO 371/27454; Lampson to Eden, despatch 67, 27 January 1941, enclosing Sirri to Lampson, 20 January 1941, J 368/368/66, FO 371/27573.
57 Bateman indicated the direction of his thinking on recognising Egypt's claim to Jaghbub when he wrote on 30 January 1941 that one day Britain might trade Libya to Egypt in return for the latter's surrender of her rights under the condominium in the Sudan. Bateman minute, 30 January 1941, FO to Lampson, tels. 458 and 459, 20 February 1941, and minutes on J 153/153/16, FO 371/27454.
58 It has been asserted by Richard Lamb, in *The Ghosts of Peace 1935–1945*, Salisbury 1987, p. 153, that Wavell and Lampson possessed in March 1941 'a strong feeling that the frontier of Cyrenaica and Egypt should be rectified in Egypt's favour as a reward for her help against Italy'. In fact Wavell and Lampson held exactly the opposite view, as has been made clear above. Lampson to FO, tel. 450, 5 March 1941, FO to Lampson, tel. 745, 15 March 1941, and minutes on J 527/368/66, FO 371/27573; Lampson to Eden, despatch 252, 21 March 1941, enclosing Lampson to Sirri, 21 March 1941, J 1011/368/66, FO 371/27573.
59 Lamb, *op. cit.*, p. 153, says that 'Woolley's views ... roughly represented the thinking in military and government circles in Cairo.' This was certainly true of the Egyptians but not of the British. Lampson and Wavell opposed Egyptian aggrandisement at Cyrenaica's expense. Woolley to Seymour, 6 February 1941, enclosing Woolley 'Libya', 6 February 1941, and minutes on J 220/220/16, FO 371/27460.
60 Woolley, *ibid.*, Gilbert, *Finest Hour*, *op. cit.*, pp. 1008–9.
61 One Egyptian was so impressed by the victorious British campaign in Cyrenaica, and especially the contribution of the 6th Australian Division, that he suggested Libya be called 'New Australia' in recognition of the valorous efforts of the Australians. This caused much amusement when broached by Lampson at a dinner for Sir Robert Menzies, Prime Minister of Australia, in Cairo in early February 1941. Killearn Diary (MS), entry for 6 February 1941.
62 Knox, *op. cit.*, pp. 279–83.
63 Gilbert, *op. cit.*, pp.1010–1; Winston S Churchill, *The Second World War.* vol. 3 *The Grand Alliance*, London 1950, pp. 14, 56–9. For criticism of the Chiefs of Staff and Churchill, see Correlli Barnett, *The Desert Generals*, third edition, London 1983, pp. 60–5.
64 Knox, *op. cit.*, pp. 278–9; Varsori, *op. cit.*, pp. 461–3; Knight, 'Italian Morale from the fall of Bardia to the attack on Tobruk', 22 January 1941, and minutes on

R 584/28/22; Knight, 'Italian Morale from the attack on Tobruk to the capture of Cyrene', 6 February 1941, R 930/28/22, FO 371/29924.
65 Lamb, *op. cit.*, pp. 148–9; Gilbert, *op. cit.*, pp. 1011–2; Varsori, *op. cit.* p. 462; minutes by Sargent and Cadogan, 11 February 1941, R 930/28/22, FO 371/29924; Prime Minister's Personal Minute, D 36/1, 11 February 1941, Annex A, WP (41) 51, 'The Formation of a Free Italian Movement in the Italian Colonies', 3 March 1941, CAB 66/15.
66 The Defence Committee (Operations) decided on 11 February 1941 that the Foreign Office should set up a committee, with an FO official as chairman (Sir Orme Sargent was appointed) and representatives from the three Service Departments, the Treasury, and the Ministry of Economic Warfare, 'to examine and report on the question of whether to attempt the formation of a Free Italian Movement in the Italian Colonies on the lines of the Free French Movement'. Defence Committee (Operations) no. 8 of 1941, 11 February 1941, CAB 69/2. Churchill instructed Eden on 12 February that, during his mission to the Eastern Mediterranean he was to ascertain 'the regime and policy to be enforced in Cyrenaica having regard to our desire to separate the Italian nation from Mussolini's system'. Churchill, op cit., p. 60.
67 For details of this bizarre plan, involving the British Embassy in Stockholm and Swedish businessmen, see Lamb, *op. cit.*, pp. 160–8.
68 The influence of Sir Leonard Woolley can be detected here. His memorandum, 'Libya', of 6 February 1941 was circulated to the committee by Sir Orme Sargent on or about 17 February 1941. Lamb is not correct (*op. cit.*, p. 151) in saying that 'Woolley's well-argued objections made little headway with the Committee', or that, as will be seen below, the committee merely 'endorsed the Prime Minister's initiative'.
69 WP (41) 51, *op. cit.*, WM 17 (41) 1, 13 February 1941, WM 19 (41) 12, 20 February 1941, CAB 65/17; WM 28 (41) 11, 4 March 1941, CAB 65/18; FO to Lampson, tel. 600, 6 March 1941, R 1317/1317/22, FO 371/29958.
70 Mitchell Diary (MS), entry for 21 February 1941.
71 Lampson conferred with Wilson about Cyrenaica on 26 February 1941. Wilson was relinquishing his command as GOC Cyrenaica in order to lead the British Expeditionary Force to Greece. Lampson told Wilson that he objected to all the options which had been put forward for Cyrenaica, that it should go to Egypt, or France, or Turkey, or should become a Free Italian state. All except for one, the suggestion that Britain should keep it, with some form of Arab autonomy, which had certain strategic advantages. 'Jumbo' Wilson agreed with him and was emphatic that Cyrenaica should not go to Egypt. Killearn Diary (MS), entry for 26 February 1941.
72 See FO 371/23388 for details.
73 On this Lampson warned, 'It seems most inadvisable to commit ourselves until after the war to any conclusion as regards the future of Libya, unless there is clear advantage in using it as a bargaining counter. Although our post-war strategical requirements cannot be adequately foreseen now, the negative strategical advantage of denying Libya to any other power is likely always to be considerable so long as the command of the Mediterranean, our communications in this part of the world by sea and air, the security of our oil supplies and the maintenance generally of our influence in the Arab countries are vital interests. There may well be strategical advantages in keeping Libya under our control for

naval and air purposes, for at least a period after the war, e.g. in the event of the Soviet Union emerging from the war as a naval, military, and air power capable, with some Western ally, of threatening our position in the Mediterranean. These considerations and the need for keeping the goodwill of the Arab world are arguments in favour of a policy of extreme caution at present, as regards the future of Libya. In so far as can be seen – and if we are prepared to face the military and political responsibility entailed – the safest ultimate solution would seem to be a mixed local government under British protection on the lines suggested ... above.' Lampson to Acting Secretary of State (Churchill), despatch 226, 14 March 1941, enclosing Lampson, 'The Future of Libya', 28 February 1941, memorandum prepared for Eden in Cairo, Baring minute, 11 April 1941, J 873/368/66, FO 371/27573. There is no evidence to suggest that Churchill saw this despatch. It was sent only to the War Office. By the time of its arrival Rommel had overrun much of Cyrenaica, which made further speculation on the future of Libya a fruitless exercise at that point.

74 Wavell reported on 20 March 1941 that he could not yet assess properly the chances of raising a Free Italian Force, but it was important to find the right leader and he thought the Force in Egypt would be a security risk. Eritrea seemed to be a better and safer choice, after it had been conquered by British forces. Wavell to WO, tel. I/50295, 20 March 1941, R 3055/168/22, FO 371/29936.

75 Eden to FO, tel. 554, 14 March 1941, R 2496/1317/22, FO 371729958.

76 Minutes on R 3055/168/22, FO 371/29936, and on R 2496/1317/22, FO 371/29958.

77 Lamb, *op. cit.*, pp. 155–7, 168; Knight, 'Internal Situation in Italy', 5 October 1941, R 8909/28/22, FO 371/29931.

78 Varsori, *op. cit.*, pp. 463–6.

79 My account of the discussion within British political and military circles of Churchill's proposal for establishing a Free Italian Movement and Force in Cyrenaica differs from that given by Richard Lamb in *The Ghosts of Peace 1935–1945*. I find it hard to agree with Mr Lamb that Churchill's 'treatment of Cyrenaica as a bargaining counter recalls, more nearly than anything appropriate to the twentieth century, Prime Minister Addington's bargaining over Malta with Napoleon in the Treaty of Amiens of 1802'. (*ibid.*, p. 149). Cyrenaica was an Italian territory, and Churchill was not suggesting a change of sovereignty, only the installation of a non-Fascist or anti-Mussolini regime. Britain was under no legal obligation to return Cyrenaica to the Sanusis. The moral obligation to release the Sanusis from Italian rule only became fully apparent in the latter half of 1941. Mr Lamb says also that 'Eden did not oppose Churchill's wild project'. Lord Gladwyn, then private secretary to Sir Alec Cadogan, told the author: 'In the Foreign Office then we thought it was a good idea and I still think so provided we could have held Cyrenaica' (*ibid.*, p. 179). As has been shown, both Eden and the Foreign Office, in co-operation with Lampson and Wavell, effectively killed Churchill's proposal for a Free Italian Cyrenaica before Rommel reconquered the territory for the Axis in April 1941.

80 Churchill *op. cit.*, pp. 173–92.

THE SECOND YEAR
1941–1942
THE DECLARATION ON THE SANUSIS

LIBYA: YEAR TWO

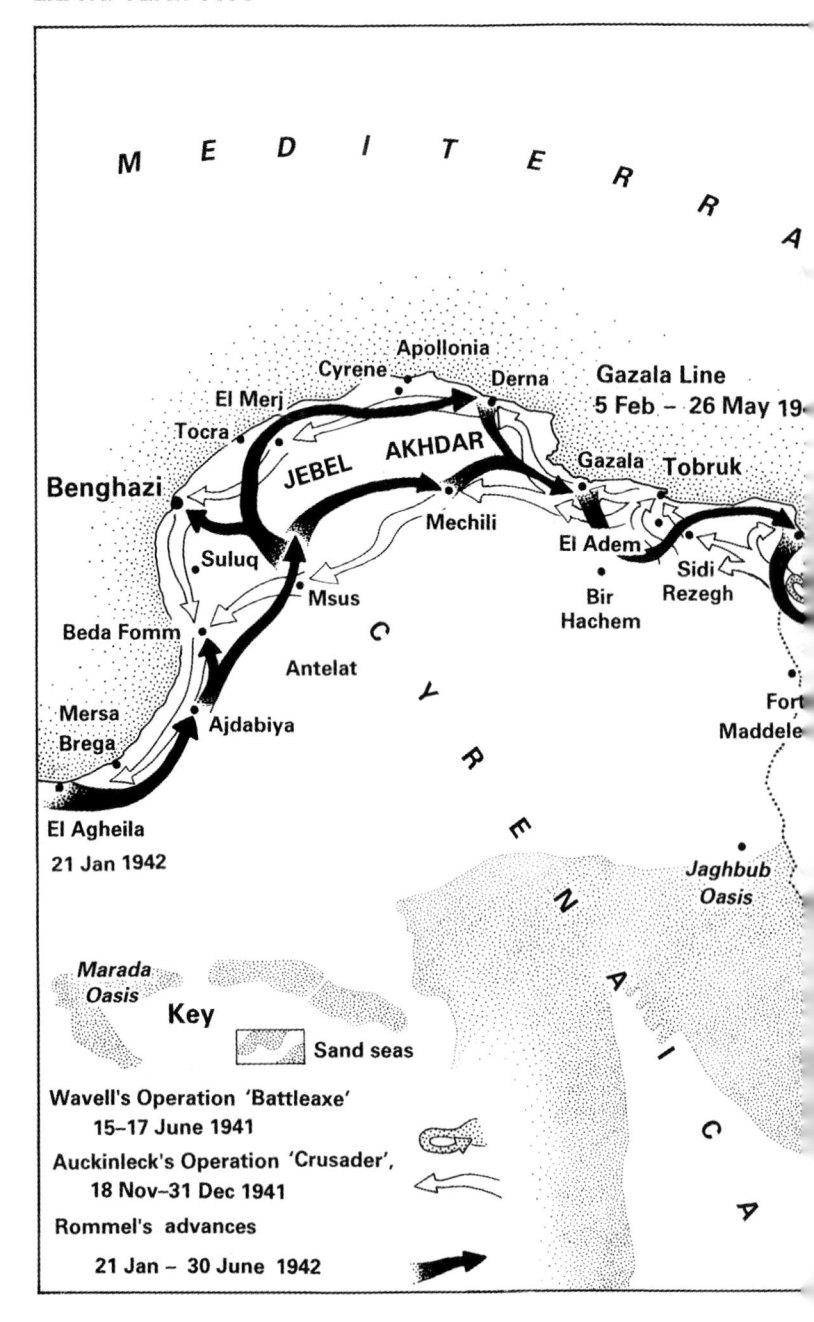

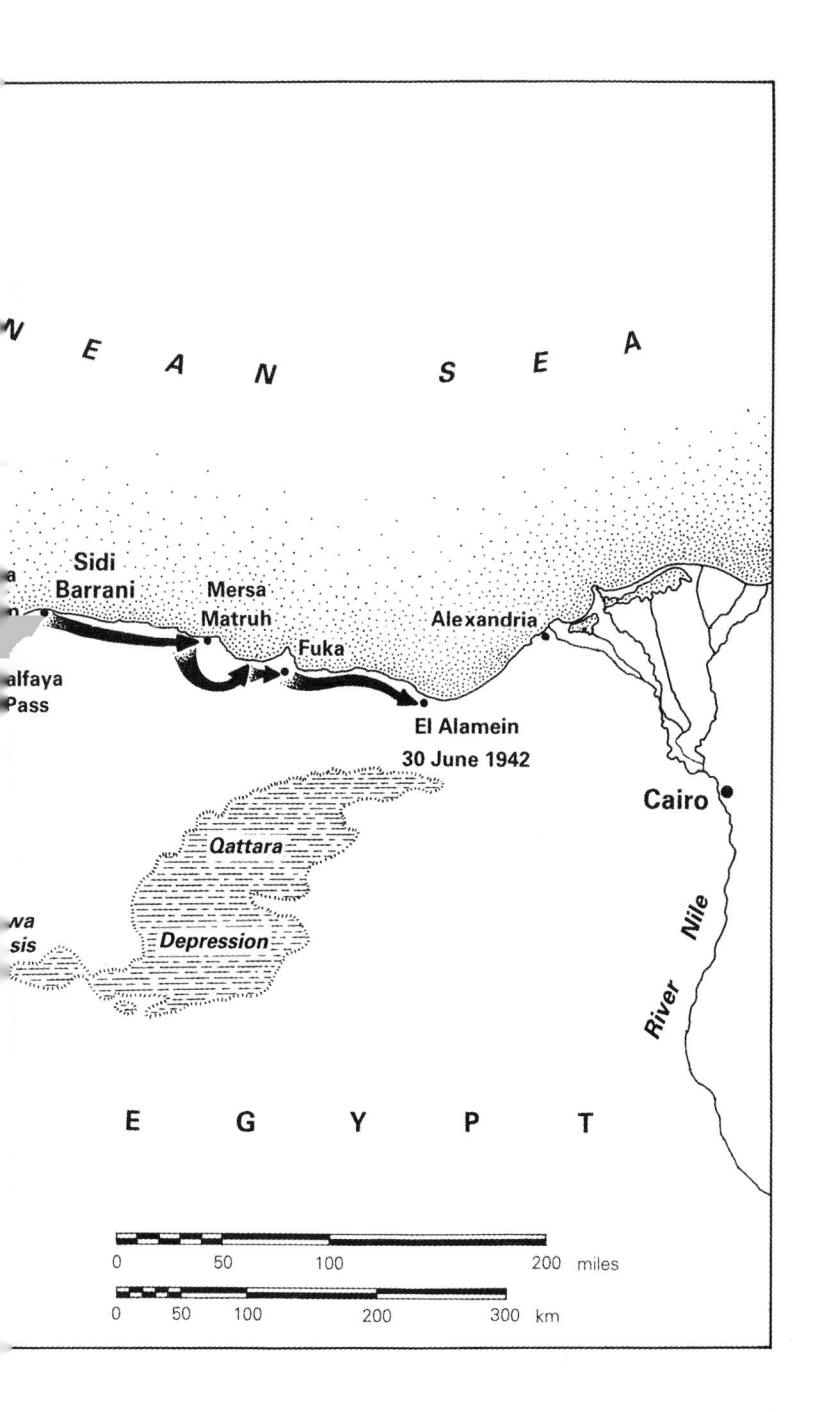

Sidi Barrani
Mersa Matruh
Fuka
Alexandria
El Alamein
30 June 1942
alfaya Pass
Cairo
Qattara Depression
River Nile
EGYPT
MEDITERRANEAN SEA

0 50 100 200 miles
0 50 100 200 300 km

overview

GERMAN INTERVENTION in the eastern Mediterranean in the spring of 1941, and the subsequent dramatic developments which occurred in the Balkans, North Africa and the Levant, demanded a strong response from Britain. It was no longer possible for the British government to avoid making decisions which would affect the political complexion of the Middle East. In the case of Libya the British government was forced by military exigency (although it made a virtue out of necessity) into making a formal commitment on the future of the inhabitants of eastern Libya, the Sanusis of Cyrenaica.

The idea of a declaration on the Sanusis was under active consideration in London and Cairo from the late summer of 1941. It was part of the process by which Britain sought to stabilise her military and political position in the Middle East in expectation of a renewed German assault. A vital element of this process was a propaganda offensive designed to palliate any adverse reactions aroused by British military actions in the region. Thus, the successive invasions of Iraq, Syria, the Lebanon, Iran and Cyrenaica by British forces were accompanied by a succession of political statements to reassure the inhabitants of these countries about their future.

The declaration on the Sanusis was to be made in conjunction with a British offensive into Cyrenaica. In the immediate run-up to the declaration, however, the military situation in the Mediterranean began to change in favour of the Axis. The effects of the build-up of German naval (submarine) and air power in the Mediterranean from the autumn of 1941 onwards began to be felt towards the end of the year. British victories in the Western Desert were accompanied by serious naval losses, which enabled the reinforcement of Rommel's forces for a counter-offensive in North Africa. In fact the declaration on the Sanusis was made the day after Panzergruppe Afrika had ended its retreat from the Egyptian frontier. On 7 January 1942 Rommel had managed to establish a front at the El Agheila defile, 'the gateway to Cyrenaica'. The military initiative thereafter passed to Rommel just as British administrators began to grapple with the problems posed by the ending of Italian rule in Cyrenaica.

Rommel's counter-attack in late January 1942 marked the beginning of a period of intense pressure by the Axis on Britain's position in the Mediterranean which was to last until the summer of 1942. Although the British were preoccupied above all with the threats to Malta, Tobruk and the Nile Delta, they were forced to devote some attention to the fate of the Sanusis of Cyrenaica. While the British military commanders in Cyrenaica found themselves having to honour the declaration on the Sanusis in an unexpected manner, the political authorities in London and Cairo worked out the administrative implications of the declaration for a future British reoccupation of Cyrenaica. These developments were to have a significant influence on British policy towards Libya in 1942–43.

It has been noted how the British military and diplomatic authorities in Cairo and the Foreign Office in London successfully prevented the British government from undertaking any definite commitment on the future of Libya during the period from June 1940 to April 1941. They dropped their opposition to a formal commitment, however, once it became clear from the summer of 1941 that there was little alternative. Instead they concentrated their attention on reducing the scope of any British obligation. As will be seen, the eventual declaration pertained only to the 'Sanusis in Cyrenaica' and made no reference to their desire for independence. The statement gave official recognition, in effect, to General Wilson's vaguely worded pledge of August 1940 that the Sanusis would be liberated from Italian rule.

Despite the limited nature of the declaration on the Sanusis, the British diplomatic, political and military authorities in Cairo continued to develop their ideas on the political future of Cyrenaica. The British Ambassador, the Minister of State and the Chief Political Officer indicated at various times from the summer of 1941 that they thought the British government should capitalise on the goodwill shown by Sayyid Idris for Britain. However, the desire of Sayyid Idris for the establishment of an autonomous Sanusi amirate in Cyrenaica under British protection ran counter to Egyptian ambitions in Libya and American objections to any prejudging of the peace settlement. The Foreign Office was reluctant to encourage Egyptian aspirations or excite American suspicions in 1941–42.

It should be emphasised that the actions of Sayyid Idris and the responses of the British authorities in Cairo and London were often influenced, from the summer of 1941 on, by events and calculations which had no direct connection with Cyrenaica. The suppression of the nationalist revolt in Iraq, the collapse of the Vichy regime in the

Levant, the Anglo-Soviet occupation of Iran, the restoration of Ethiopian independence, were all to have repercussions in Cyrenaica. Similarly, considerations of personal and national prestige in the Middle East and alliance politics helped determine attitudes towards Cyrenaica's future.

chapter 3
'AMBIGUOUS PROMISE'
MAY 1941–JANUARY 1942

> Axis broadcasts will no doubt say that this is another ambiguous promise concealing British colonising aims and that we intend either to rule [the] Senussi ourselves or to fill their country with Jews.
>
> Oliver Lyttelton, telegram to Eden, 5 January 1942[1]

LYTTLETON, THE LAF AND A COMMITMENT TO THE SANUSIS

In May 1941 the Foreign Office became alarmed at the serious decline in Britain's prestige in the Middle East owing to her defeats in Cyrenaica, Greece and Crete, and her actions in Iraq against the Pan-Arab putsch regime of Rashid Ali al-Gaylani. These events had a great influence on Arab opinion and had persuaded King Faruk, King Abd al-Aziz Ibn Saud and Syrian nationalist leaders to emulate Rashid Ali and to re-establish contacts with the Germans in order to reinsure themselves with the Axis and, if possible, to extract concessions from the latter on Arab independence, unity and Palestine. Although the Germans were willing to provide limited financial and military assistance by air to Iraq, using Vichy-controlled Syrian airfields, they could not accede to far-reaching nationalist demands without arousing the ire of Italy and Vichy France. At this stage of the war the Germans were not prepared to overrule the objections of their Allies by making concessions to Pan-Arabism. The Germans could only assure the Arabs in the most general terms of Axis sympathy with their struggle for freedom.

The British were aware of the links between the Germans and the Arab leaders, and could guess the nature of these conversations. In response to reports from Cairo and Baghdad about the devastating effects of German propaganda and activities in the Middle East, the British government in early June 1941 decided to embark upon an intensive propaganda campaign which, in conjunction with British military activity, was intended to restore Arab faith in Britain.

105

British propaganda made much of the fact that Britain on 8 June 1941 had guaranteed the Free French promise of Syrian and Lebanese independence. Certain other concessions to nationalists in the Levant were highlighted and constant reference was made to Eden's Mansion House statement of 29 May, when he had announced that he supported Syria's aspirations to independence and had great sympathy with the movement towards Arab unification. Propaganda emanating from Cairo proclaimed that certain provisions of the 1939 White Paper had already been put into effect in Palestine (even though Churchill and the bulk of the Cabinet objected to such a declaration) and that Iraq retained her sovereignty despite the routing of Rashid Ali and the Golden Square. The Arabs were largely unimpressed by British promises made at a time when Britain was hard-pressed by the Axis in the eastern Mediterranean. In any case British intervention in Iraq and Iran, the latter in concert with the Russians, during the summer of 1941, aroused the indignation of Arab nationalists.[2]

Two Arab leaders, Amir Abdallah and Sayyid Idris, were spurred by the Anglo-Free French pledges on Syrian and Lebanese independence to demand similar treatment for their countries, Transjordan and Libya. As the British authorities in London and Cairo often compared Transjordan with Cyrenaica, if not Tripolitania, it is instructive to note the differing responses to these demands.[3]

The Secretary of State for the Colonies, Lord Moyne (who had succeeded Lord Lloyd in February 1941, following the latter's death) thought Britain should accede to Abdallah's demands for independence, as a reward for his loyalty and to alleviate his disappointment at being denied the crown of Syria. However, the Foreign Office refused to countenance any change in the status of Transjordan until the British government had dealt with the much wider question of the independence and unity of all the countries of the Fertile Crescent. The Foreign Office was supported in its negative argument by the War Office and the Air Ministry who stressed the necessity of keeping an unfettered military presence in Transjordan until the war ended. Although the Foreign Office successfully opposed any concessions to Abdallah in August 1941, and again in early 1942, it followed a more conciliatory line with regard to the demands made by Sayyid Idris.[4]

It was not only events in the Levant which had prompted Sayyid Idris to ask for an undertaking from Britain that Libya would become independent. The decision of the British government to restore independence to Ethiopia played a part in convincing Sayyid Idris that he should demand similar treatment for Libya. He pointed out that the Sanusis had given Britain their aid freely, without bargaining in advance for political concessions, simply relying on the declared sympathy of the British with the aspirations of small nations. Sayyid Idris complained that the lack of a declaration on their future exposed the Sanusis to the ridicule of Egypt and the Arab world.

In an attempt to force the British government to meet his grievance, he made use of the only political weapon at his disposal, the Libyan Arab Force (LAF). In the aftermath of the costly failure to destroy Rommel's forces on the Egyptian frontier (Operation 'Battleaxe', 15–17 June 1941), it became imperative to withdraw some British units from Syria as soon as possible (Operation 'Exporter', the Anglo-Free French invasion of Vichy Syria and Lebanon, was then in progress) and despatch them to the Western Desert.

In order to fill the depleted ranks of the Allied army of occupation in Syria, the British military authorities in Egypt wanted to transfer two battalions of the Libyan Arab Force from the Western Desert to Syria. Sayyid Idris refused to agree unless he was accorded recognition as an ally of Britain and given assurances as to the future of his people. Sayyid Idris requested that the Sanusis be freed permanently from Italian rule and that an Arab amirate be established under British protection or a mandate on the model of Transjordan. Sayyid Idris did not insist on his becoming amir, but this modest disclaimer could not conceal either his ambition or the fact that there was no other candidate.[5]

It was Sayyid Idris's demands which forced the British authorities in Egypt to confront the problem of the future of Libya. They had first to consider the controversial claim by Sayyid Idris to a Sanusi amirate over all Libya. It was clear that most people in Cyrenaica (inhabited mainly by the Sanusis) would accept Idris as their amir. However, his claim to a similar position in Tripolitania was very questionable (there were about 150,000 to 250,000 Sanusis in Tripolitania out of a total population of 750,000, including 50,000 Italian colonists). Sayyid Idris had recognised this fact in private conversation and correspondence with British officials and he seemed to be prepared to limit his political ambitions to Cyrenaica.[6] Undoubtedly, the newly-appointed Minister of State in the Middle East, Oliver Lyttelton, had this in mind when he addressed the problem of the transfer of the two LAF battalions to Syria.[7]

In dealing with this question, in the latter half of August 1941, Lyttelton would appear to have been influenced by his recent experience of dealing with the problems posed by the Anglo-Free French invasion of Syria and the Lebanon. He was intent on reassuring the Arabs about

British intentions, so as to counter German propaganda which accused Britain of planning to annex all conquered Arab countries. He aimed also to safeguard British strategic interests. Lyttelton thought there was a strong case for giving satisfaction, in some form, to the desire of the Sanusis for 'recognition' and for doing so soon.

He observed that the Sanusis had suffered severely for supporting the British and had received nothing in return. The British could not very well return the Sanusis to Italian rule, even under a reformed Italy. It was reasonable, therefore, to consider granting the Sanusis some form of autonomy. This would make a favourable impression on the Arabs and the Muslims in general, and the British government could represent it as following on from Eden's Mansion House speech. It would also counter Axis propaganda which had been spreading the half-truth that Britain would make concessions to her Arab friends only when they turned against her. It would solve the immediate problem concerning the despatch of two battalions of the Libyan Arab Force to Syria and would presumably free this force for use in other theatres of war if it proved necessary in the future. Above all, Lyttelton thought that Sanusi autonomy was in Britain's short- and long-term strategic interests.

Although it was not possible to foresee the situation existing after the war, it was unlikely that Britain would allow Italy or any other potentially hostile power to become established again in Cyrenaica, as this would be a permanent threat to Egypt and the Suez Canal.[8] In friendly hands, however, Cyrenaica would form a natural bulwark for Egypt as the Sirte Desert was a readily defensible frontier. The establishment of a Sanusi amirate in Cyrenaica would enable Britain to acquire the same kind of military facilities as she enjoyed in Transjordan and neighbouring territories. Moreover, the British would avoid the responsibility, odium, and at least some of the expense, which would be incurred if they assumed the direct administration of the country.

Lyttelton quickly dismissed the weighty objections to Britain undertaking a commitment to the Sanusis during the war. He admitted that it might prove equally embarrassing for the British later on if they had to fulfil or default on their pledge: '... it may be said that we had our bellyful of contradictory promises in the Middle East during the last war and that we should avoid any advance commitments this time. But to my mind the moral of the contradictory promises of 1916–18 is not that we should adopt a policy of despair and make no promises at all, but that we should think carefully and make the right promises.'

It might also be argued that the British government should leave the future of Libya undetermined in case it proved necessary to use the country as a pawn during the negotiations for a peace treaty after the war. The Minister of State pointed out, however, that if Britain had long-term strategic interests to protect in Cyrenaica then she would not want to use the latter as a pawn in the diplomatic game. Lyttelton admitted that the presence of Italian colonists in Cyrenaica prevented the establishment of an Arab regime (a similar situation prevailed in Palestine). Lyttelton's proposed remedy was to terminate Italian rule in Cyrenaica and to transplant the Italian colonists to Tripolitania: 'They would be a permanent sore if left where they are, and in any case much of the land they occupy would be required for resettling the dispossessed Senussi.' Britain could make this the condition upon which Italy would retain Tripolitania.

The Minister of State recommended, therefore, that the British government should make an immediate public declaration to Sayyid Idris, as leader of the Sanusis. It would contain three undertakings. Firstly, Britain welcomed 'The association of his forces with their own in the task of defeating their common enemies.' Secondly, '... [a]t the end of the war he [Sayyid Idris] and his followers will in no circumstances be again placed under Italian domination'. Lastly, Sayyid Idris could be confident that 'That HM Government will follow in this, as in other matters, the policy embodied in the recent joint declaration of Mr Churchill and President Roosevelt.'

Lyttelton thought that the relevant provisions of the Atlantic Charter which applied to Cyrenaica, and could be quoted to Sayyid Idris, were Article II: 'They desire to see no territorial changes which do not agree with the freely expressed will of the people concerned,' and Article III: 'They respect the rights of all people to choose the form of government under which they will live ....' In other words, Britain would support the establishment of an autonomous Sanusi amirate in Cyrenaica after the war. Lyttelton thought that if Britain refused to become the protecting power then the Sanusis would probably prefer Turkey or Egypt, in that order, to assume the role.[9]

Lyttelton intended to raise the question of the future of Cyrenaica during his forthcoming visit to London to report to the War Cabinet on the situation in the Middle East. Accordingly, he gave the Foreign Office advance notice of his proposal. Although there is no evidence of the Middle East War Council (MEWC) having approved Lyttelton's recommendations for a declaration on Cyrenaica, it is very unlikely that the Minister of State would have proceeded in this matter without the prior agreement of Lampson and the new Commander-in-Chief, Middle East, Sir Claude Auchinleck.

Captain Oliver Lyttelton (right), the Minister of State resident in the Middle East from June 1941 to February 1942 at the British Embassy in Cairo with Sir Miles Lampson, British Ambassador in Egypt. By permission of The Imperial War Museum JAR 565.

As a newcomer to the Middle East, Lyttelton must have been heavily dependent upon his political adviser, Henry L d'Hard Alys Hopkinson (formerly private secretary to Sir Alexander Cadogan) and Lampson for guidance. Lyttelton seems to have worked well with Lampson. The latter had welcomed the idea of the Minister of State assuming the role of a 'superman' in the Middle East. As has been noted already, Lyttelton was anxious to secure the agreement of the local British authorities on a question before making a recommendation to the War Cabinet.[10]

It is hard to believe that these ideas on the future of Cyrenaica originated from Lyttelton. They bear an uncanny resemblance to the views first propounded by Lampson to Eden in March 1941, with the exception of the recommendation for a declaration on the Sanusis. It would also appear that Lampson had dropped his opposition to the British government assuming a commitment on the future of Cyrenaica during the war. His change of mind can be explained by his concern at the apparent deterioration of Britain's position in the Middle East. Since April 1941 he had stressed the need for a policy which would have some chance of countering the success of German propaganda in the Middle East; otherwise Britain would be 'in danger of reaping the world-wind of our neglect'.

Lampson had recommended the statements on Syrian and Lebanese independence and Arab unity, and had deplored the fact that there was no official declaration guaranteeing the cessation of Jewish immigration and Arab administrative predominance in Palestine.[11] In casting around for further ways of placating Arab sensibilities in the summer of 1941, Lampson probably seized upon the request by Sayyid Idris for British assurances as to the future of his country. This offered an ideal opportunity for Britain to make a direct riposte to the general thrust of Axis propaganda, which stated that only Germany and Italy could give the Arabs independence.

A declaration on the Sanusis would also maintain the good effect created in the Arab world, according to Lampson, by Eden's Mansion House speech. It is feasible to suggest that Lampson proceeded to impress upon Lyttelton, who had recently arrived in Cairo, the urgent necessity of responding in a positive manner to Sayyid Idris's demands. Perhaps the most convincing argument in favour of this interpretation lies, paradoxically, in the fact that at no time did Lampson protest to the Foreign Office about the course of action which Lyttelton was proposing should be taken with regard to Cyrenaica. The conclusion seems unavoidable both that Lampson must have approved of a declaration on the Sanusis, and that the original idea came from him rather than Lyttelton.

BRITAIN, THE UNITED STATES AND THE DECLARATION ON THE SANUSIS

The initial reaction of the Foreign Office to Lyttelton's recommendation on Cyrenaica was mixed. Bateman (head of the Egyptian Department) continued to favour Egypt's claim to Cyrenaica and attempted, therefore, to delay a decision on the proposed declaration. He pointed out that the British had yet to decide whether they were prepared to recognise Sanusi nationality, to shoulder the financial burden of supporting a Sanusi amirate, and to transfer their troops from Egypt to Cyrenaica after the war. Bateman mentioned that some officials (e.g. Woolley) favoured handing over Cyrenaica to Egypt at the peace settlement.

The Egyptian government had already put forward a claim for frontier rectification with Cyrenaica. In any case the territory could not become independent because of its mixed Italian and Arab population. Bateman held out the tantalising prospect whereby Cyrenaica might be offered to Egypt, in exchange for the latter relinquishing her share of the Sudan Condominium to Britain. Bateman thought also that offering Egypt lebensraum (*majal hayawi* in Arabic) in Cyrenaica might help ease the potentially explosive problem of overpopulation in Egypt after the war.

Sir Horace Seymour was unimpressed by Bateman's argument. On the contrary, he thought that there was 'a fairly good case' for going as far as Lyttelton's recommendation on Cyrenaica. Seymour surmised that everything would largely depend upon whether Britain resumed her former position after the war, and whether, if she had the power, she would try to prevent the surplus population of Italy expanding overseas.[12]

To a large extent, the Foreign Office was influenced in its deliberations on the future of Cyrenaica by the change in British policy towards Italy which had occurred during the summer of 1941. The possibility of securing Italy's withdrawal from the war by means of a separate peace with Britain had been rejected. There seemed little likelihood of such a development occurring until Germany had suffered a grave defeat and there had been an internal uprising in Italy against Mussolini. It seemed more profitable for the British government to concentrate instead on bringing about the collapse of Italy, the weak link of the Axis, through intensified military pressure. As Eden put it on 23 August 1941, 'We have to win a victory on land ourselves in an important theatre before we can catch one of these moonbeams.'[13]

The Foreign Office no longer felt, therefore, the same pressing need it had in the winter of 1940–41 to placate Italian opinion over the issue of the fate of the Italian colonies. As Pierson Dixon (Southern Department) pointed out on 2 October 1941, it seemed quite certain that for reasons of strategy Britain would not want to return Cyrenaica to Italy or allow it to remain under any regime in which the Italians played a part, e.g. a Free Italian Colony (Sir Orme Sargent remarked that this idea had been abandoned as impracticable). 'We must face the fact [Dixon argued] that very little of her overseas possessions will remain to Italy after the war and that any promises we may wish to make to the Italians if they show a disposition to revolt against the regime of the Germans will have to take the form of economic and colonising opportunities (point 5 of the Atlantic Charter).' Although the establishment of a Sanusi state, in any form, would be a grave setback for Italy and more unacceptable than Egypt or Britain taking over Cyrenaica, Dixon did not think this should deter the Foreign Office from accepting the Minister of State's proposals, if it was thought to be the best available solution.[14]

Eden appeared reluctant, however, to give political recognition to Sayyid Idris. Like Lyttelton he felt that while Britain might guarantee that the Sanusis should never again be placed under Italian domination in Cyrenaica, it would be unwise to go further than this.[15] Following Lyttelton's return to Cairo, Eden sought War Cabinet approval for his proposal. The Foreign Secretary pointed out that Britain had undertaken no specific political engagements to the Sanusis beyond General Wilson's pledge in August 1940 that: 'We shall co-operate ... with sincerity and loyalty so that the Arabs may be entitled to regain their freedom and take back their lands from the Italian oppressors and restore their independence once more.' The British had never given any 'official cognisance' to the resolutions adopted by Cyrenaican leaders in Cairo on 9 August 1940 in favour of the establishment of a Sanusi amirate in Cyrenaica and the formation of a temporary Sanusi government under Sayyid Idris, with the power to negotiate with the British government.[16]

Therefore, Eden and Lyttelton were prepared to meet the desire of the Sanusis for permanent freedom from Italian rule, but they thought it premature to announce the establishment of an Arab amirate in Cyrenaica under British protection, on the lines of Transjordan, as requested by Sayyid Idris. What they were prepared to recommend was that an early declaration should be made to Sayyid Idris, and that it should be limited to the simple statement: '(1) His Majesty's Government welcome the association of his forces with their own in the task of defeating their common enemies. (2) At the end of the war he and his followers will in no circumstances be again placed under Italian domination.' Such a statement, it was believed, 'would have a good effect on the Arab world generally'.[17]

Apart from a general reluctance to assume commitments during the war, it is possible that, in recommending a limited declaration to the War Cabinet, Eden and Lyttelton may have been influenced by certain political considerations. In the autumn of 1941 Britain's relations with Egypt and the United States were strained. In Egypt Lampson was anxious not to provoke King Faruk by forcing him to accept a Wafd government (although Lampson thought that only the Wafd could command enough popular support to govern Egypt properly, and thus provide the security which the British required for their major base of operations in the Middle East).

Lampson was supported by the Foreign Office who, like him, did not want an internal political crisis in Egypt while Rommel's forces still posed a threat in the Western Desert.[18] As it was, there was every likelihood that the Egyptians would exert pressure on the British government to meet nationalist demands. Eden would thus have provided a hostage to fortune if he had announced, as formerly proposed by Lyttelton, that Britain favoured self-determination for Cyrenaica. Such an announcement would have immediately raised the question of Egyptian aspirations in Libya, which in turn would have complicated Anglo-Egyptian relations at a critical juncture, something which Eden and Lyttelton were plainly anxious to avoid. Certainly Eden was aware of this danger in early January 1942, before the onset of the political crisis in Egypt.[19] It is likely that he had it in mind also in early October 1941, and persuaded Lyttelton accordingly.

Similarly, Eden would have been careful to avoid any action which might have increased American suspicion and distrust of Britain. In the late summer and early autumn of 1941 the Foreign Office and the War Cabinet had become concerned by the mood of the American people.[20] Eden may have feared that the Americans would misconstrue an announcement by the British government of self-determination for Cyrenaica after the war. Ironically, they might suspect Britain of trying to exploit the Atlantic Charter of August 1941 for her own imperialist ends.

It would have been difficult for the American public, weaned on the idea of national independence, to have grasped the idea that Sayyid Idris might actually have desired British protection for an autonomous Sanusi amirate in Cyrenaica. Indeed, some American officials did have doubts about the motives of the British government in making the declaration on the Sanusis, even in its final limited form. It is not surprising, therefore, that the Foreign Office, as early as mid-October, began to show anxiety to inform the State Department of the exact nature of the proposed declaration on the Sanusis, in case it should be interpreted as a veiled attempt at territorial aggrandisement by Britain. These considerations may well have influenced Eden's thinking in early October.

Despite these reservations, however, Eden and Seymour were disturbed by the fact that nothing was being done to formulate a comprehensive Arab policy. The chief obstacle was the continuing dispute within the War Cabinet over the 1939 White Paper on Palestine, and the role it should play in determining the Arab policy of the British government.[21] It can be argued that this stalemate, which prevented consideration from being given to Amir Abdallah's demands, persuaded Eden to look to Cyrenaica in order to demonstrate Britain's sympathy with Arab aspirations at a time when her actions in Iraq and Iran seemed to belie her stated intentions.

Although the War Cabinet on 6 October 1941 accepted the recommendation by Eden and Lyttelton for an early declaration on the Sanusis, this decision was not carried out for another three months. The issue had become less urgent when it was decided not to send the two LAF battalions to Syria, as originally envisaged. The Chief of the Imperial General Staff, Sir John Dill, had cast doubt on the wisdom of deploying Sanusi soldiers in the Levant.[22] No reasons were given for this decision but it is possible that the British military authorities in the Middle East feared disciplinary problems if the LAF battalions were exposed to the political ferment in Syria. There were strong links between the Syrian nationalists and the exiled Tripolitanian leaders. Certainly Auchinleck's decision in mid-October, supported by Lyttelton, to delay the opening of the 'Crusader' offensive from 1 to 18 November made it preferable to postpone the declaration on the Sanusis. Auchinleck seems to have been wary of giving political undertakings before a favourable outcome to the military operations had been achieved.[23]

The Foreign Office, as remarked earlier, thought it important to notify the State Department in advance of the British government's intention to issue the declaration on the Sanusis. As Sir David Scott (Assistant Under Secretary of State superintending the American Department) pointed out on 10 October, '... we promised to keep the Americans informed of any territorial etc. commitments entered into'.[24] There was concern, expressed by Neville Butler (head of the American Department) that 'The Americans might feel that we ignored their views on post-war commitments if ... [the declaration] were given in the House of Commons before anything had been said to them.'[25]

Accordingly, Sir Alexander Cadogan despatched a personal message to the US Under Secretary of State, Sumner Welles, on 15 October, which explained the purpose and the terms of the declaration. Welles agreed with the British government's proposal. As he informed President Roosevelt, the treatment accorded the Sanusis by the Italians had been 'shocking and from the standpoint of humanity alone, a statement of the kind proposed by the British Government would seem to me to be one which would be welcomed by public opinion everywhere.' Roosevelt concurred and Welles replied to Cadogan on 25 October that the Government of the United States had 'Taken due note of the contents of your message but we have no comments to offer and no suggestions to make.'[26]

The brief acknowledgment by Welles of the British government's decision to issue the declaration on the Sanusis led Scott to conclude this was 'hardly the kind of commitment that the US are interested in'. In fact the State Department began to display an interest in the Sanusis and Libya in late October 1941. Welles asked Wallace Murray (chief of the Division of Near Eastern Affairs) for more background information and the latter duly obliged on 28 October. Murray also drew attention to Egyptian ambitions with regard to Libya. Earlier in the year these had been made clear to the US chargé d'affaires in Cairo, Raymond A Hare, by Abd al-Rahman Azzam, the head of the Egyptian Territorial Army. Azzam had spoken of the natural affinity between Libya and Egypt. He advocated the union of the two countries, although with provision for the autonomy of Libya.

Azzam had said that the Tripolitanians favoured union with Egypt. He predicted that while the Sanusis were strong in Cyrenaica, their leaders would cease to exert political influence and continue merely as religious heads within a united Libya. Hare thought that the Egyptian government and the Palace would welcome an Egyptian-Libyan union if the British retained control of Libya. Murray speculated that the Egyptians wanted union between Egypt and an autonomous Libya after the war in order to demonstrate their Pan-Arab sentiments, to free Egypt from the threat posed by Italy, to increase the prestige of the country and the Crown, and to secure compensation for Egypt having been a battleground.

Murray expressed doubts, however, about the capacity of the Egyptians to govern a desert country such as Libya, which seemed to be devoid of natural resources. If Libya were put under Egyptian rule it would have to be properly arranged, otherwise it would become a heavy burden for Egypt and a source of trouble. Nevertheless, Murray and his colleagues in NEA continued to toy with the idea of union between Egypt and Libya.[27]

The inauspicious opening to Operation 'Crusader' did not discourage Sayyid Idris from demanding assurances as to the future of the Sanusis. Following the serious setback at Sidi Rezegh on 22 November (when the the Eighth Army lost much of its armour) and

General Cunningham's replacement by General Ritchie as GOC the Eighth Army, Lyttelton favoured proceeding with the declaration on the Sanusis. He thought that it would have a maximum effect on the Sanusis at that time, and that any further delay in issuing it would seriously reduce their enthusiasm. Lyttelton deferred, however, to Auchinleck's judgment on the exact timing of the declaration. The latter continued to regard the military situation in North Africa as too uncertain for the British government to make the desired announcement.

While British Commonwealth soldiers doggedly fought their way towards Tobruk, inflicting severe damage on Rommel's forces, the British authorities in Cairo and the Foreign Office in London were discussing the exact phrasing of the declaration on the Sanusis. It was confirmed that the declaration was intended to apply only to Cyrenaica, and not to Tripolitania (where the Sanusis comprised a third of the population). There was a difference of opinion, however, about whether the declaration should cover all the inhabitants of Cyrenaica, including the small non-Sanusi element, or simply the Sanusis, who constituted the overwhelming majority.

Brigadier Longrigg (who had been reappointed as DCPO Cyrenaica) and Lyttelton favoured the former statement which would definitely commit Britain to removing Cyrenaica from Italian rule. The Foreign Office thought that this was probably the War Cabinet's original intention but it had not been stated categorically. Cadogan's statement of 15 October to Welles had made it clear that the declaration would be limited to the 'Sanusis in Cyrenaica', and the Foreign Office preferred this to the Cairo formula, which was seen as an embellishment. Furthermore, the Foreign Office hoped that there was sufficient ambiguity in a declaration that the 'Sanusis in Cyrenaica' would not again be subjected to Italian rule, to defuse Italian criticism of Britain's action. It would also allow the British government some leeway in determining the future of Cyrenaica.[28]

As the outcome of 'Crusader' was still in the balance in the first week of December 1941, Auchinleck persuaded Eden against making the desired declaration on 4 December in the House of Commons, before Eden's departure for a conference with the Soviets in Moscow.[29] It was not until 22 December, after the the Eighth Army had finally won 'Crusader' and Rommel's Panzergruppe Afrika had been forced to retreat, first to Ain al-Gazala and then to Ajdabiya, that Auchinleck gave his permission. By then the House of Commons had risen for Christmas and would not sit again until 8 January 1942, and then only for one day.

A British Crusader tank passes a burning German Mark IV tank during Operation Crusader, November 1941. By permission of The Imperial War Museum E 6751.

   This further unavoidable delay led to renewed agitation by Sayyid Idris for the British government to give an assurance on the future independence of the Sanusis. As the Eighth Army proceeded to occupy Cyrenaica (Benghazi fell on 24 December), Sayyid Idris came under increasing pressure from his followers to secure a pledge from Britain. Earlier Sayyid Idris had made it clear to the British authorities in Cairo that unless they were prepared to make such a concession his position would become intolerable and he would have to withdraw from active collaboration with Britain. In order, no doubt, to prevent this from occurring, Lyttelton favoured informing Sayyid Idris immediately of the terms of the declaration and communicating it to the local press. The Foreign Office had decided, however, that Sayyid Idris was not to be informed in advance of the precise content of the declaration, although he could be told that Eden would make a statement on 8 January 1942.

The Foreign Office wanted to avoid both premature publicity and the danger that Sayyid Idris might try to discuss the terms of the draft declaration. As Sir Horace Seymour pointed out on 23 December, 'We are not promising to set him up as ruler of a state and he might want alterations made.' Consequently, the Minister of State simply informed Sayyid Idris on 1 January 1942 that the Secretary of State for Foreign Affairs was to make a statement on the Sanusis in the House of Commons on 8 January, and that there should be no prior publicity. Sayyid Idris was also told not to expect too much from Eden's declaration.[30]

The Minister of State attempted to calm the anxiety expressed by Sayyid Idris that the declaration might prove to be wholly inadequate. Lyttelton urged the Foreign Office to give assurances to Sayyid Idris regarding the administration of Cyrenaica and to concede Allied status to the Sanusis. The Foreign Office was reluctant, however, to make any statement to Sayyid Idris which might be interpreted as a British commitment to the independence of the Sanusis and Cyrenaica. It was thought wiser not to go beyond the terms of the draft declaration for the moment.[31] However, on 5 January the Foreign Office did agree to Lyttelton's suggestion that a copy of the text of Eden's statement, with a translation, should be conveyed to Sayyid Idris before it was generally published. It was agreed that the declaration should be given prominence in the Arabic press, in radio broadcasts throughout the Middle East, and in pamphlets to be distributed in Cyrenaica.

Lyttelton was concerned, however, that Axis propaganda might exploit the rather negative language in which the British declaration had to be couched for reasons of policy. It could be said that this was 'another ambiguous promise concealing British colonising aims and that we intend either to rule Senussi ourselves or to fill their country with Jews. Sayyid himself would be particularly sensitive to this kind of insinuation.' The Minister of State feared that unless such innuendo could be forestalled by informed comment then much of the declaration's value would be lost.

Lyttelton proposed to avoid this danger by giving adequate guidance (along the lines of the abortive letter to Idris) to British Information Officers in the Middle East. The background to the declaration would be explained to these officers. They would be told that although an open promise of autonomy for the Sanusis had to be avoided, in inspiring comment on the pledge that the Sanusis would be freed permanently from Italian rule, they could refer to the principles of the Atlantic Charter and hint that some form of autonomy would be a natural development after the war. Although the

Anthony Eden, the British Foreign Secretary, who issued the Declaration on the Sanusis, January 1942. By permission of The Imperial War Museum HU 49409.

Foreign Office approved Lyttelton's suggestion, it was on the condition that it would not be published or conveyed in written form to Sayyid Idris.[32]

In early January 1942 the Eighth Army was unsuccessful in its attempt at Ajdabiya to rout Rommel's forces and capture the 'fortified bottleneck' at El Agheila, 'a position which in British hands would serve either as a sally-port for a renewed offensive into Tripolitania or as a barbican for captured Cyrenaica.'[33] On 5–6 January the second British offensive in Libya had come to a temporary halt while preparations were made for the advance into Tripolitania, Operation 'Acrobat'. Auchinleck and Ritchie had recovered the ground which had been lost to Rommel in April 1941.

It was an appropriate moment for the British Foreign Secretary to make a statement on the future of the inhabitants of Cyrenaica. In response to an arranged question in the House of Commons on 8 January 1942, Eden declared that: 'The Sayyid Idris al-Sanusi made contact with the British authorities in Egypt within a month of the collapse of France at a time when the military situation in Africa was most unfavourable to us. A Sanusi force was subsequently raised from those of his followers who had escaped from Italian oppression at various times during the past twenty years. This force performed considerable ancillary duties during the successful fighting in the Western Desert in the winter of 1940–41, and is again playing a useful part in the campaign now in progress. I take this opportunity to express the warm appreciation of His Majesty's government for the contribution which Sayyid Idris al-Sanusi and his followers have made and are making to the British war effort. We welcome their association with His Majesty's forces in the task of defeating the common enemies. His Majesty's government is determined that at the end of the war the Sanusis in Cyrenaica will in no circumstances again fall under Italian domination.'[34]

chapter 4
'A NATIVE STATE'
JANUARY–JUNE 1942

> ... in short, the administrative policy will be so orientated as to give the general complexion of a native state, as opposed to that of a native territory under the subjugation of a European power.
>
> Brigadier H R Hone, memorandum of 9 May 1942.[35]

THE SECOND BRITISH OCCUPATION OF CYRENAICA

THE DECLARATION on the Sanusis does not seem to have had the effect in Italy, the Middle East and the United States which the British government originally desired, although it is impossible to be completely sure because of a paucity of information. (The relevant Foreign Office file is missing. It would seem to have been destroyed, rather than retained under statute.)

In the case of Italy this was due, in part, to a change of mind by the Foreign Office. After the declaration received publicity in Britain, the Political Warfare Executive and the Foreign Office (Southern Department) decided on 10 January to mention it only briefly and objectively in propaganda to Italy. There was no attempt to exploit the declaration. The Foreign Office was convinced by 21 January that it was better not to go on record with 'a statement in black and white' that Italy had lost Cyrenaica forever. In Italy the government-controlled press played down the declaration. The Foreign Office (Political Intelligence Department) thought that this was done for reasons of political prestige, in view of the recent Axis reverses in Cyrenaica and Russia.[36]

Eden's declaration appears to have met with an equally limited response in the Middle East. It must have been noted by the Arabic press (it was mentioned by the French-language newspapers in Beirut, the *Revue du Liban* and *Le Jour*) although in Egypt the food shortage and the growing political crisis monopolised the attention of the public. (On 6 January the Egyptian government had announced its decision to 'suspend' diplomatic relations with Vichy France, in accordance with the policy of rupturing relations with all states at war with Egypt's ally, Britain.) The Egyptian Foreign Minister had, however, referred to Egyptian aspirations in Cyrenaica (probably à propos of the declaration on the Sanusis) during the closed session of the Foreign Affairs Committee of the Egyptian Chamber of Deputies on 20 January. He may have raised the subject in an attempt to propitiate his critics, who demanded his resignation following the cutting of diplomatic ties with the Vichy regime.

Above all, the declaration disappointed Sayyid Idris and his followers because it made no reference to the future independence of Libya, an omission which was sharply criticised by the exiled Tripolitanian leaders. However, this discontent was not immediately apparent to the British authorities in Egypt. In mid-January 1942 Sayyid Idris issued his own declaration to the Sanusis in Cyrenaica, congratulating them on being freed from Italian oppression and expressing his appreciation for Britain's action.[37]

Eden's statement aroused suspicion among American officials in Cairo and Washington about British intentions in Cyrenaica. The US Minister to Egypt, Alexander Kirk, informed the State Department of the declaration on 16 January. He interpreted it as precluding Cyrenaica from being returned to Italy after the war. Although he was unaware of any move to determine the permanent future of Cyrenaica, he thought it might be significant that the British Military Administration in Cyrenaica was said to be modelled on the shaikhdoms under British protection in the Persian Gulf.

The State Department was interested in this and on 21 January asked Kirk for the terms of Eden's declaration (although the Foreign Office had informed the State Department of the essential details in October 1941) and whether it was compatible with the possibility of Cyrenaica being granted to Egypt. Kirk duly obliged on 29 January and answered in the affirmative on the latter point, adding that he did not think that either the British, the Egyptians or even the Sanusis had come to any definite decision on the post-war future of Cyrenaica.[38]

This would seem to indicate that the State Department, or rather the Division of Near Eastern Affairs, was still considering the idea of a union of Egypt and Libya, or at least of Cyrenaica, after the war. Undoubtedly, this should be interpreted within the context of American policy towards Egypt. The State Department's attitude was characterised by the desire to compete with Britain at all levels. Whenever the British appeared to be weakening or in a conciliatory mood in Egypt, as during the period of King Faruk's bid for direct rule from 1937 to 1942, the NEA was quick to detect any opportunities which could be exploited to increase American influence.

The steady deterioration of Anglo-Egyptian relations in January 1942 encouraged some American officials, such as the US Military Attaché in Cairo, Colonel Bonner Fellers, to press for closer ties between the United States and Egypt. The NEA was even prepared to capitalise on the political crisis in Egypt in early February.[39] It is just possible that the anglophobe chief of NEA, Wallace Murray, entertained the thought of American support for an eventual union of Egypt and Libya because it would not only thwart suspected British designs in Cyrenaica but also win the favour of the Egyptians at Britain's expense.

The State Department need not have worried. The British were in occupation of the greater part of Cyrenaica for too short a time in early 1942 to allow the British Military Administration to work out the

Generalfeldmarshschall Erwin Rommel at a staff conference in the Western Desert, 1942. By permission of The Imperial War Museum E 4061E.

Italian farmers and their families talking at Fort Maddalena, Cyrenaica, January 1942 and lining up for food and broth issued by the occupying British forces.
By permission of the Australian War Memorial: Negative 023044.

administrative implications of the declaration on the Sanusis. Longrigg and his staff seem to have concentrated on trying to persuade the Italian agricultural colonists in the Jabal Akhdar, who had concentrated in the village centres for mutual protection against the Sanusis, to return to their farms to resume cultivation.[40]

Any progress the British administrators might have made was cut short by Rommel's counter-offensive on 21 January 1942. In a series of brilliant manoeuvres Rommel outwitted the British commanders of the Eighth Army and, having mauled another British armoured division, forced them to abandon Benghazi on 29 January and retreat to Ain al-Gazala. By 4 February Panzergruppe Afrika had overrun the Jabal Akhdar and established a position running from Timini on the coast to Makili on the south-eastern flank of the Jabal. Rommel had regained control of western Cyrenaica.

The British found themselves having to honour their pledge to the Sanusis in a manner they had not seriously anticipated. As the Eighth Army withdrew east of the Jabal Akhdar at the end of January, thousands of Sanusis accompanied them. No doubt the Sanusis feared Italian reprisals for their co-operation with the British forces and for carrying out acts of revenge against Italian colonists during the second British occupation of the Jabal. Many tribesmen sought refuge in eastern Cyrenaica, which continued under British military administration until May 1942. However, large numbers of Sanusis were evacuated to Egypt, where they were accommodated in a camp near Alexandria. The ablebodied youth were drafted into the Libyan Arab Force or the Palestine Regiment, or sent to the Cyrenaica Police School, which was intended to provide the nucleus of a police force for the next British occupation of Cyrenaica proper, the Jabal Akhdar.[41]

In the aftermath of the reverse suffered by the Eighth Army in western Cyrenaica and the political crisis in Egypt, Sayyid Idris expressed

The agricultural centre of d'Annunzio at the mouth of the Barce valley, where Italian farmers took refuge, January 1942. By permission of the Australian War Memorial: Negative 023043.

his dissatisfaction with the negative content of Eden's declaration. The Sanusi leader appears to have interpreted it as promising the liberation of Cyrenaica, but at the same time he was disappointed by the absence of a positive assurance as to the future independence of the territory. Undoubtedly, Sayyid Idris was under great pressure at that time from his followers, many of whom had recently fled to Egypt and were demanding some reassurances as to their future.

In addition, the exiled Tripolitanian leaders criticised him for not securing a promise from the British that Tripolitania would be freed from Italian rule. They were angered also by Eden's reference in his declaration to the Sanusis, which the Tripolitanian shaikhs saw as implying British recognition of Sanusi overlordship in Libya. In order to quell the growing sense of unease, and the potential threat it posed to his leadership, Sayyid Idris submitted a series of demands about the political future of Libya to the Minister of State on 23 February 1942. These required the British government to: '1 Declare the complete independence of Libya in its internal affairs and recognise a Muslim ruler as its head of government; 2 Guarantee Libya against foreign attack; 3 Conclude a treaty with Libya, the terms of which would be agreed upon; 4 Appoint a joint Anglo-Libyan Committee to lay the foundation of a Libyan regime.'[42]

Oliver Lyttelton's days as 'the Satrap of the Middle East' had come to an end following the setback in Cyrenaica.[43] Churchill thought Lyttelton 'had failed badly' in not ensuring beforehand that the Eighth Army was capable of holding Cyrenaica. He was accused of 'taking too much interest in local politics and foreign affairs and not enough in what he was intended to do'. Churchill recalled Lyttelton to London to become Minister of Production (Munitions) in the War Cabinet.[44]

Before his departure from Cairo on 26 February, Lyttelton seems to have indulged his penchant for oriental intrigue one last time. Although he was not prepared to give any written guarantee on the future status of Libya, he appears to have made an oral pledge to Sayyid Idris that his country would be granted its freedom after the war (it is not clear whether Lyttelton was referring to Cyrenaica or all Libya). This gave Sayyid Idris enough of an opening to defuse the criticism of his leadership. The leading Cyrenaican shaikhs in exile were made to realise that they had little choice but to accept the British government's verbal promises to the Sanusis. It was agreed that their continuing contribution to the war effort was necessary in order to ensure the redemption of Britain's pledge after the war.[45]

Nothing better illustrates the growing strategic importance of Cyrenaica in British eyes than the acrimonious debate which took place between Churchill and Auchinleck in the spring of 1942 on the timing of the next British offensive in North Africa. Churchill and the War Cabinet began in late February to press Auchinleck to take advantage of the relative weakness of Panzergruppe Afrika, and attack Rommel before he could be reinforced in his Mechili-Timini position, 89 km west of Tobruk. It was thought imperative that the Eighth Army regain control of the Jabal Akhdar and the Martuba airfields (24 km south-east of Derna) in order to enable the RAF to provide air cover for the supply ships to reach Malta from Alexandria.

Malta had been under intensive air bombardment since 21 December 1941 and the supply situation on the island had become serious. Churchill believed that the fall of Malta would be catastrophic and probably fatal in the long run to the defence of the Nile Valley, since it would deprive British aircraft and submarines operating from the island fortress of the ability to interdict Axis supply lines across the Central Mediterranean. This, in turn, would permit the unimpeded build-up of the Axis forces for the invasion of Egypt.[46] Moreover, it was hoped that an early offensive in North Africa would help the Russians by forcing the Germans to despatch units from the Eastern Front to the war in the desert.

Auchinleck did not dispute the urgency of the situation but he was not prepared to launch even a limited offensive in Cyrenaica until the Eighth Army had the requisite superiority in cruiser tanks (3 to 2) over the Afrika Korps to give it a reasonable chance of success. He doubted whether this would be feasible before early June 1942.

As Commander-in-Chief Middle East, Auchinleck feared that if his armoured formations were destroyed in a premature offensive he would be unable to hold the defensive position in Marmarica (between Ain al-Gazala and Bir Hakaim) and on the Egyptian frontier (from Sallum to Maddalena), and would have to retire to the prepared position at El Alamein, within 112 km of Alexandria. The 'peril in which Egypt would then stand would probably have worse results than if Malta were to succumb'. Auchinleck had also to consider the possibility of remaining on the defensive in North Africa and reinforcing the Northern Front, in the event of a German thrust through the Caucasus, or the Southern front, if the forces of Imperial Japan continued to make significant advances in the Indian Ocean region. Churchill was unimpressed by such reasoning and Auchinleck was forced to agree to provide a 'distraction in Cyrenaica in time to allow the passing of a convoy from Alexandria to Malta in early June'.[47]

Lieutenant General Ritchie, Commander in Chief Eighth Army, with his corps commanders, Generals Norrie and Gott, during the Battle of Gazala, May 1942.
By permission of The Imperial War Museum E 12602.

It was becoming painfully clear to the British that just as the defence of Egypt from the west depended on holding the port of Tobruk, the continued effectiveness of Malta in contesting enemy control of the Central Mediterranean could be maintained only if the RAF was able to provide the additional air cover needed for the protection of supply convoys. This necessitated the use of airfields in western Cyrenaica. The Chiefs of Staff and the Foreign Office took these considerations into account when they began, in the winter of 1942, to assess Britain's post-war defence requirements in the Mediterranean.

Churchill's edict to attack was overturned as soon as it was realised that Rommel was about to resume his drive towards Tobruk. In the latter half of May 1942 General Ritchie concentrated on preparing the Eighth Army to fight a defensive battle based on the quadrilateral position Ain al-Gazala–Tobruk–Bir al-Gobi–Bir Hakaim. Plans were drawn up for the evacuation of all Sanusis from eastern Cyrenaica to Egypt.[48] Ironically, the British commanders now regarded the Sanusis as a security risk, potential enemy agents who could operate undetected from tribal encampments located almost in the midst of the Eighth Army. It was thought undesirable to concentrate the tribes on the coast north of the main road from Gambit to Bardia, where there was adequate grazing and water for the flocks. Auchinleck thought the only solution to this problem was to remove the whole Arab population from the area of operations. Permission was sought and gained from the Egyptian government to bring the tribes east of Sidi Barani, where there was suitable pasturage and they would be away from British troops.[49]

REFLECTIONS ON THE FUTURE OF CYRENAICA

While the rapidly deteriorating situation at the battlefront dictated the need for drastic measures, the relative calm of Cairo allowed time for reflection on the future in Cyrenaica. There is an air of unreality about these deliberations which were predicated upon a successful offensive by the Eighth Army in western Cyrenaica.

Following his appointment as Chief Political Officer North in February 1942, Brigadier H R Hone made it one of his first tasks to try and settle the administrative consequences of Eden's declaration. In mid-May he presented his conclusions to the Middle East War Council (MEWC). Like others in Cairo concerned with conducting relations with the Sanusis (e.g. Major Anderson and Brigadier Longrigg), Hone interpreted the declaration to mean that 'Cyrenaica shall in no circumstances again fall under Italian domination.'[50]

In view of this commitment Hone did not think it would be possible to justify the maintenance of the façade of Italian administration, in accordance with a strict interpretation of international law, following the next British occupation of Cyrenaica. This would arouse suspicion and dissatisfaction among the Sanusis, as seen during the two previous occupations. Hone realised, however, that it was necessary to have a clear idea as to what should replace the Italian system. Above all, the Occupied Territories Administrations (OTA) had to avoid, in any administrative action, giving a wider meaning to Eden's declaration than it in fact possessed, especially as the British government had deliberately, for obvious reasons, given no hint as to what it thought the political destiny of Cyrenaica might be.

Hone began by sketching the outlines of a possible new administrative structure in Cyrenaica, under British control. Italian sovereignty over Cyrenaica would be regarded as having ended and therefore 'the Arabs of Cyrenaica' would no longer owe allegiance to the King of Italy.

Free French Foreign Legionnaires leap up from the desert to rush an enemy strong point. Bir Hacheim, 12 June 1942. By permission of The Imperial War Museum E 13313.

Italian laws would be steadily repealed and replaced by laws more suitable to 'an Arab system of government'. Italian courts would be abolished. New courts would be established, with Arab judges where suitable, under the authority of the military governor. Italian fiscal laws would no longer operate; it was proposed that the British would have the right to set up 'a new system of taxation designed primarily for Arab needs and mode of life'. The military administration in Cyrenaica would be kept entirely separate and distinct from that intended for Tripolitania.

'In short,' concluded Hone, 'the administrative policy will be so orientated as to give the general complexion of a native state, as opposed to that of a native territory under the subjugation of a European power whose primary object is to exploit the resources of the country for the enhancement of its own wealth and prestige.'

There was also the problem of the disposal of Italian property in Cyrenaica, mainly the agricultural settlements situated in the most fertile areas of the Jabal Akhdar. It was presumed that a considerable number of Italian settlers would remain in Cyrenaica following the British occupation. The early removal of the Italian colonists would be naturally popular with the Sanusis, who desired to reclaim their lands (although it was observed that their euphoria might turn to disappointment and dispute once the lands were divided).

However, there were practical difficulties in removing the Italians, such as lack of transport and a suitable place to accommodate them. Moreover, there would be a marked decrease in the production of vital foodstuffs in the Jabal Akhdar if the Sanusis replaced the Italians. 'The conclusion is that willy-nilly we must face the fact that for some time after our occupation of Cyrenaica the Italian colonists must be kept on their farms and the possession of their land safeguarded.' This would have to be adequately explained to the Sanusis, although the latter would be convinced only by 'some promise with regard to future action'. Therefore, the British government would have to declare that the land would be restored eventually to its legitimate Arab owners, and in the meantime it would work out an 'Arab settlement scheme'. Hone suggested also that 'a non-committal explanation of immediate policy' on Cyrenaica should be given to British political officers so as to enable them to answer questions from the inhabitants about the future of Cyrenaica.[51]

In the latter half of May 1942 there was some disagreement among the interested authorities in Cairo – OTA, the Middle East Intelligence Centre (MEIC), Security Intelligence Middle East (SIME) and the Propaganda Directorate – about the question of the removal of the Italian colonists from Cyrenaica. Whereas economic considerations determined OTA's attitude, the other agencies held that political and security requirements should be of paramount concern. The ensuing stalemate was resolved only by the intervention of the chairman of the MEWC, R G Casey, who had recently arrived in Cairo to take up his appointment as Minister of State in the Middle East (Walter Monckton had been acting Minister of State since Lyttelton's departure in February).

After consulting Auchinleck and other authorities, Casey concluded that the basic changes in administrative policy for Cyrenaica proposed by Hone were justified. Casey maintained, however, that as long as the Italian colonists remained in undisputed possession of the land in the Jabal Akhdar 'it would be useless to look for stability in the administration, now or after the war, of a Cyrenaica liberated from Italy'. The Minister of State thought that 'the most practicable and advantageous solution would be to announce, as the the Eighth Army advanced into the Jabal Akhdar, that the Italian colonists would be removed as soon as possible'. This would satisfy the Sanusis and might encourage many Italians to flee to Tripolitania. Any remaining colonists could be repatriated by arrangement with the Italian government.[52]

Casey despatched his recommendation on the future British military administration of Cyrenaica to London on 26 May 1942. His timing left much to be desired. On the evening of 26 May Rommel launched his offensive against the Eighth Army's defensive position in eastern Cyrenaica. By 18 June, following the destruction of his armoured formations, General Ritchie (GOC Eighth Army) had ordered the remnants of his demoralised forces to withdraw behind the Egyptian frontier defences. Tobruk had been abandoned to its fate (it fell on 21 June) despite Auchinleck's instruction to Ritchie to defend it by holding Rommel on a line through Akrama and al-Adem.

The Eighth Army was thus unable to evacuate the native population of eastern Cyrenaica. Those Sanusis who could flee to Egypt did so, but many were left behind to face the wrath of the Italians. On 25 June the Panzergruppe Afrika had reached Mersa Matruh. Ritchie had failed to put distance between himself and Rommel and to rally the Eighth Army. He was relieved of his command before he could preside over its destruction by making a stand at Matruh. Auchinleck's determination to preserve the Eighth Army at all costs, and his bold decision to withdraw it to the El Alamein position, proved crucial for the defence of Egypt and the Middle East.

Whilst these dramatic events had been occurring, the Foreign Office had been considering the Minister of State's recommendation on administrative policy for Cyrenaica. Eden demonstrated a remarkable confidence in the outcome of the struggle then taking place in the Western Desert, when he informed Casey on 25 June that 'though no explicit statement to that effect has been made, or will be made for the present, it is in fact the intention of His Majesty's Government that "Cyrenaica shall in no circumstances again fall under Italian domination", and the position as regards the populations of Tripolitania and Cyrenaica is clearly understood by them. On this assumption, and on the further assumption that once Cyrenaica has again been effectively occupied, that occupation will continue uninterruptedly until the end of the war ....'

Eden agreed to the course of action proposed by Casey, with one qualification. Although the British should do what they thought right when they reoccupied Cyrenaica, they should avoid making public statements of their intentions towards either the Italian colonists or with regard to the administration in general. This would embarrass the British government as it maintained that the Axis powers had no right, in territories occupied by them, to act 'on the basis that there would be a permanent change in the political status of the countries concerned'.

Moreover, Eden (or rather the Legal Adviser of the Foreign Office) did not think it either desirable or necessary for the British government to make out a case theoretically justifying its action in Cyrenaica. Italy would retain sovereignty over the territory until denied it either by annexation, which would not bind Italy, or at the peace settlement. What was important was not whether the Sanusis were still formally Italian subjects, but whether the Italians would ever be able to take revenge for Sanusi actions during the British occupation.[53]

The Foreign Office's decision to approve a new administrative policy for Cyrenaica effectively ended the speculation in London and Cairo about the proper interpretation to be given to Eden's declaration on the Sanusis. It was clear now that, in order to ensure that the Sanusis did not again come under Italian domination, Cyrenaica would have to be freed from Italian rule. It was intended to remove the Italian colonists and 'to develop local rural and municipal government on native lines' in Cyrenaica under the 'benevolent administration' of Britain.[54]

This policy was to be implemented in secret as the British government might otherwise be accused of behaving in the same manner as the Axis powers in territories occupied by them. It was to be six months, however, before OTA was able to carry out the new policy in Cyrenaica. In late June 1942 British military fortunes in North Africa had reached their nadir.

Even Sayyid Idris despaired of the future. He had asked the Minister of State to arrange for the evacuation from Egypt of several thousand Sanusis, whose lives would be in jeopardy for having collaborated with the British if the Axis forces reached the Nile Delta. As in August 1940, it was only possible to promise to evacuate the most important Sanusi shaikhs and their families, several hundred in number, who had been compromised by their support for the British. It would appear that Sayyid Idris intended to take ship to the Hijaz, where Ibn Saud was prepared to grant him and his followers asylum on the condition (accepted by Idris) that they would not spread the teachings of the Sanusis. In the event it proved unnecessary to take these emergency measures. In early July 1942, however, not even the wildest optimist could have foreseen that in the winter of 1942–43 the Sanusis would return to Cyrenaica, in the wake of the Eighth Army's victorious advance to the Mareth Line and beyond.[55]

summary

THE PERIOD from the late summer of 1941 to the early summer of 1942 represents an important stage in the development of the Libyan problem. The overriding desire of the Sanusis of Cyrenaica to be freed from Italian rule was gratified, at least in theory, by Eden's announcement of 8 January 1942. In the short term it proved difficult to implement this declaration. It was not until the winter of 1942–43 that the Sanusis of Cyrenaica were finally liberated from Italian tutelage.

Sayyid Idris was unsuccessful, however, in his attempts to extract a pledge from Britain on the future independence of Cyrenaica or of Libya as a whole. He was severely criticised for this failure by the exiled Tripolitanian leaders. Moreover, the latter remained vehemently opposed to Sanusi leadership in Libya, although they were not averse to securing any benefits which might accrue from the Anglo-Sanusi connection.

If it had been decided to free Cyrenaica from Italian rule, there was no agreement among the parties concerned about what should replace it and what should happen to Tripolitania. It was known that the Egyptians desired to control Cyrenaica and possibly Tripolitania for reasons of prestige and security. There were doubts, however, about the capacity of the Egyptians to administer even Cyrenaica. This was a desert country, devoid of natural resources, having only a small cultivable area, and a nomadic hinterland. There was an indication also that, despite assurances to the Sanusis, the Egyptians hoped to deny effective political power to Sayyid Idris by favouring the Tripolitanians within a united Libya under Egyptian suzerainty.

Both the Near Eastern Division of the State Department and the Egyptian Department of the Foreign Office displayed an interest at this time, although for different reasons, in meeting Egyptian aspirations in Libya, or at least Cyrenaica. The NEA seems to have been motivated by a desire to reduce British influence in North Africa. The Egyptian Department appears to have regarded the 'land west of the Nile' as a useful pawn which could be traded to Egypt in exchange for the latter relinquishing her share of the Sudan Condominium to Britain. While the war raged in the Western Desert, however, neither the State Department nor the Foreign Office showed any inclination to encourage Egyptian ambitions in Libya.

The alternative to Egyptian rule in Libya seemed to be some form of British control. Sayyid Idris demanded the establishment of an autonomous Sanusi amirate in Libya, or at the very least Cyrenaica, under British protection. Sir Miles Lampson and Oliver Lyttelton had shown an interest in this plan, as it offered the inviting prospect of setting up British air and naval bases at Tobruk and Benghazi after the war, to defend the western approaches to Egypt.

The Axis onslaught against Britain's position in the eastern Mediterranean had demonstrated the strategic importance of Cyrenaica to the defence of Egypt and Malta. However, the Foreign Office refused to undertake any formal commitment about the political future of the territory. Apart from continuing doubts about the existence of a Sanusi nationality, it was feared that Britain might be seen as an expansionist power. The Foreign Office wanted to avoid further complicating Britain's relations with the United States and Egypt at such a critical stage of the war.

It proved impossible, however, to avoid taking some decisions which would affect the political future of Cyrenaica and Libya. In order to maintain the co-operation of Sayyid Idris and the Sanusis it was necessary to reassure them as to their future. In addition to Eden's declaration that the Sanusis in Cyrenaica would not be returned to Italian rule, the British authorities in the Middle East were prepared to hint that the Sanusis would receive autonomy after the war, an outcome which was implicit in the decision 'to develop local rural and municipal government on native lines' in Cyrenaica following British reoccupation. The Foreign Office recognised the inexorable logic of the situation in Cyrenaica but was anxious about acknowledging it openly lest Britain be accused of trying to predetermine the peace settlement.

NOTES

1 Cairo to FO, from Minister of State, tel. 51, 5 January 1942, R 357/96/22, FO 371/33226.
2 Hirszowicz, *op. cit.*, pp. 150–3, 184–8, 211–3, 232–6; Porath, *op. cit.*, pp. 192–4, 244–9.
3 It was observed that conditions in Cyrenaica were not unlike those in Transjordan: 'a small belt of settled country with a nomadic hinterland, a relatively homogeneous population, and a local eminent family'. Draft MEWC, 'The Senussi. Memorandum by the Minister of State', 21 August 1941, received by FO 5 September 1941, J 2841/368/66, FO 371/27573.
4 Porath, *op. cit.*, pp. 208–14.
5 Draft MEWC, 'The Senussi ...', *op. cit.*
6 Anderson to Secretary to Minister of State, 11 September 1941, with enclosures, J 2841/368/66, FO 371/27573; Khadduri, *op. cit.*, pp. 34–5.
7 This was done in a draft paper for the Middle East War Council of 21 August 1941. Lyttelton's task, as the representative of the War Cabinet in the Middle East, was to give the local commanders-in-chief 'that political guidance which has not hitherto been available locally...', as well as relieving them of the 'extraneous policies with which they have hitherto been burdened' (Gilbert, *op. cit.*, p. 1125). The latter policies included relations with the Free French, the administration of occupied enemy territories, propaganda, subversive warfare and supervision of the activities of the new Intendant-General, including matters connected with supplies from the United States. Lyttelton was given the authority to co-ordinate the policy of British representatives throughout the Middle East. This was achieved through the agency of the Middle East War Council (MEWC) and its various sub-committees, the most important being the Middle East Defence Committee (MEDC). The MEWC rarely met in full session because of the difficulty of assembling its members in Cairo at the same time (the members included all British representatives in the region. In contrast the MEDC met daily. It consisted solely of the British authorities resident in Egypt: the British Ambassador, the three Commanders-in-Chief and the Intendant-General under the chairmanship of the Minister of State (George Kirk, *The Middle East in the War. Survey of International Affairs 1939–46*, RIIA, London 1952, pp. 160–1). The MEDC was regarded as 'the heart and soul of the fighting machine in the Middle East' (Lord Birkenhead, *The Life of Lord Monckton of Brenchley*, London 1969, p. 200). It was desirable whenever possible for the Minister of State to send a recommendation to the War Cabinet which had been agreed first by the MEWC or MEDC (*The Memoirs of Lord Chandos*, London 1964, pp. 227–8.). It is important to remember that it was now the Minister of State, rather than the Commander-in-Chief, Middle East, who was responsible for giving guidance to the Chief Political Officer, OETA, on all important questions of policy affecting the Italian colonies, although the CPO remained responsible in his military capacity to the C-in-C ME.
8 Lyttelton had been struck, soon after his arrival in Cairo, by how vulnerable the Nile Delta and British communications were to air attack. Chandos, *op. cit.*, pp. 241–2.
9 Draft MEWC, 'The Senussi', *op. cit.*
10 Chandos, *op. cit.*, pp. 231–2; Trefor E Evans, ed., *The Killearn Diaries 1934–46*, London 1972, pp. 184–5, 199–220.

11 Porath, *op. cit.*, pp. 245–6.
12 Minutes by Bateman and Seymour, 20 September 1941, J 2841/368/66, FO 371/27573.
13 Varsori, *op. cit.*, pp. 463–6.
14 Minutes by Dixon and Sargent, 2 October 1941, J 2841/368/66, FO 371/27573.
15 Minute by Bateman, 3 October 1941, J 2841/368/66, FO 371/27573.
16 No official committee on Sanusi government had been set up in accordance with the declaration of 9 August 1940. Instead there was an Arab bureau where both Sayyid Idris and Major J N D Anderson (British liaison officer with the Sanusis) had offices. A considerable sum of money had been given to Sayyid Idris for his personal use, smaller sums to certain members of the Sanusi family and yet smaller sums to many of the Cyrenaican shaikhs, who were assisting in recruitment and other work. Five thousand Libyan POWs had been released by the British in 1941. It had been possible to absorb only about one thousand into the Libyan Arab Force or the Libyan Working Battalions. Tripolitanian POWs seem to have been excluded from the LAF because of their questionable loyalty. Anderson to Secretary to Minister of State, 11 September 1941 with enclosures, J 2841/368/66, FO 371/27573.
17 WP (41)232, 'The Senussi and Cyrenaica', memorandum by the Secretary of State for Foreign Affairs, 4 October 1941, CAB 66/19.
18 Charles D Smith, '4 February 1942: Its Causes and Its Influence on Egyptian Politics and on the future of Anglo-Egyptian Relations 1937–45', International Journal of Middle East Studies, vol. 10, 1979, pp. 463–7.
19 FO to Cairo, For Minister of State, tel. 71, 5 January 1942, R 357/96/22, FO 371/332260.
20 Christopher Thorne, *Allies of a Kind*, London 1978, pp. 96–109.
21 Porath, *op. cit.*, p. 251.
22 WM 100(41)8, 6 October 1941, CAB 65/19; FO to Cairo, For Minister of State, tel. 3490, 10 October 1941, J 2841/368/66; Cairo to FO, From Minister of State, Personal and Secret, 15 October 1941, J 3296/368/66, FO 371/27573; WPIS, no. 106, (W 12301/53/50) 15 October 1941, p. 16, Great Britain. Foreign Office Weekly Political Intelligence Summaries, vol. 4, July–December 1941, London 1983.
23 Auchinleck's subordinates were less circumspect, however, about undertaking prior commitments in Libya. General Cunningham, GOC Eighth Army, favoured an active propaganda campaign in Tripolitania in preparation for the eventual British advance into that territory (Operation 'Acrobat'). In order to cultivate the goodwill of the Tripolitanian tribes, and persuade them to pass on military information, as well as to hide agents and escaped POWs, Cunningham proposed using the Long Range Desert Group. LRDG patrols would distribute food and money, and at the same time spread propaganda and rumours to mislead the enemy. Cunningham sought permission from the MEWC in mid-October 1941 for assurances to be given to the Tripolitanians concerning their future. But Brigadier I G Clayton (head of the Middle East Intelligence Centre) preferred that the Tripolitanians should remain under Italian rule and therefore opposed the spread of propaganda to the tribes. Nevertheless, the MEWC decided on 17 October that it should not be assumed that Tripolitania, if conquered by Britain, would be returned to Italy after the war. Moreover, in order to mitigate the

Tripolitanians' distrust of Britain, the MEWC favoured giving them assurances that they would not be handed over to the Sanusis. There is no evidence to suggest that this propaganda policy was ever carried out during the winter campaign of 1941–42. MEWC (41)48 'Policy in Libya', 14 October 1941, with enclosures, AIR 23/1297; MEWC (41)17th Conclusions, 17 October 1941, Air 23/1340.

24 Scott was referring (minute of 10 October 1941, J 3299/368/66, FO 371/27573) to Cadogan's pledge of 9 August 1941 to Welles at the Argentia Conference, that 'should the British government at any time intend to make any commitments of this character, the Government of the United States would be advised prior to the making of such commitments'. Welles to Roosevelt, 21 October 1941, 740.0011 European War 1939/1590T–2/3, Foreign Relations of the United States (FRUS),1942, vol. Ill, p. 34.

25 Minute by Butler, 12 October 1941, J 3299/368/66, FO 371/27573. During the ABC staff talks in Washington between 29 January and 27 March 1941 and in mid-July (in a telegram from Roosevelt to Churchill and at a private meeting between Hopkins, Winant and the Prime Minister) the Americans had conveyed their anxiety to the British government about Britain's undertaking territorial commitments during the war which would prove binding at the peace settlement. The lack of response from the Foreign Office and Churchill led Welles and Roosevelt to seek specific assurances from the British at the Argentia Conference in August 1941. (See COS(41)304, 12 May 1941, with enclosures, A 4175/384/45, and further material on A 4176/A 4866/ A 5425/384/45, FO 371/26221, A 5911/384/45, FO 371/26222; Welles to Winant, For Former Naval Person from the President, no. 2600, 14 July 1941, 740.0011 European War 1939/13132b, telegram, FRUS 1941, vol. 1, p. 342; David Reynolds, *The Creation of the Anglo-American Alliance 1937–41. A Study in Competitive Co-operation*, London 1981, pp. 256–8.) On 9 August Cadogan reviewed all British commitments for the benefit of the US Under Secretary of State and reassured him 'that the British Government had entered into no commitments which had to do with the frontier or territorial readjustments, with one possible exception'. This was a vague verbal statement about Istria to the Yugoslavian government prior to the coup in March 1941. Welles to Roosevelt, 21 October 1941, *op. cit.*, 'In fact it committed us to nothing.' Minute by Cadogan, 20 August 1941, W 10301/426/49, FO 371/28904. On 12 August Churchill joined Roosevelt in an Eight Point Declaration (the Atlantic Charter) which rendered superfluous 'a formal statement by His Majesty's Government to the effect that they were clear of (territorial) commitments...' (*ibid.*). The declaration of 'certain common principles in the national policies of Britain and the United States' included pledges by the two leaders that: 'Their countries seek no aggrandisement territorial or other' (Article I); 'They desire to see no territorial changes that do not accord with the freely expressed wishes of the people concerned' (Article II); 'They respect the right of all peoples to choose the form of government under which they will live, and they wish to see sovereign rights restored to those who have been forcibly deprived of them' (Article III). Brierly, 'Note on the Atlantic Declaration', 3 September 1941, FRPS HR I/59/iii, CAB 117/58. In order 'to avoid future misunderstandings with the Americans' (minute by Malkin, 14 October 1941, J 3299/368/66, FQ 371/27573) the Foreign Office drew up a full list of all 'Commitments entered into by His Majesty's Government with certain foreign governments which may affect the conduct of the war or the post-war settlement. 'These comprised the treaties and

other agreements concluded by Britain with other countries over the years, from Afghanistan to Yugoslavia. (FO memorandum, 16 February 1942, W 4334/27/49, FO 371/32425).

26 *The Diaries of Sir Alexander Cadogan 1938–45, op. cit.,* give the impression that the subject of the declaration on the Sanusis was raised at the Argentia Conference. The editor of the Diaries, David Dilks, supplemented the diary entry of 9 August 1941 with information from Cadogan's 1962 record of the 'Atlantic Meeting'. The latter erroneously states that Cadogan informed Welles on 9 August 'that the Senussi had been told that they would be freed from Italian rule...' (*Diaries* , p. 397). In fact it was not until mid-October that Welles learnt from Cadogan of the intention of the British government to issue the declaration on the Sanusis. The latter statement was made by Eden in the House of Commons on 8 January 1942. FO to Washington, Cadogan to Welles, tel. 5602, 15 October 1941. J 3299/368/66, FO 371/27573; Halifax to Welles, 18 October, Welles to Roosevelt, 21 October, Welles to Halifax, 25 October 1941, 740.0011 European War 1939/15907 1/3, 15907 2/3, 20758, FRUS 1942, vol. 11, pp. 33–5; Halifax to Cadogan, 30 October 1941, J 3722/368/66, FO 371/27573.

27 Minute by Scott, 10 October 1941, J 3299/368/66, FO 371/27573; Murray, 'Libya and the Senussi Movement', 28 October 1941, memorandum for Welles, 865C.00/98, Hare to Secretary of State, despatch 2364, 4 March 1941, 865C.00/96, RG 59/Box 5059.

28 The declaration was capable of two interpretations: either the Sanusis were to be removed from Cyrenaica or Cyrenaica was to be removed from Italian rule. As only the latter solution was practicable it was assumed by Cadogan, among others, that Britain had decided to follow this option. This was not stated categorically, however, until June 1942. Cairo to FO, From Minister of State, tel. 3726, 26 November 1941, FO to Cairo, For Minister of State, tel. 4221, 1 December 1941, and minutes on J 3721/368/66, FO 371/27573.

29 The Dominion Governments had been notified on 28 November 1941 that the War Cabinet was considering making a declaration on the future of the Sanusis. On 29 December the Dominions were informed of the content of the declaration. Cairo to FO, from Minister of State, tel. 3811, 3 December 1941, J 3783/368/66, DO to Dominion Governments, tel. 714, 28 November 1941, J 3623/368/66, DO to Dominion Governments, tel. 781, 29 December 1941, J 4031/ 368/66, FO 371/27573.

30 Cairo to FO, From Minister of State, tel. 4036, 22 December 1941, FO to Cairo, For Minister of State, tel. 4592, 24 December 1941, and minutes on J 4031/368/66, Cairo to FO, From Minister of State, tel. 4074, 26 December 1941, FO to Cairo, For Minister of State, 28 December 1941, J 4103/368/66, FO 371/27573; Cairo to FO, From Minister of State, tel. 8, 1 January 1942, R 357/96/22, FO 371/33226; Khadduri, *op. cit.*, pp. 34–5.

31 Lyttelton on 1 January 1942 had passed on to the Foreign Office a proposal by Longrigg that the Minister of State should follow up his talk with Sayyid Idris by means of a letter (the content of which would be kept secret). The British government could reiterate its appreciation of the efforts of Sayyid Idris in helping to form the Libyan Arab Force and congratulate the Sanusis on their achievement. The Sanusis would be told also that the British would not object to this force being called the 'Free Libyans' (Lyttelton preferred 'Free Libya Arab Force'). Longrigg recommended also that assurances be given to Sayyid Idris regarding

the administration of Cyrenaica, saying 'that every sympathy would be shown for the rights of the inhabitants and their freedom would only be restricted as far as was inevitable under our military requirements and international law'. The letter would repeat the assurance that the Sanusis of Cyrenaica would not again come under Italian rule and that any future administration for which the British government was responsible 'will place [the] well-being and interests of the inhabitants themselves in the forefront of its efforts and will include provisions for [the] full freedom of worship and settlement for followers of Senussi sect and will reserve a distinguished place for the person and family of the leader thereof'. The Foreign Office refused to sanction this letter. Eden thought that Sayyid Idris might misinterpret several passages in the draft letter with embarrassing consequences for the British. In particular, Eden preferred the current title of the Sanusi forces, 'Libya[n] Arab Force', to 'Free Libyans'. It was feared that Sayyid Idris would read too much into the word 'Free'. Moreover, the assurance which the DCPO Cyrenaica and Minister of State proposed giving Sayyid Idris might not be welcomed by the Egyptian government. Lyttelton was instructed, therefore, not to say anything further to Sayyid Idris. For the present the British government did not intend to go beyond the limited terms of the declaration on the Sanusis to be made on 8 January 1942. The Foreign Office held out the prospect, however, of expanding Eden's statement following the development of the situation in Libya. The Foreign Office objected also to Lyttelton's suggestion that the vague phrase 'allied war effort' be substituted for 'British war effort' in the text of the declaration, because the latter implied that Sayyid Idris and the Sanusis were only British mercenaries. The Foreign Office disagreed with this interpretation and felt that the statement should be as unambiguous as possible. The phrase 'allied war effort' hinted also at an independent status which it would be inappropriate to discuss. The Foreign Office did agree, however, to revise the text of the declaration to include mention of the useful role played by the Libyan Arab Force in the campaign then in progress, as well as during the winter campaign of 1940–41. Cairo to FO, from Minister of State, tel. 8, 1 January 1942, FO to Cairo, For Minister of State, tel. 71, 5 January 1942, Cairo to FO, From Minister of State, tel. 41, 4 January 1942, FO to Cairo, For Minister of State, tels. 72 and 73, 5 January 1942, R 357/96/22, FO 371/33226.

32 FO to Cairo, For Minister of State, tel. 73, 5 January 1942, Cairo to FO, From Minister of State, tel. 51,5 January 1942, FO to Cairo, For Minister of State, tel. 83, 6 January 1942, Cairo to Jerusalem, from Tweedy for Information Officer, tel. 3, 8 January 1942. Rpt.'d. to FO, Baghdad, Aden, Khartoum, Beirut, R 357/96/22, FO 371/332260.

33 Barnett, *op. cit.*, p. 128.

34 One sentence which was struck from Eden's parliamentary statement (Parl. Debs., 5th ser., H of C, vol. 377, cols 77–78.) referred to the terrible suffering the Sanusis in Cyrenaica had experienced at the hands of the Italians. Longrigg denied that the Sanusis had been severely punished for helping the British raise the Libyan Arab Force, (Cairo, to FO, from Minister of State, tel. 3726, 26 November 1941, J 3721/368/66, FO 371/27573). This is contradicted by Kennedy-Shaw who was Intelligence Officer to the Long Range Desert Group from July 1940 to February 1943 (immediately following which he wrote an account of the LRDG's activities, which was published in 1945. See W B Kennedy-Shaw, *The Long Range Desert Group. The Story of its Work in Libya, 1942*, London 1945, pp. 149–150.

He says that the Sanusis did suffer badly from Italian retribution as a result of helping British forces operating in Cyrenaica. Kennedy-Shaw was probably in a better position to judge as the LRDG was operating in the Jabal Akhdar in 1941. While Kennedy-Shaw was at the LRDG advance base at Siwa and then Kufra, Longrigg was in Cairo for most of 1941.

35 Rucker to Eden, 26 May 1942, enclosing extract from MEWC (42)21 9 May 1942 and extract from MEWC(42)12th mtg., Item 3, 13 May 1942, FO 1015/71.

36 *The Times*, 9 January 1942, p. 5; Minutes by Dixon, 10 and 21 October January 1942, R 357/96/22, FO 371/33226; WPIS no. 118 (W 349/21/50) 7 January 1942, p. 18, WPIS no. 119 (W757/21/50) 14 January 1942, p. 11, vol. 5, January–June 1942, *op. cit.*; Review of the Foreign Press, 1939–45, Series A, (RFP), vol. VI, 5 January 1942–29 June 1942, RIIA, Chatham House, London 1980, no. 12, 2 February 1942, p. 82, no. 124, 16 February 1942, pp.116–7.

37 RFP, Series B, vol. V, 2 January 1942–18 December 1942, no. 122, pp. 73–5, no. 123 pp. 84–5, no. 130 pp. 173–4; WPIS no. 123, 11 February 1942, p. 16, vol. 5, *op. cit.*, Kirk to Hull, tel. 168, 29 January 1942, 365A.11/10, FRUS 1942 vol. III, p. 37; Khadduri, *op. cit.*, p. 35–6; *Oriente Moderno*, January 1942, pp. 55–6.

38 Kirk to Hull, tel. 95, 16 January 1942, Hull to Kirk, tel. 660, 21 January 1942, 865D.01/604, Kirk to Hull, tel. 167, 29 January 1942, 365A.11/9, Kirk to Hull, tel. 168, 29 January 1942, 365A.11/10; FRUS, 1942, vol. III, pp. 35–7.

39 Philip J Baram, *The Department of State in the Middle East, 1919–45,* University of Pennsylvania 1978, pp. 187–9; Barry Rubin, *The Great Powers in the Middle East 1941–47,* London 1980, pp. 133–5.

40 Kirk, *op. cit.*, p. 396; Segre concludes that: 'The second British occupation delivered a final crushing blow to the settlements on the Gebel. The colonists suffered 42 dead and 26 wounded and another round of rapes, murders and robberies. Many of their houses had become uninhabitable; the families had lost most of their household necessities; their agricultural machinery was destroyed or requisitioned, and the livestock was lost. Even the oldest and most experienced colonist families, those who left their houses under direct threat from armed Libyans, no longer had the courage to return to their isolated farms.' Segre, *op. cit.*, p. 167. The Italian authorities seem to have decided about February 1942 on the withdrawal of the Italian colonists from the Jabal. By spring 1942 half the population (of 8,426) had been evacuated to the comparative safety of Tripolitania.

41 Rennell. *op. cit.*, pp. 246–7.

42 Khadduri, *op. cit.*, pp. 35–6.

43 Chandos, *op. cit.*, p. 278.

44 Harvey, diary entry for 9 February 1942, John Harvey, ed., *The War Diaries of Oliver Harvey,* London 1978, p. 930.

45 Majid Khadduri asked King Idris in an interview on 31 August 1961 why the British had been reluctant to give a written guarantee of Libya's future independence in 1942. According to the King: 'The British pointed out that they had given (written) pledges to King Husayn (of the Hejaz) during World War I which they could not fulfil; they accordingly did not want to give such pledges, but preferred to extend their utmost assistance to their allies after they had won the war.' I have relied on Khadduri, *op. cit.*, pp. 35–7, for this account of the events of February 1942. He has used the documents contained in *The White Book on the Unity of Tripolitania and Cyrenaica,* Cairo 1949. The relevant FO file is missing

(J 8/8/66 for 1942). Fortunately, as will be seen, the views of the Foreign Office on relations with Sayyid Idris in 1942 can be divined from the War Office files.
46 Admiral Cunningham, C-in-C Mediterranean Fleet, observed that: 'Malta was really the linchpin of the campaign in the Mediterranean. As the island served as the principal operational base for the surface ships, submarines and aircraft working against the Axis supply line to North Africa, its maintenance had a direct bearing on the progress of the battle in Cyrenaica, a fact that is not always appreciated.' Lord Cunningham, *A Sailor's Odyssey*, London 1951, p. 421.
47 C-in-C ME to AOC in C, ME, 22 March 1942, enclosed 'Libya. March 1942', Auchinleck, 21 March 1942, AIR 23/1332; Kirk, *op. cit.*, pp. 213–5; Barnett, *op. cit.*, pp. 137–8; Martin Gilbert, *Road to Victory. Winston S. Churchill 1941–45*, London 1986, pp. 102–4.
48 On a visit to the front in early May, HRH the Duke of Gloucester had attended, with General Ritchie, a tribal *darbar* at Zanzur organised by the British Political Officer (Rennell, *op. cit.*, p. 247). In response to a plea from a Sanusi shaikh that the royal visitor 'do justice' to Sanusi aspirations for freedom from Italian rule, Gloucester reassured the assembled shaikhs 'that they would receive, after the defeat of the Axis, all the aid and consideration due to them.' RFP , Series B, vol. V, *op. cit.*, no. 138, 5 June 1942, p. 281.
49 MEWC(42)24, 'evacuation of Arabs from Eastern Cyrenaica', Note by C-in-C, ME, 12 May 1942, MEWC(42)12th mtg., item 6, 13 May, 13th mtg., item 5, 27 May 1942, AIR 23/1298.
50 Rucker to Eden, 26 May 1942, extract from MEWC(42)21, 9 May 1942 and extract from MEWC(42) 12th mtg., item 3, 13 May 1942, FO 1015/71.
51 *ibid*.
52 MEWC(42) 12th mtg., item 3, 13 May, 13th mtg., item 4, 27 May 1942, AIR 23/1298; report by Chief Political Officer of 17 August 1942 on the work of the Political Branch. GHQ, MEF and the OTA of Cyrenaica and Eritrea to 30 June 1942, enclosure 3, 'Administrative Policy in Cyrenaica', memorandum by the Chief Political Officer Middle East, May 1942. WO 230/88; Rucker to Eden, 26 May 1942, extract from MEWC (42)21, 9 May 1942 and extract from MEWC(42) 12th mtg., item 3, 13 May 1942, FO 1015/71. It should be noted that the amended version of Hone's memorandum 'Administrative Policy in Cyrenaica', to which Rucker referred Eden is contained on WO 230/88. The original version is on FO 1015/71.
53 Report by the Chief Political Officer of 17 August 1942. *op. cit.*, enclosure 4, Eden to Casey, 25 June 1942, WO 230/88.
54 *ibid.*, enclosure 3, Hone memorandum, May 1942.
55 Richard Casey, *Personal Experience 1939–46*, London 1962, pp. 112–3; Great Britain. Foreign Office. Index to General Correspondence, 1942. Part IV, p. 9, entry under 'Said Idris el–Senussi , "Proposed visit to Hejaz with party owing to military situation in Egypt, undertaking given to King Ibn Saud not to spread Senussi doctrine. Plan abandoned." ' J 4374/J 5020/8/66. This file is missing. It has probably been destroyed.

THE THIRD YEAR
1942–1943
THE CONQUEST OF LIBYA

LIBYA: YEAR THREE

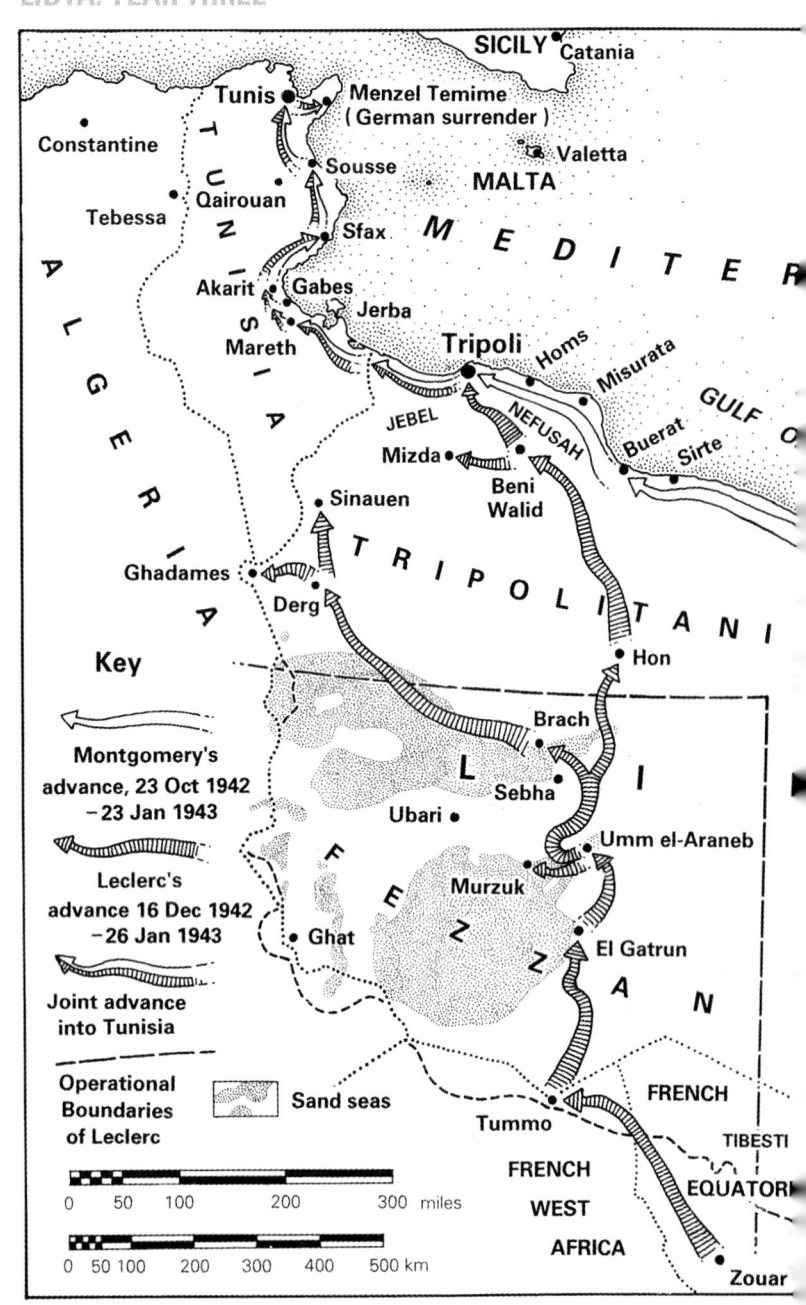

Key

⇐ Montgomery's advance, 23 Oct 1942 – 23 Jan 1943

⇐ Leclerc's advance 16 Dec 1942 – 26 Jan 1943

⇐ Joint advance into Tunisia

--- Operational Boundaries of Leclerc

Sand seas

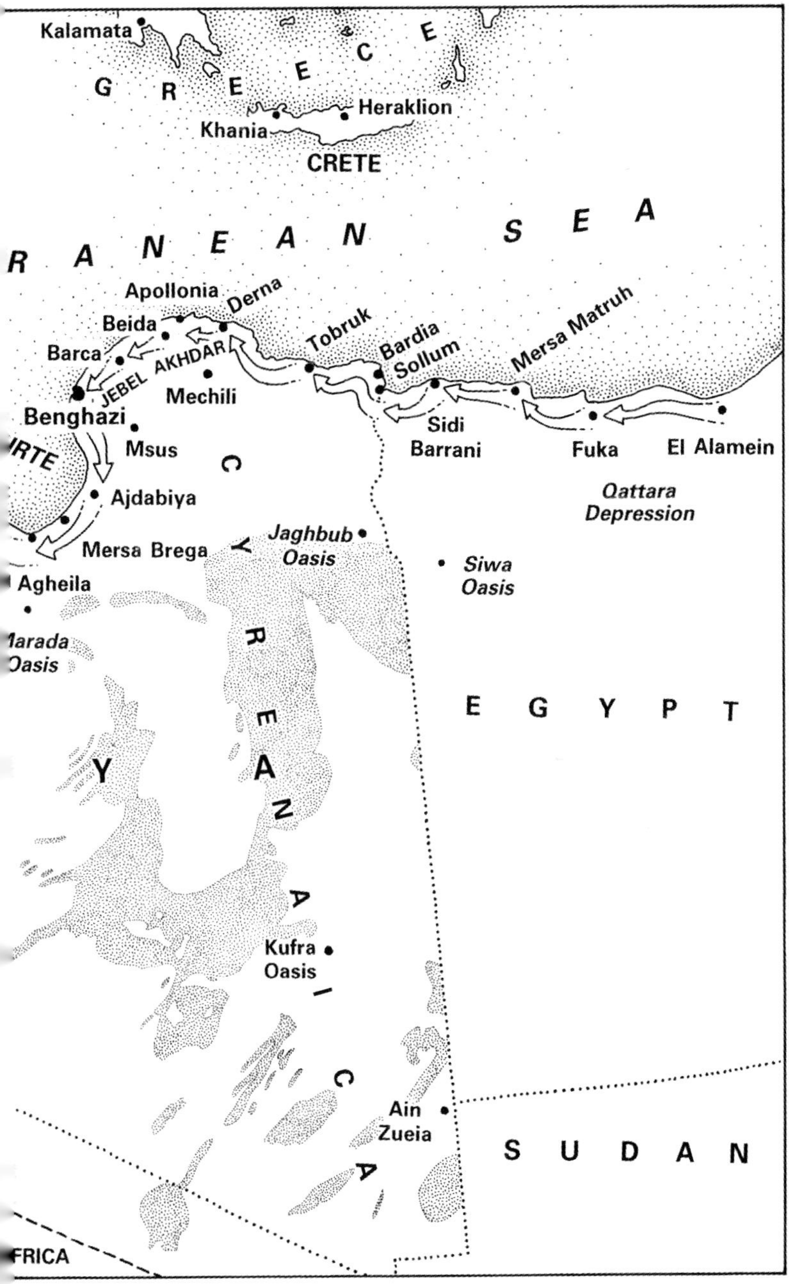
Kalamata
G R E E C E
Heraklion
Khania
CRETE
R A N E A N S E A
Apollonia
Derna
Beida
Barca
JEBEL AKHDAR
Benghazi
Mechili
Tobruk
Bardia
Sollum
Mersa Matruh
Sidi Barrani
Fuka
El Alamein
Msus
Ajdabiya
Mersa Brega
Agheila
Qattara Depression
Jaghbub Oasis
Siwa Oasis
C Y R E N A I C A
E G Y P T
Kufra Oasis
Ain Zueia
S U D A N
FRICA

overview

THE LAST act of the Desert War was played out during the period from July 1942 to February 1943. Rommel's failure to break through at El Alamein in the summer of 1942 led to a reversal of Axis fortunes in North Africa. The decision to launch Operation 'Torch', the Allied invasion of French North Africa, in combination with a British offensive 'to take or destroy at the earliest opportunity the German-Italian Army commanded by Field-Marshal Rommel, together with all its supplies and establishments in Egypt and Libya', spelled the end of Panzerarmee Afrika.[1] Following the Eighth Army's victory at Second Alamein in late October–early November 1942 and the Allied landings in Morocco and Algeria, Rommel was forced to evacuate Egypt and Cyrenaica and fall back on the Axis bridgehead in Tunisia before his forces were cut off and annihilated in the Sirte Desert by the numerically superior Allied armies.

However, the check suffered by Eisenhower's forces in Tunisia in December 1942 and Montgomery's cautious pursuit of the Panzerarmee Afrika enabled Rommel to slow down his retreat. After fighting successive delaying actions at the El Agheila defile and Buerat, Rommel's forces fell back to Tripoli. Montgomery's advance was so dilatory that he lost contact with the enemy. His long march of 2,250 km (1,400 miles) from El Alamein (the distance from London to Moscow) may have driven the German forces 'from pillar to post', as Churchill put it, but it failed in its original objective which was to destroy the Panzerarmee Afrika and capture the port of Tripoli intact.[2] Rommel was allowed to withdraw into Tunisia after wrecking Tripoli harbour as he had done Benghazi port.

The Eighth Army arrived in Tripoli on 23 January 1943, only three days ahead of General Leclerc's small Free French force which had advanced some 2,250 km (1,400 miles) in six weeks from its base in Chad, admittedly against lighter opposition than the Eighth Army had encountered. Leclerc's achievement allowed the French to claim a share in the control of Libya pending a decision on the future of the country at the peace settlement. This cut across the plans of the

British and American commanders in North Africa for putting Libya exclusively under British military administration, and it was to complicate the search for a satisfactory solution to the question of Libya's future.

In Cyrenaica, however, the Eighth Army had redeemed the pledge which Eden had made in January 1942 that the Sanusis would never again be subject to Italian domination. Eden had made clear in June 1942 to the British authorities in Cairo that this entailed the end of Italian rule in Cyrenaica. He had approved a plan for the administration of Cyrenaica which would give the country 'the general complexion of a native state'. This plan was duly carried out by the Military Government following the third and final British occupation of Cyrenaica. The War Office and the Foreign Office stressed, however, that Sayyid Idris was not to be installed as head of a native state in Cyrenaica during the war as Britain would be accused of prejudging the peace settlement.

Apart from the requirements of international law there were strong doubts about the administrative capability of Sayyid Idris. Thinking in London on the future of Cyrenaica continued to centre on the idea of a nominal Egyptian suzerainty with Sanusi autonomy. The Foreign Office gave further consideration to the possibility of executing a barter deal with Egypt after the war, whereby the latter would receive Cyrenaica in exchange for surrendering her 'rights' in the Sudan to Britain.

The principal stumbling-block to this plan proved to be Lampson's reluctance to revive the dormant issue of the Sudan during the war, or to make concessions to Egypt in Cyrenaica. It is possible to detect the signs of a different line of approach from the newly-established Military Government in Cyrenaica. The idea of a British-protected state in Cyrenaica along the lines of Transjordan, which had been raised by Lampson and canvassed by Lyttelton in 1941, was revived in a tentative fashion by the military administrators Cumming and Hone in late 1942.

Sayyid Idris and the leading Tripolitanian exiles in Cairo had more ambitious plans. They desired nothing less than the creation of an independent amirate in Libya, with Idris as amir. The Tripolitanians remained opposed to the Sanusis but they hoped, by renewing the idea of a Sanusi amirate, to secure the support of Sayyid Idris in their campaign to extract the same concessions for Tripolitania as the British had made in Cyrenaica. For his part Sayyid Idris was quite content to draw any political benefits he could from the Tripolitanian initiative but was less anxious to help his rivals escape from their predicament.

However, the British military administrators in Libya, the Chief Political Officer and the Minister of State in Cairo were too absorbed by their task of establishing law and order and reviving the devastated economies of Cyrenaica and Tripolitania to give more than passing attention to the political demands of Sayyid Idris or the exiled Tripolitanian leaders. Tripolitania was *terra incognita* for Britain as the Eighth Army never advanced beyond the Sirte Desert until late December 1942. Little attention had been devoted to the problem of military administration, following British occupation, let alone to the question of the future of Tripolitania.

The divided state of Tripolitanian politics, combined with the continued presence of a large Italian minority, discouraged the British from making any commitments on the future of the territory. In contrast to Cyrenaica it was decided to maintain the Italian administrative structure in Tripolitania intact. The country was to be administered in accordance with a strict interpretation of international law on the occupation of enemy territories, on a 'care and maintenance' basis.

The situation in Tripolitania was complicated by Free French actions in the Fezzan. The Free French leader, General de Gaulle, had territorial designs on southern Libya. The Fezzan was intended to be Free France's share of the fruits of the Allied victory in North Africa. This objective clearly ran counter to the plans of the British military administrators for British administrative control throughout Libya. Developments in French North Africa, however, were to dictate the British response. Eden and the Foreign Office were anxious to build up de Gaulle's political position *vis-à-vis* his political rival General Giraud in order to encourage the formation of a united front for the liberation of France. The Foreign Office succeeded in persuading the War Office that if the British government pressed de Gaulle to make concessions over the administration of the Fezzan it would only create 'bad blood' between the British and the Free French and undermine de Gaulle's growing prestige. The British military and political authorities in Cairo were forced to concede that considerations of *haute politique* must take precedence over local administrative concerns. This was further evidence of the powerful influence of outside events in determining political developments within Libya.

chapter 5
'USE THEM JUSTLY AND GRACIOUSLY WITH SUFFICIENT GUARD NEVERTHELESS'
CYRENAICA, JULY 1942–DECEMBER 1943

> If you plant where savages are, do not entertain them with trifles and gingles, but use them justly and graciously with sufficient guard nevertheless.
>
> Sir Francis Bacon, quoted by D C Cumming in memo. of 9 December 1942[3]

THE CYRENAICA-SUDAN BARTER PLAN

THE FALL of Tobruk on 21 June 1942 and the headlong retreat of the Eighth Army into Egypt led to a revision of Axis strategy in the war in the Mediterranean. Hitler and Mussolini decided to postpone the planned seizure of Malta, Operation 'Hercules', and to allow Rommel to concentrate on the pursuit and destruction of the demoralised British forces, thus opening the way to Alexandria and Suez.

The alluring prospect of a triumphal entry into Cairo spurred Mussolini to depart for Cyrenaica on 29 June 1942 with a large retinue, including a white horse, in anticipation of Rommel's final victory. As Panzerarmee Afrika assaulted the Eighth Army's defensive position at El Alamein, Mussolini planned the Italian occupation of Egypt. He intended that Italy should inherit Britain's position in Egypt and the Sudan. Thus the Axis declaration of 3 July, which called for an 'Egypt for the Egyptians', did not state categorically that the Axis would respect the 'complete independence and full sovereignty' of Egypt, as they had pledged to do in Iraq. Moreover, the declaration made no reference either to general Arab aspirations or to the chief Egyptian demand for the unity of the Nile Valley.

It did not inspire either the Egyptian nationalists or King Faruk to repudiate the British connection. The former were more hostile to Italy than to Britain and the Wafd government gave as much support as could be expected to the British authorities in Egypt. Ali Mahir and other pro-Axis elements were rounded up and interned, thus eliminating the internal challenge to Britain's position in Egypt at a critical juncture. King Faruk was too wary of British intervention to do more than send secret greetings of goodwill to Hitler. The great mass of Egyptians maintained a placid indifference to the Axis invasion of Egypt.[4] If, by making the declaration on Egypt, Mussolini sought to take revenge for the British declaration on the Sanusis in Cyrenaica, he was to be sorely disappointed.

Mussolini's plans for Egypt were thwarted by the Eighth Army's spirited defence of the El Alamein position in the first half of July 1942. Auchinleck defeated Rommel's attempt to take Alexandria and Cairo. Although the British counter-attack proved unsuccessful, owing to the lack of enough fresh well-trained troops, the Panzerarmee Afrika had been forced onto the defensive. Rommel had lost the initiative in the Desert War. After waiting three weeks at Derna, Mussolini, the 'Protector of Islam', returned to Italy.

Auchinleck's defensive victory at First Alamein proved to be the turning point. Encouraged by this decisive success Churchill and Roosevelt had decided on 24 July that Anglo-American forces should invade French North Africa in the autumn of 1942 (Operation 'Torch'). The objective of 'Torch' was defined as 'to gain control of the whole coast of Africa up to Tunis'. In retrospect Rommel recognised that this decision 'spelled the end of the Army in Africa'. His unsuccessful offensive at Alam Halfa in late August and the continued stubborn defence of its El Alamein position by the Panzerarmee Afrika should be seen as essentially bloody and futile attempts to deny the inevitable.[5]

The Wafd government acquitted itself well during the critical summer of 1942 and the Egyptian Prime Minister, Mustafa al-Nahhas, intended to make full political capital out of his loyalty to Britain. He had attempted to raise the question of the revision of the 1936 Anglo-Egyptian Treaty and the problem of the Sudan with Lampson on the 11 June, at the height of the Ain el-Gazala battle. Nahhas had also referred in vague terms to the issue of Egypt's representation at the peace conference. Lampson had told Nahhas in reply 'that these matters should be left alone during the war', and this line was approved on 17 June by the Foreign Office.[6]

On reflection, however, and in the light of Egyptian co-operation during the military crisis, the Foreign Office decided to agree to support Egyptian participation in the peace conference on matters of direct concern to Egypt. This was, no doubt, an attempt to sidetrack the discussion of Egyptian nationalist claims during the war. Although

Nahhas privately expressed disappointment at the limited nature of this concession, he used it to some effect, in his Speech from the Throne of 16 November, to outflank a clumsy manoeuvre by the political opposition to seize the nationalist mantle.[7]

Nahhas's initiative led the Foreign Office to speculate on what progress, if any, could be made at the end of the war towards a settlement of the status of the Sudan. In order to break the Anglo-Egyptian deadlock over sovereignty in the Sudan, the new head of Egyptian Department, P J Scrivener, suggested on 1 September 1942 that Egypt might be given sovereignty over Cyrenaica in return for Egyptian recognition of exclusive British sovereignty over the Sudan. Scrivener thought that, at first sight, this was an attractive arrangement, especially as it was the best solution for Cyrenaica. It would possibly be welcomed by most of tribal Sudan, although it would not really affect them, and many of the intelligentsia. The barter depended, however, on Egypt's willingness to accept it and on the colonial policy to be worked out by the United Nations, and especially by the United States and Britain, in the light of the Atlantic Charter. Britain's assumption of sole sovereignty in the Sudan might also stir up the more extreme Sudanese nationalist movements. Scrivener regarded as portentous the call by the recent 'Graduates Congress' in Khartoum for the grant of self-determination to the Sudan at the end of the war.

It was felt that the Sudanese were not sufficiently advanced in political development or education to become independent (they were in a pre-national stage). Moreover, if the Sudan were to be granted independence the Arab North would overwhelm the Pagan/Christian South. The British government could not allow this and Scrivener thought that the future probably lay in creating an independent Arab state in the northern Sudan and incorporating the southern part of the country within a 'British East African system'.

In view of the uncertainties involved in an Anglo-Egyptian barter over the Sudan, the only concrete suggestion that the Egyptian Department could make was for Britain and Egypt to redefine their intentions towards the Sudan, if and when the Anglo-Egyptian Treaty came under review. They could state that the Sudan would become fully independent when circumstances permitted, and that in the meantime the administration of the Sudan would be directed towards the fulfilment of this aim. It was thought that it would be difficult for the Egyptians to reject this proposal.[8]

Scrivener's proposal met with a mixed reception within the Foreign Office. J Coulson (Economic and Reconstruction Department) held that the Anglo-Egyptian Condominium in the Sudan had worked 'tolerably well' and should continue if possible. Coulson expressed reservations about both the proposed declaration on Sudanese independence, which would complicate the North/South divide, and the handing over of Cyrenaica to Egypt. He thought 'the woolly-headed idealists, who will be our chief critics whatever post-war settlement is reached, would be very disturbed by this sort of political barter which might appear purely opportunist'.[9] On the other hand, the new Assistant Under-Secretary, superintending Egyptian, Eastern and Far Eastern departments, Sir Maurice Peterson, did not seem to be worried that the Atlantic Charter might restrict Britain's freedom of action in the Sudan and Cyrenaica. In any case, he did not regard the question of the future of the Sudan as having a high priority at this stage of the war. He was prepared only to allow Scrivener to consult the British authorities in Khartoum and Cairo.[10]

The Governor-General of the Sudan, H J Huddleston, thought that the proposal 'that Egypt should receive Cyrenaica in exchange for her "rights" in the Sudan is ingenious and attractive, and, if Egypt could be induced to accept the exchange, we should be only too glad. But I fear the historic connection with the Sudan and the dependence of Egypt on the Nile waters make their agreement most unlikely.' Moreover, Huddleston pointed out, prior to such an agreement responsible Sudanese opinion would have to be consulted over any alteration in the status of the Sudan, in view of the qualified pledge of 29 April to this effect made by the Sudan Government in reply to a manifesto of 3 April from the Graduates Congress.

The educated Sudanese had felt that they should have been consulted over the Anglo-Egyptian Treaty of 1936 and this feeling had been intensified as a result of the war and the growth of nationalism. Huddleston surmised that a majority of Sudanese would probably welcome a complete political separation from Egypt, although he could not be definite about this. The educated minority would demand safeguards for the future independence of the Sudan and possibly a cultural and commercial treaty with Egypt. They did not desire British colonial status unless 'some sort of colonial charter on partnership lines had by that time been evolved'.

Huddleston concluded that it would be inopportune for Britain and Egypt to make an early declaration of interest on Sudanese independence. The Sudan could not become fully independent for many years and the country's future might lie in Dominion status within the British Commonwealth or 'in autonomous membership (with or without its Southern Provinces) of a Near Eastern Federation (Egypt, Arabia, Palestine, Syria and Iraq)'.[11]

Lampson was in general agreement with Huddleston. They had conferred together on this matter in Cairo, and both had reached the conclusion that the exchange of Cyrenaica for the Sudan was 'quite outside the sphere of practical politics'. Lampson said that there was no doubt that the Egyptians would like to be given Cyrenaica or at least the frontier region, up to and including Bardia. Occasionally they had advanced claims to this region, based on proposals alleged to have been considered when Lord Kitchener was Consul-General in Egypt. Lampson felt, however, that the Egyptians were not 'seriously interested' in Cyrenaica 'and would certainly not regard it as in any sense comparable to their loss of interest in the Sudan. The Sudan has for Egypt practical, historical and sentimental associations which will I surmise never be eradicated ... I do not believe any Egyptian Government could ever agree to give up its claim to share in the control of the Sudan in return for any territorial concession however large.'

Lampson made it clear that he was loath to comment on any detailed proposal for a new statement by Britain and Egypt over the Sudan. He pointed out that the question of sovereignty remained dormant, and the British should attempt to maintain this situation, at least until the end of the war, by refusing to listen to any Egyptian agitation. The Sudan Government intended to encourage Sudanese nationalism by associating the Sudanese with the central government, as a counterweight to Egyptian pressure. This would make it much easier for Britain to avoid making concessions over the Sudan to Egypt after the war. The longer Britain could 'put off a showdown with the Egyptians the stronger will be our position'. Moreover, the attitude of British public opinion towards Egyptian demands on the Sudan and the progress made with Sudanisation would not become clear until after the war.[12]

The pessimism of Lampson seemed to have a sobering effect on the Foreign Office. E A Chapman-Andrews denied that the Egyptian Department had ever seriously believed that Egypt would be prepared to exchange their rights in the Sudan in order to acquire control of Cyrenaica. Scrivener and Peterson felt that they had at least clarified their thinking on this matter and that it was not possible to take it any further for the present.[13] Despite these reservations, however, the Foreign Office continued to show an interest in the idea of a barter arrangement with Egypt involving Cyrenaica.

THE THIRD AND FINAL BRITISH OCCUPATION OF CYRENAICA

While the Cyrenaica-Sudan question was being considered in London and Cairo, the immediate fate of Cyrenaica was being determined by force of arms. The Eighth Army triumphed over the Panzerarmee Afrika at Second Alamein (from 23 October to 2 November). General Montgomery failed, however, to exploit the victory by pursuing and annihilating Rommel's forces before they escaped into Libya. The Eighth Army proceeded to shepherd the Panzerarmee through Cyrenaica. Montgomery proclaimed to 'the people of Barqa' on 11 November that the British military occupation of Cyrenaica would continue until the end of the war. This meant the conclusion of the peace treaties and not merely the cessation of hostilities in Cyrenaica or North Africa.

He stated: 'The military government will not enter into questions relating to political affairs of the future but will endeavour to rule with firmness, justice and consideration for the interests of the people of the country.' There followed the usual warning against disturbing the peace or hindering operations, and the need to obey the orders of the military. Supplies would be provided when the army could transport them. Montgomery reiterated that the British government had thanked Sayyid Idris for his assistance to the Allied cause and had promised that the Sanusis would not again be subject to Italian rule. 'While the British Army rules the country it wishes to establish friendly and cordial relations with the people.'[14]

In conjunction with Montgomery's proclamation of 11 November the new DCPO Cyrenaica, Lt. Colonel D C Cumming, issued instructions to his political officers which set the guidelines for the third British occupation of Cyrenaica. Cumming pointed out that the British government faced a complicated problem in Cyrenaica. Although it recognised Italian sovereignty over the country, its Arab inhabitants could not be classed as enemies of Britain. In fact the Sanusis had helped the British and Eden had given them an assurance that they would not be returned to Italian rule. It had to be borne in mind that the military government was temporary, until the future of the country was determined at the peace settlement, its primary task being to ensure that the civilian population did not hinder operations or endanger the safety of the occupying army. At the same time it was incumbent upon the British administrators to provide 'good government'. This was also the best practical solution as it would ensure that Cyrenaica remained quiet.[15]

Cumming learnt soon after his arrival in Cyrenaica, following the fall of Tobruk to British forces on 13 November, that the Italian government had withdrawn its remaining nationals from the territory.[16] Cumming embarked upon a rapid tour of the Jabal Akhdar following the Eighth Army's capture of Benghazi on 20 November. He impressed upon the Sanusis he encountered that the British were in full accord with Sayyid Idris, that the tribesmen should not hinder military operations and that civilian food supplies could not be brought up while the Eighth Army needed all the transport. If the tribes wished to help they were to keep quiet, protect the abandoned Italian farms and plough as much as possible.[17]

At first the full co-operation of the Sanusis was not forthcoming. This changed once it was realised, following Rommel's withdrawal by 24 November to his old position at the El Agheila defile, that the Panzerarmee Afrika was in no fit condition to return and that the British would remain in Cyrenaica. The supply situation was satisfactory as the Axis forces had distributed food to the population before they had evacuated the territory. The tribesmen showed no inclination to occupy the farms on the Jabal Akhdar. Two LAF battalions were deployed to act as gendarmerie outside the towns while the newly-formed Cyrenaica Police Force operated in the towns.[18]

By the end of November British political officers were present in all the major centres of population in Cyrenaica. Because he found Benghazi too congested Cumming opened his headquarters at Barce on 23 November and later moved to Beda Littoria. The title of the British military administration was changed from 'Occupied Territories Administration' (OTA) to the 'Military Government of Cyrenaica', thereby removing the element of speculation attached to the former title. In March 1943 the title was changed again, as Cyrenaica was no longer an operational area, to the 'Military Administration of Cyrenaica'.[19]

Cyrenaica presented a grim spectacle after two years of war. The coastal towns had been devastated and were virtually uninhabitable because of the lack of housing, essential utilities and a precarious food supply. The scene in the hinterland was less dismal. Although military operations had restricted their movements, destroyed many of their wells and closed their normal markets, the native agriculturalists and pastoralists had had sufficient resources to survive, even though the crops had been poor and the herds had been depleted.

It was discovered, however, that as a result of war and Fascist colonial policy the native and animal population in Cyrenaica had been reduced to a level below that existing before the Italian occupation of the country.[20] There was also the problem of the abandoned Italian farms, only 1,700 of which were capable of being resettled. The British administrators were confronted with a novel situation in Cyrenaica. As has been pointed out, 'Cyrenaica suffered more than other Italian-occupied territories: Eritrea and Tripolitania were better endowed materially than their economic capacity warranted and an Italian system of government was allowed and able to continue without interruption under British military control. Cyrenaica, as a wholly native country, was the only one of the three likely under normal circumstances to be able to support itself, but inherited practically no benefits from the Italians, and the Administration had the task of starting up a completely new though temporary government with virtually no assets and no chance of getting any.'[21]

After three weeks in Cyrenaica, Cumming attempted to assess the political and economic prospects of the territory. He observed that the Italians had done much damage to the social and moral institutions of the Arab population of Cyrenaica. 'The Arabs have been introduced to European civilisation by the least creditable of mentors and they are suspicious and unresponsive to other Europeans.' The Arabs could not exploit the material benefactions of Italian rule because they were still limited by the social psychology of nomads. The Italians had made little attempt to train Arab technicians who could maintain the public works, services and utilities which had been provided at great expense for the Italian colonists in Cyrenaica.

Moreover, there were political problems, due in part to the Turkish legacy. The Turks had brought the Sanusi Order into contact with the Pan-Islamic movement and by flattering treatment had given the Sanusi leaders an exaggerated view of their own power. Cumming thought that while on the one hand the Sanusis had set relatively high moral standards of behaviour and had achieved a considerable degree of political unity among the anarchical tribes of Cyrenaica, on the other hand they had been a reactionary influence. They lacked also a sense of political responsibility as a result of exercising their influence in partnership, first with the Turks and then with the Italians (from 1920, and the Pact of Al-Rajma, to 1923). 'The Senussia have acquired a taste for living beyond their political means.' The Cyrenaican refugees, led by Sayyid Idris, were an important factor but they suffered from 'irresponsibility, a romantic detachment from the political realities of their country, and a taste for intrigue' (some were in contact also with Arab nationalists). Cumming described Sayyid Idris as 'a childless hypochondriac with an acute political instinct but few of the attributes of an administrator'.

He had lost much of the austere sanctity with which he was surrounded when he arrived in Egypt in 1922, but 'he still has a firm hold over the Arabs in Cyrenaica. To the feckless Arab he bears the essence of sanctity; to the politically minded townsman, or exile, he is a convenient peg on which to hang vague ideas of Cyrenaican independence.'[22]

Cumming made clear that by creating the Libyan Arab Force and making a declaration that the Sanusis in Cyrenaica would be freed from Italian rule, Britain had entered into a commitment which could not be discharged, in Arab eyes, without the establishment of a sovereignty acceptable to the people and without some relatively generous treatment as a reward for services rendered during the war. Cumming thought it would be useless to expect the Arabs of Cyrenaica to take a rational view either of their sacrifices or their small contribution to the defeat of the Axis in Libya. They saw themselves as allies of Britain and gave a literal interpretation to the terms of the Atlantic Charter which was favourable to their vaguely-defined aspirations. However, Cyrenaica would be under military government until the peace settlement and in the meantime it would suffer considerable hardship.

As to the future, 'Cyrenaica will be incapable of supporting itself as a purely Arab state and no country that must satisfy its strategic requirements by controlling the eastern Mediterranean and Egypt can afford to see it under the control of any other interested and potentially hostile power. One cannot forecast the post-war settlement, but assuming that Britain, or some league in which Britain is a leading partner, continues to control the strategic danger zones, it is reasonable to suppose that naval and air bases will be established in Cyrenaica. The future of the country may, therefore, be under British influence in some form or other.'

Cumming considered that Cyrenaica might become a British colony, probably under some form of international supervision. He admitted, however, that as British colonies were expected to be self-sufficient, Cyrenaica could soon become 'as lustreless a jewel in the crown as, for instance, Somaliland'. Alternatively, Britain 'could establish sovereignty over the strategic bases and leave the rest to an indigenous sovereignty with which treaty relations are established, as in Aden...' or 'enter into a treaty relationship with an indigenous but ineffective sovereignty, as in Zanzibar'.[23]

Cumming prophesied that if the Cyrenaican Arabs were left to their own devices, social and economic retrogression would occur for which the British would be severely criticised. European investment was needed although this might be seen as exploitation. Cumming laid emphasis on the fact that as long as the majority of the population was nomadic it would be impossible to educate them to civilised standards.

'The nomad psychology is one of waste, lawlessness and irresponsibility, and it is inimical to civilisation in the modern world.' Cumming suggested that 'if the population can be concentrated or settled, hope might be entertained of applying the forces of education and social guidance to introduce a form of civilisation into the country which would have a reasonable prospect of keeping pace with modern developments. Otherwise, we must be content with a decaying nomadic society.'

However, more settled conditions in the Jabal Akhdar were only possible if a year-round supply of drinking water was available. It was this which had dissuaded the Jewish Territorial Organisation from taking up the offer of the Turkish government in 1907 for the Jews to colonise Cyrenaica. The Italians had recognised the problem and they had begun laying the Ain Mara pipeline. Further progress on any appreciable scale was dependent on completion of this project. Cumming held out the prospect of the Military Government and the people of Cyrenaica forming a partnership to farm the arable land of the Jabal Akhdar on a communal basis.

Although these problems were mainly in the future, Cumming warned that the actions of the Military Government would have an effect upon future policy. If the British failed to restore to the Arabs at least the degree of participation in government that they had enjoyed under the Turks, or maintained less than the social services provided by the Italians, or introduced foreign settlers without the consent of the inhabitants, then the Cyrenaican Arabs, and eventually the rest of the Arab world, would accuse the British of duplicity. Moreover, if Britain wanted strategic bases in Cyrenaica then it was advisable to secure the confidence of the Arabs in British administration.

Cumming quoted Sir Francis Bacon with approval, 'If you plant where savages are, do not entertain them with trifles and gingles, but use them justly and graciously, with sufficient guard nevertheless.'[24] This could be achieved through good administration, allowing the Arabs a greater say in the government of their country and restoring the morale of the people and inculcating a sense of responsibility in their leaders.

Cumming's analysis of the administrative problems facing the Military Government in Cyrenaica was fully endorsed by the Chief Political Officer, Brigadier Hone, who visited Cyrenaica in early December 1942. Hone was insistent about the dangers of an uncontrolled influx of foreigners and foreign capital into Cyrenaica and the exploitation of the country by undesirable means. He sought War Office approval to permit only the entry of a few reputable traders from Egypt and elsewhere into Cyrenaica to supply local Arab needs in manufactured goods. He wanted to maintain Cyrenaica 'as a purely Arab state like Transjordan', at least until the end of the war.[25] In order to achieve this Hone pleaded for more Arabic-speaking officers with a good knowledge of the Arabs to be sent to Cyrenaica.

It was feared in London that Hone might be going beyond the terms of Eden's declaration on the Sanusis in Cyrenaica. The War Office, with the agreement of the Foreign Office, sought a reassurance from Hone on 9 January 1943 that his intention to maintain Cyrenaica as a purely Arab state like Transjordan did not imply some form of British indirect rule through Sayyid Idris or any recognition of his temporal power. Hone was also instructed that the Military Government of Cyrenaica was to refrain from making any statement about future policy. Cyrenaica was to be governed as occupied enemy territory in accordance with international law, qualified only by Eden's declaration (and commentary of 25 June 1942). Hone was given permission, however, to 'temper existing criminal and civil laws and regulations which are partial to Italian interests at expense of Arab interests'. He could also exclude 'undesirables including immigrants and traders'.[26]

Hone swiftly disavowed any intention of establishing a system of indirect rule through Sayyid Idris in Cyrenaica. The latter had not yet raised the question of his return from exile and Hone made clear

Sayyid Idris's triumphant return to Cyrenaica, 1944. By permission of Faraj Najem Collection.

Sayyid Idris in Soluch, on his return to Cyrenaica, 1944. By permission of Faraj Najem Collection.

that the head of the Sanusi Order would remain in Egypt. He would be permitted a short visit to Cyrenaica in the near future as a matter of courtesy and to aid in the establishment of British military rule, but his speeches would be carefully vetted.

The Foreign Office objected to Hone's proposal for restricting Sayyid Idris's freedom of movement and speech. As Gilbert Mackereth (Egyptian Department) pointed out, 'We must not revert to a practice of pin-pricks, which had done no good in the past.' Sayyid Idris should be put on his honour not to raise political matters which could be exploited by Axis propaganda. If this did not work then other methods could be tried. However, Mackereth opposed publicising any such visit to Cyrenaica as it 'would go to Sayyid Idris's head'.

In fact Sayyid Idris did not visit Cyrenaica until 1944. A visit planned for April 1943 was called off because Hone refused to allow Idris to take his large retinue with him. Apart from logistical difficulties, Hone feared that a 'royal progress' through Cyrenaica would cause political problems.[27] Despite this treatment Sayyid Idris agreed to use his influence with the Cyrenaican Arabs on behalf of the Military Government. He called upon the Sanusis to keep the peace and to co-operate with the British authorities. The tribes heeded this advice.

Although the tribesmen remained armed there were only sporadic outbreaks of tribal violence. In order to prevent the Sanusi-dominated LAF from becoming a focus of patriotic activity in Cyrenaica, thus rivalling the authority of the British Military Government, the two remaining battalions were disbanded and amalgamated with the Cyrenaica Police Force to form an armed gendarmerie, the Cyrenaica Defence Force. However, Sanusi influence remained strong in this new force.[28]

In the winter of 1942–43 Hone and Cumming began to implement the policy of freeing Cyrenaica from the vestiges of Italian rule, in accordance with Eden's directive to Casey of 25 June 1942. Their task had been simplified by the fact that the Italian population of Cyrenaica had fled to Tripolitania. As the Italian government had removed both their administrative records and their officials in Cyrenaica the British administered the territory by proclamation law on lines suitable for the Arab population. They had now 'to develop local rural and municipal government on native lines ...' under the 'benevolent administration' of Britain. This had to be accomplished in secret, however, in order to avoid the accusation that Britain was trying to predetermine the peace settlement.[29]

It was decided that the most useful and practical method of governing the tribal community in Cyrenaica was to revive traditional tribal authority and to encourage tribal chiefs to settle tribal disputes. However, this proved to be a long and arduous task because of the disintegration of the tribal system under Italian rule. The authority of the tribal chiefs had declined and only two tribes, the al-Ubaydat and the al-Bara'sa, had recognised shaikhs. The other tribes had split into numerous sub-divisions.

By the end of 1943 some progress had been made in reducing the great number of petty shaikhs in Cyrenaica by cutting subsidies, in order that the few legitimate shaikhs could re-establish their authority (some paramount shaikhs returned from exile in Egypt and the Sudan). Meanwhile, a municipal council was set up in Benghazi composed of native notables, and Sayyid Abu al-Qasim al-Sanusi, a cousin of Sayyid Idris, was appointed as *qaim maqam* (later he became Secretary of the Interior). In addition, the British began to establish a native civil service in Cyrenaica in order to encourage the Arabs to fill responsible positions.

In 1943, Bardia and Tobruk remained closed for operational reasons to the population of Cyrenaica, and the Benghazi municipal council proved to be the sole organ for the expression of urban political opinion. It soon complained to the Military Government about the utter stagnation of Cyrenaican trade, the lack of public utility services and the small scale of educational and medical services. The British administrators managed by the end of 1943 to create rudimentary medical and educational services but the lack of funds, equipment and skilled personnel prevented the restoration of the worst war damage in the towns (only the rubble was cleared from Benghazi in 1943). The shortage of shipping and motor transport, which was beyond the Military Government's control, prevented anything more than a trickle of goods from Egypt and Tripolitania from being imported into Cyrenaica.[30]

In an attempt to revive trade and restore agricultural production, a 'Hill Farms Scheme' was set up whereby Arab tenants operated, under British control, the oldest Italian settlements in the Jabal Akhdar (Luigi Razza, Beda Littoria, Luigi Savoia and Giovanni Berta). It proved a difficult task, as Sir Hugh Foot makes clear: 'The Arabs were incapable of cultivating the Italian farms and our efforts to teach them to care for the cattle and prune the vines and prevent the goats from eating the fruit trees was only very slowly effective. Usually they would pitch their tents alongside an Italian farm and use the farmhouse as a store or stable.'

However, by the summer of 1943 a grape crop had been harvested and wine produced, presumably for export. A more important development occurred on the Barce Plain where, following the summer harvest, by the end of 1943 nearly 4,450 hectares had been ploughed and sown, mostly with wheat, as part of a Middle East Supply Centre plan for increasing food production in the Middle East.

Foot has vividly described the novel method, of cultivation: 'The large Barce Plain was covered with little white farmhouses but since there was no-one to run the farms we organised a vast and motley line of tractors and damaged tanks and ploughed the whole plain for wheat in one operation, the tractors and tanks making detours to avoid the houses and then proceeding in line abreast across the twenty-mile (32 km) plain.' This was indeed a case of turning swords into ploughshares!

With the encouragement of the Military Government the Arabs of Cyrenaica proceeded in 1943 'to occupy the abandoned shell of Italian colonisation'. In particular the tribal shaikhs began to re-establish the Sanusi system of *zawias* in the old Italian villages, which were well-suited for use as religious and administrative centres. This development may be said to symbolise the earnestness of Eden's pledge that 'His Majesty's Government is determined that at the end of the war the Sanusis will in no circumstances again fall under Italian domination.'[31]

chapter 6
'TRIPOLITANIA IS NOT ON ALL FOURS WITH CYRENAICA'
NOVEMBER 1942–FEBRUARY 1943

> Tripolitania is not on all fours with Cyrenaica, for there the Senussi element represents only a small minority, and the declaration made in Parliament does not apply.
>
> Sir James Grigg, in memorandum for Cabinet of 24 February 1943[32]

PLANNING THE OCCUPATION OF TRIPOLITANIA

IN CONTRAST to the relative ease with which the British occupied Cyrenaica, the occupation of Tripolitania proved to be an altogether more complicated and protracted affair. Originally, it had been thought that General Eisenhower's forces would capture Tripoli from the west. After the 'Torch' landings on 8 November and five days of desultory fighting and hectic negotiating, the Allies gained Morocco, Algeria, and later French West Africa. The French Fleet had been scuttled at Toulon but 'the big prize', Tunisia, eluded the Allies. Units of General Anderson's First Army advanced to within 24 km of Tunis and 32 km of Bizerta but increasing German resistance prevented them from making further gains. It was to be six months before the Allies overran Tunisia.

By mid-December it was clear that Tripoli would fall to the Eighth Army. Even before this, however, General Eisenhower had been amenable to the idea of a British military administration in Tripolitania. He had agreed that a team of British political officers should accompany the First Army during its advance through Tunisia. If any units of the First Army had entered Tripolitania from the west, the British political officers would have issued the same proclamations of British military rule that the Eighth Army intended to use.

Eisenhower sought official sanction for this policy from the Combined Chiefs of Staff in early December 1942. He stressed the importance of having separate systems of military government for occupied Italian and French territory in North Africa. He proposed that the

British should administer Libya and that American civil government should stop at the eastern border of Tunisia.

However, this proposal did not satisfy President Roosevelt. He felt that Tripolitania should be included within the American sphere of responsibility in North Africa because of the territory's close economic and social ties with Tunisia. (Roosevelt may have had in mind the large Italian community in both territories.) The President left it to the State Department to settle the matter with the Foreign Office, although he admitted that he was not prepared to press his view against the opposition of the British and General Eisenhower.[33]

The Foreign Office was not impressed by Roosevelt's views. There was only a slender social and economic relationship between Tunisia and Tripolitania, communications were bad and Franco-Italian enmity in North Africa had to be taken into account. Sir William Strang (Assistant Under-Secretary of State superintending the French Department) felt it was illogical, both on political and administrative grounds, to divide Tripolitania from Cyrenaica. These territories had been under the same colonial administration and it was desirable to have one power occupying them in order to avoid any divergence of local policy.

According to the Treasury there were serious financial objections to a division of Libya. Strang felt that these difficulties probably could be overcome if there were pressing military reasons for placing Tripolitania under American control but, as the War Office confirmed, these did not exist.[34] In fact, in the opinion of the Chiefs of Staff (based on the findings of the Joint Planning Staff, the JPS) the balance of the military argument lay in favour of making the border between Tunisia and Tripolitania the dividing line between the American and the British spheres of responsibility in North Africa.

As far as land operations and communications were concerned, Tripolitania might equally well be under the Allied Commander-in-Chief, North Africa, or the Commander-in-Chief, Middle East, but from the point of view of internal security and economic stability it was thought that the administrative boundary should be fixed on the Tripolitania-Tunisia frontier.

The JPS opposed the division of Libya between two occupying powers with dissimilar methods of control because this might well lead to internal dissatisfaction and unrest among the inhabitants, who were used to a single dominion. In addition, the oasis of Hon was the centre of economic life in the hinterland of Libya. It had contacts with both Cyrenaica and Tripolitania, and it was undesirable for a political division to sever these contacts. Moreover, there were closer economic

Curtiss Kittyhawks of No. 239 Wing RAF fly into Marble Arch landing ground, December 1942, past the Arco dei Fileni ('Marble Arch'), a monument erected in 1937 on the Via Balbia, the coastal road in Libya between the provinces of Tripolitania and Cyrenaica, to celebrate the completion of the road and the foundation of the (New Roman) Empire. By permission of The Imperial War Museum ME (RAF) 7245.

links between the coastal areas of Tripolitania and Cyrenaica than between Tripoli and Tunis.

These considerations, coupled with the necessity of having airfields in Tripolitania in order to allow the Middle East air forces to carry out operations in the Central Mediterranean, outweighed the slight but unimportant advantage in making the line El Agheila-Corfu the division between the naval commands in the Mediterranean (i.e. the Central Mediterranean would be included in the Western Command for operations against Italy).[35] This reasoning convinced Secretary of State Hull that the Tripolitania-Tunisia frontier was the logical division between the American and British spheres of responsibility in North Africa. Accordingly, he recommended it to the White House Chief of Staff, Admiral William B Leahy on 23 December. At a meeting with the President on 7 January 1943 the Joint Chiefs of Staff approved this recommendation.[36]

While the question of military jurisdiction in Tripolitania was being worked out by the Combined Chiefs, Brigadier Hone had pressed the Minister of State in the Middle East and the Foreign Office and War Office in London for a decision on the administrative policy to be followed in Tripolitania in the event of a British occupation. Eden had indicated to Casey on 25 June 1942 that the military administrations in Cyrenaica and Tripolitania should be kept separate and distinct. Tripolitania was to be administered as occupied enemy territory in accordance with a strict interpretation of the appropriate provisions of international law. Therefore, the Italian administrative structure would be kept largely intact.

Hone wanted to know whether Eden still approved of this policy. The Chief Political Officer predicted that the Tripolitanian Arabs would press the British government to issue a pledge that Tripolitania, like Cyrenaica, would be 'released from the Italian yoke'. (The term 'Arab' in Tripolitania has a linguistic rather than a racial connotation. The majority of the native population of about 650,000 were of Berber origin, and 23% were still Berber-speaking.)

Curtiss Kittyhawk Pilots of No. 239 Wing RAF report to their Commanding Officer's tent at Marble Arch, Tripolitania, after a sortie against retreating Axis forces in Libya, December 1942. By permission of The Imperial War Museum CM 4231.

Hone warned that the Tripolitanians would be likely to follow the Cyrenaican example and demand the restoration of their lands. Under international law, however, Britain was precluded from dispossessing the Italian colonists in Tripolitania and returning the land either wholly or in part to the Arabs (even in Cyrenaica, following the Italian exodus, the abandoned farms were controlled by the Custodian of Enemy Property although leased to the Arabs, pending a final decision on ownership at the peace settlement). Hone thought that the sharp contrast between British policy in Cyrenaica and Tripolitania, especially on the land question, would arouse adverse comment among Tripolitanian Arabs which might have serious repercussions throughout the Arab world.[37]

For these reasons Hone was convinced that it would be unwise for the British government, for the sake of temporary political expediency, to bow to demands from the Tripolitanian Arabs for a declaration on the future of Tripolitania. He was opposed in general to the idea of making declarations on occupied territories during the war as it was 'apt to be dangerous'.[38] He pointed out that Britain had made an exception in the case of Cyrenaica because of the need to retain the confidence and assistance of the Sanusis in the war against Italy by rewarding them for their efforts in support of the British cause.

However, the declaration on the Sanusis had been made in general terms and was restricted in scope. Tripolitania differed from Cyrenaica in that the Sanusis constituted about a third of the population and there was no recognised leader. Moreover, as the British had had no direct contact with Tripolitania, it was impossible to gauge the opinion of the overwhelming majority of Tripolitanian Arabs. It was thought, although it could not be confirmed, that the Cyrenaican Arabs were more hostile to the Italians than the Tripolitanians.

It was recognised that the French had political aspirations with regard to Tripolitania but not as regards Cyrenaica, with the possible exception of Kufra. There was also the possibility that, in a bid for Italian friendship in the future, Britain might think it desirable to restore Tripolitania to Italy. These considerations led Hone to propose a short and uncompromising reply to any demand from the Tripolitanian Arabs for a declaration on their future. The reply should merely state that Britain intended to maintain the status quo in Tripolitania and would preserve private rights in land at least until the end of the war. Hone also wanted permission to evict any Arabs who tried to occupy abandoned Italian farms in Tripolitania. The Italian colonists would be encouraged to continue farming in order to support themselves and to maintain the food production of the country.[39]

Thinking in London had been moving on parallel lines to that in Cairo. As the Eighth Army prepared to assault the Panzerarmee's position at Buerat, the War Office and the Foreign Office had ordered Hone to adhere to a strict interpretation of international law in the administration of Tripolitania.[40] As the Secretary of State for War, Sir James Grigg, later made clear to the Cabinet, 'Tripolitania is not on all fours with Cyrenaica, for there the Senussi element represents only a small minority, and the declaration made in Parliament does not apply. We propose, therefore, that in Tripolitania the normal principles of military government and the requirements of international conventions shall be observed without any specific qualification as in Cyrenaica.'

An important factor in the equation was that whereas there were no longer any Italian colonists in Cyrenaica, many still remained in Tripolitania. It was expected that one of the major problems facing the British administrators would be the return of these colonists to their farms in Tripolitania.[41]

Hone proved accurate in predicting that the Tripolitanian Arabs would demand the same treatment as Britain had accorded the Sanusis of Cyrenaica. The British authorities in Cairo learnt from Sayyid Idris in early January 1943 that he had been approached by an Egyptian Senator of Cyrenaican descent, Abdul Sattar Bey al-Basil, on behalf of the Tripolitanian shaikhs in exile. It will be recalled that the latter had refused to co-operate in the formation of the Libyan Arab Force owing to their opposition to the political aspirations of Sayyid Idris. However, the advance of the Eighth Army into Tripolitania, following Rommel's withdrawal from El Agheila to Buerat, persuaded the Tripolitanian shaikhs of the need to make up their differences with the Sanusis.

The Tripolitanian shaikhs wanted Sayyid Idris to convince the British of the essential unity of all Libya and to urge that the policy being applied in Cyrenaica should be applied also in Tripolitania. In return the Tripolitanian shaikhs, who had formed a Tripolitanian Committee, were prepared to agree in writing to Sayyid Idris becoming Amir of Tripolitania as well as of Cyrenaica.

The Tripolitanian initiative met with a cool response from Sayyid Idris, but it is worth noting that he did not categorically reject the idea of becoming Amir of a united Libya. It was his enemy, Abdul Rahman Azzam, he learned, who had advised the Tripolitanian shaikhs to approach Abdul Sattar Bey al-Basil. Sayyid Idris told the Egyptian Senator that he had no need of a further written statement offering him the amirate of Tripolitania (following the written offers in 1922 and 1939). He reminded Abdul Sattar Bey al-Basil that the Tripolitanians had declined

'TRIPOLITANIA IS NOT ON ALL FOURS ...': NOVEMBER 1942–FEBRUARY 1943

A Vickers Wellington of No. 1 General Reconnaissance Unit, flying south-west over the harbour at Tripoli, during a mine-clearance operation soon after the occupation of the town by the Allies on 23 January 1943. By permission of The Imperial War Museum CM 5201.

the British offer to co-operate in the formation of the LAF in 1940 and that any attempt at a rapprochement should be made directly to the British authorities and not through him.

In conversation with British political officers in Cairo, Sayyid Idris did not show any enthusiasm for the Tripolitanian proposal possibly because he was unsure how much public support he could raise in Tripolitania. Yet at the same time he seemed anxious to avoid being seen to foresake his Tripolitanian followers (Sanusi influence was strong in eastern Tripolitania). In correspondence with the British authorities, as will be seen, he was careful always to avoid renouncing his interest in Tripolitania by stating his claim to Libya rather than Cyrenaica alone. Sayyid Idris was mainly interested in re-establishing himself in Cyrenaica but until his future was finally determined he could not afford to reject outright any Tripolitanian approaches.[42]

Lieutenant General Bernard Law Montgomery, GOC Eighth Army, returns the salute of Eighth Army tank crews as he drives into Tripoli, 26 January 1943. By permission of The Imperial War Museum E 21589.

The Tripolitanian initiative aroused some interest in the Egyptian Department of the Foreign Office. Gilbert Mackereth thought that it might contain the germ of a solution to the problem of Tripolitania's future, and that a close watch should be kept on Sayyid Idris's success in reconciling the Sanusis with the Tripolitanian shaikhs: 'The possibility of such unity is not without its attractions, for an Arab shaikh under our trusteeship (on behalf of the United Nations, of course) may well provide the means of satisfying the strategic desiderata of the fighting services and increase the protective cushion for the Suez Canal.'

However, both Mackereth and Scrivener agreed that it would be a mistake for the British government to take any initiative at this stage: 'The movement, if it is to grow into anything substantial, must progress naturally.' The British military administrators were to be told to refrain from 'meddling in this sort of thing on their own. It was just the sort of game the political officers enjoyed playing with such devastating effect.' Sir Maurice Peterson seemed to think, however, that any 'shaikhdom' in Libya would be under Egyptian rather than British suzerainty.[43]

Sayyid Idris was quick to capitalise on the British conquest of Tripolitania and the evidence of Tripolitanian support for a united Libya under a Sanusi amirate. On 25 January, following the entry of the

Eighth Army into Tripoli two days before, he congratulated both Casey and Churchill on the triumph of Allied arms in North Africa and the expulsion of all Axis forces from Libya (a similar message was sent to Roosevelt). Sayyid Idris requested, on behalf of the Libyan people, 'that the future of their country should be decided now and its position and form of government declared on the principle put up by the leaders of the country to the British Government on 9th August, 1940, when they decided for co-operation with Great Britain and the Allies against the Axis in order to set free their country.'

The Libyans had co-operated faithfully with Britain and her allies, and this had been recognised by the Foreign Secretary in his statement on the Sanusis of 8 January 1942. According to Sayyid Idris, the Eden Declaration and the Atlantic Charter required that the Allies should treat Libya not as occupied enemy territory, like Eritrea, but 'as (the) territory of a friend ... whose rights and freedom had been stolen and to whom Great Britain and her Allies had come in order to destroy their common enemy and give victory to the oppressed.'

He had in mind the example of Haile Selassie in Ethiopia who had been restored to his throne in 1941 by the British, following the conquest of Italian East Africa. Sayyid Idris thought that the Libyans had an even greater claim than the Ethiopians to their immediate independence because of their longer struggle against the Italians, which involved such heavy sacrifices. He stated that the Libyans wanted 'a free, national Arab government' to be formed in Libya without delay. Libya should be regarded as an Arab state. 'This nation is an Arab nation which desires that its future should not fall short of the future of its brother Arabs, such as Iraq, Transjordan, Syria and all the Arab lands.'

Sayyid Idris demanded that Libya should be represented at the peace conference. In an attempt to reassure the British, he said that the formation of a National Government would not conflict with the maintenance of the military administrations in Libya during the war. In fact the former would aid the latter by ensuring the loyal co-operation of the Libyan population, who would 'see that their efforts are truly appreciated and the promise of freedom to the weak has been proved and actually put into execution. The effect in all the Arab lands, too, will without doubt be beneficial.'[44]

Casey considered it undesirable to deal in any detail with the controversial questions raised by Sayyid Idris. He kept his reply to Sayyid Idris brief, simply referring him to his (Casey's) own statement of 26 January 1943 on Tripolitania. Following the capture of Tripoli, the Minister of State had informed the press that the British government had decided that Tripolitania, purged of its Fascist elements, would be administered as occupied enemy territory until the end of the war when its destiny would be determined by the United Nations.

Casey told Sayyid Idris that the British government had no intention of following the example of the Axis powers in flouting 'the canons of international law' in countries occupied by them. Therefore, military administrations would be maintained in Cyrenaica and Tripolitania during the war, 'after which the ultimate destiny of these territories would be decided by the United Nations.'[45]

Gilbert Mackereth was not surprised by Sayyid Idris's request for a 'National Government' in Libya. It highlighted the desirability, in Mackereth's view, of the British government clarifying its own mind about Libya not so much because of the need to declare British policy but because it was necessary to prepare the way for the future. Mackereth suggested that the Prime Minister, in replying to Sayyid Idris, should evade the latter's polemical points and state that the future of Libya could only be decided at the peace settlement. Until then Italian North Africa would remain under British military administration in accordance with international law.

It should also be pointed out to Sayyid Idris that Libya bore no comparison with Ethiopia, where an existing sovereignty had been restored. Sayyid Idris had suggested the creation of a new sovereignty in Libya. Churchill agreed to these points and Casey was instructed to reply to Sayyid Idris that the Prime Minister was in complete agreement with the Minister of State's reply of 8 February and that there was no parallel between the position in Ethiopia and that in Libya. Casey conveyed this message to Sayyid Idris on 19 April 1943.[46]

THE BRITISH OCCUPATION OF TRIPOLITANIA

The British Military Administration in Tripolitania made it clear from the outset that it was a temporary authority concerned only with the care and maintenance of the territory until the peace settlement, in accordance with international law, and with the security and needs of the Allied forces. The requirements of the Eighth Army were paramount during the Tunisian campaign and the invasion of Sicily.

The main military need, following the British occupation of Tripoli, was to reopen the blocked harbour for use as a base for the advance into Tunisia. This task was carried out after considerable delay, which was severely criticised, by Major General Sir Brian Robertson, who in late February 1943 became GOC Tripolitania Base. Tripoli had sustained

25-pdr field guns and 'Quad' artillery tractors parade past British Prime Minister Winston Churchill during his visit to Tripoli to thank the Eighth Army for its success in the North African campaign, 4 February 1943. By permission of The Imperial War Museum E 4141E.

much less bomb damage than Benghazi or Tobruk. In fact Tripolitania had not suffered the material devastation which had occurred in Cyrenaica as a result of the Desert War. However, typhus was prevalent in Tripolitania, especially in Tripoli City and among the two thousand Jews found in a concentration camp at Garian.[47]

The epidemic was soon brought under control with the help of Italian doctors and nurses who had remained behind. Eventually the Italian medical service was restored to its former efficiency, but with an essential difference: it was now available to Tripolitanian Arabs and Jews as well as to the Italian community. The shortage of foodstuffs in Tripolitania made it hard for the British military administrators to meet the requirements of both the Eighth Army and the civilian population. The scarcity of food in Tripoli was particularly serious and a strict rationing system had to be introduced (it was calculated that there was only a two-month supply available and this had been distributed to the population by the Axis authorities before they evacuated the city). It was discovered that about two-thirds of the livestock had been slaughtered in 1941 to feed and provide leather for Rommel's Panzerarmee Afrika.

Moreover, agricultural production on the Italian farms in Tripolitania, which was heavily mechanised, had declined dramatically owing to the shortage of transport, spare parts and fuel and the systematic destruction of irrigation ditches, water pumps and the electric power stations by the retreating Germans.

In the first six months of its existence the British Military Administration (BMA) of Tripolitania concentrated its efforts on acquiring grain and reviving agricultural production. The latter task was made easier by the fact that many Italian farmers remained in Tripolitania (some 15,000 out of a total Italian community of about 50,000). During Rommel's retreat along the Tripolitanian coast the Italian colonists abandoned the outlying agricultural settlements and concentrated in the village centres for safety. There was never any danger of a wholesale massacre of Italian civilians by the Arabs, and only isolated incidents of violence were recorded. But widespread looting occurred and this was only brought under control by the units of the Sudan Defence Force who assumed internal security duties pending the establishment of a native police force (a police school was opened at Tarhuna in March 1943).

In accordance with the British government's decision to maintain the Italian agricultural settlements, the Italians returned to their farms under British protection. The Italian colonisation companies came under the supervision of the BMA's Department of Agriculture and the colonists eventually produced food for the towns and the British armed forces and made good profits. But it took until the spring of 1944 before living conditions appreciably improved in Tripoli and the other coastal towns. There was no trade with neighbouring countries in 1943, except for a limited wool and date trade with Cyrenaica. In order to encourage trade a customs union was established between Cyrenaica and Tripolitania.[48]

Although the population of Tripolitania suffered considerable privation in 1943, the vast majority accepted British military occupation and were prepared to co-operate with the BMA. The British presence was particularly welcomed by the long-established Jewish community (of about 26,000) which had been actively persecuted by the Italian authorities since 1941.[49] In order to mark the end of Fascist rule in Tripolitania, the Vice-Governor, his Secretary and the two prefects of Tripoli and Misurata were arrested and interned. In accordance with the decision to maintain the Italian administrative structure intact, however, the British used Italian law supplemented by proclamations, while the services of Italian judges, doctors and minor officials who had remained behind were employed. The latter worked well under British supervision and this set-up was accepted by the majority of Tripolitanian Arabs, with the exception of the politically-aware minority.

The 21 municipal councils in the towns and agricultural village centres continued to function and the local British administrators were assisted by Italian and Arab advisory councils in the districts. The political behaviour of the Italian community never posed a threat to Allied operations in Tunisia or Sicily. While taking the salute at the march-past of the 51st Division in the main square of Tripoli on 4 February 1943, Churchill noticed that 'the Italians were second to none in their enthusiasm'. The Italian colonists, concerned above all with eking out an existence under the harsh wartime conditions, had little time for politics and quickly shed their allegiance to Fascism. It was deemed unwise to excite the suspicion of the BMA when the latter was acting as the sole protector of Italian interests against Arab claims.

Winston Churchill greets an officer of 51st Highland Division during his visit to Tripoli, 4 February 1943. By permission of The Imperial War Museum E 4136E.

Winston Churchill with military leaders during his visit to Tripoli. The group includes: General Sir Oliver Leese, General Sir Harold Alexander, General Sir Alan Brooke and General Sir Bernard Montgomery, 7 February 1943. By permission of The Imperial War Museum E 22271.

Evidence of the change of political climate in Tripolitania can be seen in the fact that two Italian anti-fascist parties made separate approaches to the BMA in April 1943 in an attempt to secure official recognition. They failed to elicit a satisfactory response. Leading Arab dignitaries in Tripoli had also called on the British authorities to allow the formation of political parties but had met with similar discouragement. It proved much harder for the Tripolitanian Arabs to reach agreement on their political aims because of the traditionally fragmented nature of Tripolitanian politics.

Moreover, the tribal system in Tripolitania had been disrupted to an even greater extent than in Cyrenaica because of the Italian tendency to split up the tribes (*cabilas*) on an arbitrary basis. Apart from several nomadic or semi-nomadic tribes, there were few large tribes in existence in 1943. As has been pointed out, 'It was not to be expected that, in such a tribal system or disintegration of a system, any unanimity would be forthcoming or any persons of consequence found to take the lead. It was not until the late summer of 1943 that Tripolitanian Arab politicians began to demand that all Italian officials, especially Italian judges, be removed from the BMA, that Italian land be returned to the Arabs and that Arab schools be established to educate the Tripolitanians in order that they might govern themselves.'[50]

In late February, following the conquest of Libya, Sir James Grigg defined British policy in Cyrenaica and Tripolitania for the benefit of the War Cabinet. 'In both these territories we propose to act on the assumption that no policy has been formulated by HM Government regarding their post-war status, although with regard to Cyrenaica we are committed to the non-return of this predominantly Senussi country to Italy. We shall, therefore, proceed to administer the area as occupied enemy territory according to the appropriate provisions of the Manual of Military Law. Military Administrators and Political Officers have been warned to eschew all discussion about the political future of these North African territories and to abstain from any declaration on the subject.'[51] What Grigg did not indicate, however, was that British plans for Tripolitania had had to be significantly revised because of the Free French *fait accompli* in the Fezzan.

chapter 7
'CE FRUIT SAVOUREUX DU DÉSERT' THE FEZZAN, SEPTEMBER 1942–JUNE 1943

> Ainsi était enfin cueilli, à force d'audace et de méthode, ce fruit savoureux du désert. (*So, through our daring and method, we plucked this tasty desert fruit.*)
>
> Charles de Gaulle's description of the Free French conquest of the Fezzan.[52]

GENERAL LECLERC'S CONQUEST OF THE FEZZAN

IN CONTRAST to its active opposition to the idea of an American administration in Tripolitania, the Foreign Office refused to intervene in order to prevent the establishment of a Free French military administration in the south-west region of Libya known as the Fezzan. The latter development occurred as a result of the activities of 'la colonne Leclerc' (the Leclerc column). The Free French forces in Chad under General Leclerc de Hauteclocque had been carrying out hit-and-run raids against Italian forces in southern Libya since January 1941, and in March of that year they captured the Kufra oases.[53]

It was the intention of the Free French leader, General de Gaulle, that Leclerc should take advantage of any successful British offensive into Tripolitania and embark upon the conquest of the Fezzan. Rommel's counter-offensives in April 1941 and January and May 1942 effectively thwarted Free French plans.[54] But when it became clear from September 1942 onwards that the Eighth Army was about to undertake the offensive at El Alamein, and that a major Allied operation was in the offing in French West or North Africa, the Free French were spurred into action.

De Gaulle visited Chad in mid-September and instructed Leclerc to prepare his forces to operate against the Vichy regime in Niger (should the Allies invade French West Africa), to undertake an offensive in southern Libya 'en vue d'occuper d'abord la région du Fezzan avec exploitation éventuelle, soit vers Tripoli, soit vers Ghadames, en combinaison avec des opérations alliées en Cyrenaique et en Tripolitaine' (with the

It was a patrol of the Long Range Desert Group such as this which navigated General Leclerc's Free French force across the desert from Zouar to Hon, pointing them towards Tripoli, September 1942. By permission of The Imperial War Museum HU 16666.

aim of first occupying the Fezzan region, and exploiting it later, either in the direction of Tripoli or Ghadames, in conjunction with the Allied operations in Cyrenaica and Tripolitania), and to participate in Allied operations in French North Africa.[55] In the event Leclerc was called upon only to execute the operation in Libya. De Gaulle had stressed, however, that although Leclerc should co-operate with the Allied forces he should not subordinate himself to a foreign military command.

De Gaulle's insistence on this point stemmed from his realisation that if Leclerc came under British command from the outset then the Fezzan would fall under British military administration. This would have thwarted de Gaulle's aim of a liberated France annexing the Fezzan after the war. He regarded southern Libya as a purely French front and the Fezzan as the reward for the Free French military effort.[56] This would seem to be the key to de Gaulle's subsequent intractable behaviour.

Although there was some doubt at General Headquarters, Middle East about the value of operations in the Fezzan, General Alexander realised that nothing should be done to discourage the enthusiastic Leclerc from carrying out his plans. The higher British military authorities in Cairo and London seemed to be unaware at this point of the political purpose behind the proposed operation. Alexander welcomed Leclerc's co-operation although he pointed out that the British would not be able to keep Leclerc's forces supplied or to provide air cover as far south as the Fezzan.

De Gaulle informed an appreciative General Alan Brooke (Commander of the Imperial General Staff, CIGS) on 15 November 1942, following the fall of Tobruk to the Eighth Army, that Leclerc's forces would be ready to attack by 5 December but that they would not do so until Montgomery reached the Gulf of Sirte. Alexander informed Leclerc on 21 November that his operational boundaries should be 27 Degrees Latitude and 18 Degrees Longitude, the northern boundary moving finally to 28 Degrees Latitude (see map, pp. 198–9). In any case, it was not thought that Leclerc's supplies would allow him to operate north of the Fezzan.[57]

Belatedly, it was realised that no provision had been made for the administration of the Fezzan. Alexander tried to redeem the situation on 27 November by requesting Leclerc to allow two British political officers (POs) to accompany his column. They would be responsible for the territory occupied by the Free French until such time as it was brought under British military administration. Leclerc was asked to issue proclamations, brought by the political officers, which were identical to those used by Montgomery, and to follow British currency policy (lire and BMA notes but no francs).

As time was short the two British POs, Lt. Colonel P B E Acland and Lt. West, were appointed and sent to Fort Lamy, with a letter of introduction from Alexander. Leclerc, however, had already replied to Alexander on 29 November, saying that, because administrative matters, and therefore international law, were involved, he had referred the matter to General de Gaulle.[58]

The C-in-C Middle East and the Minister of State urged the War Office and the Foreign Office respectively on 30 November to press de Gaulle to accept British administrative arrangements in Tripolitania, including the Fezzan, as Eisenhower had done. Casey added that this was especially important 'in view of possible French aspirations to territory on [the] southern border of Tripolitania'.[59]

The Foreign Office at first was reluctant to raise this question as a political issue with de Gaulle, preferring that the War Office deal with it as a purely military matter. However, it proved advisable for Eden to make a direct request to de Gaulle to allow British political officers to accompany Leclerc's expedition. De Gaulle refused to accede to this demand but on 2 December, to calm British fears, he told Charles Peake (British representative to the French National Committee) and Lt. Colonel O A Archdale (head of No. 20 Military Mission to the Free French) that he did not envisage Leclerc advancing further than the Fezzan. If Leclerc did enter Tripolitania then he would of course come under Alexander's command. Leclerc would also issue proclamations in the Fezzan which were similar to those used by the Eighth Army. Lastly, de Gaulle alluded to his intentions in the Fezzan by stating that whereas in Kufra he had handed over authority to the British, because he did not wish to stay there, the operation in the Fezzan was different (i.e. he intended to stay there).[60]

De Gaulle telegraphed to Leclerc ordering him to resist Alexander's demands: 'Le Fezzan doit être la part de la France dans la bataille d'Afrique. C'est le lieu géographique entre le Sud-Tunisien et le Tchad. Vous devez repousser purement et simplement toute immixtion britannique dans cette région sous n'importe quelle forme, politique, administrative, monétaire, etc.'[61] (The Fezzan must be France's share in the battle for Africa. It is geographically sited between southern Tunisia and Chad. You must simply reject any kind of British interference in this region, whether political, administrative, monetary, etc.) Despite appeals from Sir Frederick Bovenschen (the Permanent Under-Secretary at the War Office), his counterpart at the Foreign Office, Sir Alexander Cadogan, would not force de Gaulle's hand over the Fezzan because of the situation in North Africa.

Anglo-Free French relations were in a sensitive state as a result of British support for American policy in French North Africa, which involved the exclusion of the Free French not only from Operation 'Torch', but also, and more particularly, the last-minute murky deal with Vichy Commander-in-Chief, Admiral Darlan.[62] As de Gaulle remained adamant in his opposition to the idea of British political officers accompanying 'la colonne Leclerc', even after a second approach by the Foreign Office on 5 December, Alexander recalled Acland and West to Cairo on 7 December. Leclerc interpreted this as British agreement to French administration of the Fezzan, though even Alexander suggested that they should postpone the discussion of political problems in order not to prejudice military operations.[63]

There were those in Cairo who wanted to disabuse the Free French of this notion. On 12 December the Deputy Minister of State, Lord Moyne, voiced his fear to the Foreign Office that a French occupation of much of the Fezzan would lead to a French claim to retain administrative control of this long-coveted area. If this was conceded it would allow the French an opportunity to put forward their long-term claim for a corridor to the sea.

In order to block this Moyne thought that de Gaulle should be forced to agree that all Tripolitania, including the Fezzan, should, when occupied, be placed under British military administration, like Kufra. The Chief Political Officer, Brigadier Hone, supported this course of action and warned General Headquarters, Middle East on 17 December that the Free French would occupy a considerable area of Tripolitania unless the Eighth Army sent out patrols south of the line of Rommel's advance along the coast.[64] The War Office agreed that it was necessary to correct Leclerc's misconception. It would be greatly embarrassing to the C-in-C Middle East to have two kinds of military administration in the same area, and there were serious technical objections to the introduction of French currency into the Fezzan.

But on 24 December (the day of the assassination in Algiers of Darlan), Strang informed Casey, who was visiting London, 'that it would be useless to reopen with General de Gaulle the question of his agreeing in advance to hand over any territory occupied by Leclerc to the Commander-in-Chief Middle East. De Gaulle has already refused to do this and if ... this is a "long-coveted area" he is clearly unlikely to change his mind and sign it away for nothing. To press him further at this stage would only create friction without achieving anything.'[65]

The Foreign Office proposed to wait and see how Leclerc's operation progressed. When the latter reached his objectives, which were unknown, he might decide to contact the Eighth Army. Alexander could then use the powers at his disposal to persuade Leclerc that all occupied enemy territory should come under the control of Middle East Command.[66]

'La colonne Leclerc' (a motorised force of 2,300 men) began its advance from Zouar in the Tibesti mountains on 16 December, as the Eighth Army approached Nofilia on the Gulf of Sirte. The previous day Montgomery had declared that Tripolitania was thenceforth under British military occupation. While the Free French forces fought to establish a foothold in the southern Fezzan, Alexander informed Leclerc that his column was not to operate beyond Mizda. Hone warned the War Office on 30 December that the Free French would make strenuous efforts, for political reasons, to reach Mizda and to occupy as much Italian territory as possible. This would severely hamper the work of the British DCPO Tripolitania, Brigadier Lush.

Hone proposed that, whenever Leclerc came under British command, then that should be the point at which the limit of French administration would be fixed. Hone was worried about French aspirations on the southern frontiers of Libya.[67] His anxieties must have been increased by French military successes. The Axis stronghold in the Fezzan, Umm el-Araneb, fell to the Free French on 6 January 1943 after bitter fighting. The same day the garrisons at El Gatrun and Brach surrendered and Italian resistance in the Fezzan crumbled. Leclerc's forces entered the old trading capital of Murzuk and the military capital of Sebha on 8 January. The Fezzan had been conquered and on 9 January a Free French military administration was established with Lt. Colonel Delange as Military Governor. The Sanusi shaikh Ahmad Saif al-Nasir, who had been in exile in Chad since 1930 and had accompanied 'la colonne Leclerc', was installed as *Mutasarrif* in Murzuk to advise the French authorities on the administration of the territory.[68]

De Gaulle was ecstatic. On 13 January he broadcast the news of Leclerc's exploit to occupied France and invested it with an almost mystical significance: 'Mais, peut-être, l'effort de ces bon soldats a-t-il quelque peu consolé la misère de la France ... tous les hommes purs et forts qui en ont porté le poids, depuis leur jeune et glorieux General jusqu'au plus obscur soldat, en ont fait un humble don, offert de toute leur ferveur à la douleur et a la fierté de la France.'[69] (But perhaps the efforts of our fine soldiers have done something to console France in her misery ... all those pure and strong men who bore the burden, from their young and glorious general to the lowliest soldier, have made us a humble gift, offered most fervently to the suffering and pride of France.) To the liberated inhabitants of the Fezzan de Gaulle declared, 'Au Fezzan, comme partout ailleurs, la France est et demeurera l'amie sincère et eprouvée des musulmans. Grâce à la défaite de notre ennemi commun, le Fezzan va trouver sous l'autorité française l'ordre et la paix. S'il plaît à Dieu!'[70] (In the Fezzan, as everywhere else, France is and will remain the sincere and tested friend of the Muslims. Thanks to the defeat of our common enemy, the Fezzan will find order and peace under France's authority. Thanks be to God!)

BRITAIN ACCEPTS THE FREE FRENCH *FAIT ACCOMPLI*

The British military and political authorities in Tripolitania and Cairo reacted swiftly to Leclerc's conquest of the Fezzan. Brigadier Lush warned Hone on 12 January that the situation could not be allowed to drift any longer as Leclerc's force would soon come into contact with the Eighth Army (this occurred at Hon on 13 January).[71] It was necessary to frame a clear-cut administrative policy for Tripolitania and the Fezzan which would be, as far as possible, in the best interests of the Arab inhabitants. Accordingly, Hone recommended to the War Office on 14 January, with the backing of Alexander and Moyne, that both the DCPO Tripolitania and the French Military Governor in the Fezzan should come under the command of the C-in-C Middle East. It was important not to divide western Libya into two separate jurisdictions as this would cause administrative difficulties.

Hone heeded Lush's advice that the Fezzan should be regarded as an integral part of Libya. The Arab inhabitants of this barren province looked to Hon as the centre of administration and to Murzuk as the

The Free French leader, General Charles de Gaulle. By permission of The Imperial War Museum D 1966.

centre of trade (the caravan routes from the Tibesti and Ghat to Murzuk, on to Brach and Hon, and thence to Tripoli and Misurata, carried the trade of the Sahara, although this had dwindled considerably in the previous twenty years). From Hon the Arabs looked to Tripoli as the centre of government.

Consequently, Hone proposed to continue the Italian system whereby the *Territorio Militare del Sud*, with its administrative headquarters at Hon, came directly under the Governor-General in Tripoli. If the Allies followed the Italian example, they would avoid the danger of being suspected of planning the partition of western Libya and allowing the French to add the Fezzan to their Central African territories. It would also stifle Arab attempts to play the British off against the French. The British could stress the interim nature of the military administration in Libya in order to allay Arab fears of their ultimate intentions. These were the lines along which Cairo wanted the Foreign Office to reach a practical working arrangement with de Gaulle in London.[72]

The Foreign Office was convinced, however, that de Gaulle would reject the solution proposed by Cairo. As Eden explained to Sir James Grigg, the Secretary of State for War, on 22 January (the day de Gaulle arrived in Morocco to meet his political rival, General Giraud), the Free French leader 'clearly regards the Fezzan as a valuable asset which will increase his credit with General Giraud and, taking a longer view, will enhance France's bargaining power at the peace settlement. He can therefore be expected to do all in his power to retain direct control of it and to make a major issue out of any attempt to force his hand.'[73]

The Foreign Office thought it would be better if Alexander were to reach an *ad hoc* working arrangement with Leclerc over the Fezzan, excluding de Gaulle completely from these negotiations. This would allow the C-in-C Middle East to use what leverage he had over Leclerc, in particular on matters of finance, to reach a satisfactory settlement.

Moreover, Eden disputed the contention that it was administratively essential for one authority to control both Tripolitania and the Fezzan until the end of the war. He understood 'that the Fezzan is more or less isolated from Tripolitania by desert and was always administered separately by the Italians as a military area. Large sections of it were actually French until shortly before the war when Laval ceded them to Mussolini and the whole area could, I should have thought, just as well be linked for the time being with the Chad territory as with Libya proper. As regards the Arab question, my impression is that the Fezzan is mainly peopled by Tuaregs, who are quite a separate race from the Arabs and that the Arab world as a whole is little concerned with their doings. As regards the economic aspect, I should have thought that the Fezzan scarcely presented a serious problem. The few thousands of primitive Tuaregs who live there must require very little in the way of currency or imported goods and there can be virtually no trade with them.' In short, Eden's view was that the Fezzan was not of sufficient military importance to Britain, once the Axis had been driven out of Libya, to warrant 'a row with de Gaulle in order to get our own way there'.[74]

The War Office had expected this negative response from Eden. The Vice-Chief of the Imperial General Staff, General Sir Archibald Nye, explained to the C-in-C Middle East on 23 January that while the Secretary of State for War agreed with Alexander, Moyne and Hone on this question, he did not feel that he could press the Foreign Office further. Grigg hoped that Alexander could come to a satisfactory arrangement on administrative matters with Leclerc, but if he strongly disagreed with this course of action he should raise it with Churchill (who was in North Africa at this time).[75]

Alexander seems to have accepted the Foreign Office's argument, for on 29 January Hone instructed Lush to reach a working arrangement with Leclerc. But it was stressed that this should be a *modus vivendi* rather than an agreement on the general issue of whether the French would continue to administer the Fezzan. It was still believed that this could only be dealt with in London.[76]

The situation became more complex when it was learnt in Cairo that 'la colonne Leclerc' had arrived in Tripoli on 26 January (the Eighth Army had entered the city on the 23rd) and Leclerc had placed his small force under Montgomery's command for the advance into Tunisia. Leclerc had also accepted that the Italian boundary of the Fezzan military province should be the northerly limit of French administration. Yet on the same day a Free French flying column had seized Derg and Ghadames (Sinauen was captured on 29 January) and de Gaulle ordered Leclerc to take over the administration of these border oases. Previously they had been administered by the Italians as part of the Nalut province of Tripolitania. In addition, the Free French had occupied Mizda and the entire Ghibla area of 56,325 sq km, previously in the Garian province of Tripolitania.[77]

Alexander and Casey immediately protested to London that Leclerc had breached the agreement of 26 January and that the matter should be taken up with de Gaulle. It was important for operational and administrative reasons that all of Tripolitania north of the Fezzan should be under British control and it was most desirable on operational and security grounds that Hon and Zella should remain under British jurisdiction. The northern limit of French administration should be 28 Degrees Latitude and 16 Degrees Longitude, as previously agreed with Leclerc.[78]

The Foreign Office was unmoved by Cairo's protest at Leclerc's *fait accompli* on the Tunisian border. Gilbert Mackereth and R L Speaight (French Department) wanted to avoid any discussion with de Gaulle. It was feared that if pressed on this issue the Free French leader would probably make difficulties over the British retention of Kufra, Hon and Zella, which had come under the *Territorio Militare del Sud*. Moreover, Mackereth and Speaight seemed to be under the mistaken impression that Laval had ceded these 'Tunisian' oases (of Ghadames, Derg and Sinauen) to Mussolini before the war and that the French would do their utmost to reclaim them at the peace conference.[79]

The British would unite de Gaulle and Giraud against them if they insisted on the French relinquishing control of the border oases. It was doubted whether there was any strong military reason for occupying Ghadames and Derg. (Ghadames stood at the northern end of one of the great Trans-Saharan routes, via Air and Ghat, which led into Tunisia; Derg and Sinauen were transit points on the route from Ghadames to the north.) Mackereth and Speaight thought that the C-in-C Middle East and the Minister of State should accept Leclerc's occupation of Ghadames and Derg. These border oases were isolated, and a more exact definition of boundaries between the British and French zones of administration was regarded as unnecessary. While the Foreign Office tried to persuade the War Office of this, however, the issue of the administrative frontier brought the whole question to a head.[80]

Brigadier Lush and Lt. Colonel Delange had reached a *modus vivendi* on administrative matters on 10 February, thus reducing the chance of friction between their separate administrations. They could not agree, however, on the administrative frontier west of Hon. Lush wanted to follow the old Fezzan boundary (i.e. the northern boundary of the Italian *Territorio Militare del Sud*) while Delange favoured a new frontier line which, he claimed, the Italians had been considering in 1940 but had not implemented. This would include Ghadames and Derg, but not Sinauen, within the Fezzan. Delange contended that Ghadames and Derg looked towards Algeria, and that the main trade routes from the south ran from Ghat along the Algerian/Libyan frontier to Ghadames (although he admitted that Ghadames and Derg had always been supplied from Tripoli and were currently in need of food). Leclerc and Montgomery agreed that this matter should be resolved in London and that in the meantime a compromise arrangement would prevail in the three oases under dispute, whereby proclamations establishing British jurisdiction would be posted but the French political officers would remain in practical charge of the administration.[81]

Although it was aware of the weakness of the British case, the War Office on 22 February requested the Foreign Office to put pressure on de Gaulle to instruct Leclerc to withdraw his political officers from the border oases.[82] Several days later, however, the War Office decided to support the Minister of State in the Middle East's suggestion that the French political officers should be allowed to administer the three oases provided that they were attached to the staff of the DCPO Tripolitania so as to ensure overall British control. This solution had a double advantage: 'It would save French face and sidetrack discussions on basis of map which may lead to difficulties if we wish to retain Hon and Zella which we occupied and which are both definitely inside the old Italian military zone.'[83]

But the Foreign Office remained unconvinced, and by 6 March Mackereth had persuaded the Occupied Enemy Territories branch of the War Office (MO 11) that Casey's proposal would not work but would only create friction and trouble. Mackereth believed that the new Fezzan boundary was practicable and that it suited the British military administration, as the latter would retain control of Hon, Zella and Kufra. Moreover, Ghadames and Derg were Tuareg centres and therefore should be included within the Fezzan.

As Sinauen was inhabited by Arabs it could be handed over temporarily to the DCPO Tripolitania. As it belonged more naturally to Tunisia, Mackereth thought that in any readjustment of the Tunisian-Tripolitanian frontier at the peace settlement it probably could be attached to the territory of the Bey of Tunis. According to Nye, Mackereth explained to the War Office: 'Only if important operational issues were at stake (and none had ever been advanced) would it be worthwhile trying to force the French to relinquish authority where they had already established themselves. De Gaulle would violently oppose any such proposition and the raising of it would create much bad blood between him and us, with no advantage, and at a time when that is the one thing we want to avoid in view of the Anglo-American-Giraud-de Gaulle problem at the moment.'[84] This was a reference to the difficult negotiations to establish a single authority in French North Africa which would replace the French National Committee and Giraud's administration.

Although the War Office preferred Casey's solution, it found it hard to refute Mackereth's argument. As a consequence, therefore, both the C-in-C Middle East and the Minister of State were instructed on 23 March to accept the new Fezzan boundary, as defined by Lt. Colonel Delange, on condition that Leclerc's forces evacuated Sinauen and the British military administration retained Hon, Zella and Kufra.[85] The C-in-C Middle East appealed in vain, on behalf of the Minister of State in the Middle East and the Chief Political Officer, against this decision on the grounds that Ghadames and Derg were Arab, not Tuareg, centres and that the French would claim them at the peace settlement. There were fears also that smuggling would flourish across a border uncontrolled by the BMA Tripolitania.

The Foreign Office believed, and the War Office reluctantly agreed, that there were no strong operational reasons for a British occupation of Ghadames and Derg. The political disadvantages in pressing de Gaulle and Giraud to evacuate the oases, which it was thought the French would claim at the peace conference, outweighed any local administrative inconvenience suffered by the British in Tripolitania.[86] In the final analysis it did not matter, in the eyes of the Foreign Office, whether the oases were inhabited by the Tuareg or Arabs.[87]

The British military and political authorities in Cairo and Tripolitania finally agreed in mid-May 1943 to accept the new Fezzan boundary. No serious difficulties, apart from smuggling, were anticipated.[88] The Foreign Office view had prevailed. Its validity seemed to be confirmed when in Algiers on 3 June, after seven months of discussion and conflict, it was agreed to set up a French Committee of National Liberation with de Gaulle and Giraud as co-presidents.[89] No doubt the Foreign Office thought that allowing de Gaulle a free hand in the Fezzan was a small price to pay for the re-establishment of French unity, no matter how fragile that might be.

It soon became clear that the French intended to isolate the Fezzan and the oases on the Tunisian border from the rest of Libya. The French evacuated Mizda and the Ghibla but not Sinauen. There was no close liaison between the British military administration in Tripolitania and the French military government in the Fezzan, which meant that the British were largely ignorant of developments in southern Libya. There was little trade between the two territories and the French tried to restrict the movement of the border tribes across the administrative frontier. No attempt was made by the French administrators to act in concert with the British military administration in Tripolitania on currency matters or legal affairs.[90]

In mid-June 1943 it was observed that the French were disarming the Fezzanese in order to reduce their garrison. The French were reluctant to accede to the British wish to supply the French garrison in the Fezzan from Tripoli instead of Chad, which in turn had to be supplied from Brazzaville at British expense. Eventually, following the fall of Tunisia to the Allies, a compromise was reached whereby the French ran a fortnightly supply convoy from Tunis to the Fezzan. The French had gone to great lengths to avoid using the direct route from Tripoli Port via Mizda and Brach, preferring the much longer route from Tunis via Tripoli, Misurata and Hon. Similarly, the French preferred to supply Ghadames via Fort Flatters instead of Tripoli. They did not want to weaken their claims to the Fezzan and the border oases at the peace settlement.[91]

This raised another problem. If the French were to retain their hold on the Fezzan they would have to contend with Sayyid Idris's claim to the territory, whose tribes had long been connected by religion and kinship with the Cyrenaican tribes. The presence in the Fezzan of Sanusi tribes ready to agitate for inclusion in a Sanusi amirate under Sayyid Idris would embarrass both the French and British military administrations in Libya. If the French Army proceeded to suppress a Sanusi revolt in the same way they had vanquished the Sanusis in Equatorial Africa at the turn of the century, this would strain Anglo-French relations. In addition, de Gaulle's insistence for political reasons on maintaining a token garrison in Kufra, the former headquarters of the Sanusis (and the burial place of Sayyid al-Mahdi, the father of Sayyid Idris), made the Sanusis uneasy.[92]

Ironically, Hon lost its operational and strategic significance to the British at this time. It was soon discovered that the vicinity of the aerodrome was heavily mined and the facility was little used. It proved expensive and difficult to maintain a British political officer in Hon because of the poor communications from the coast. Nevertheless, it was judged to be unwise to raise the question of an alteration of the administrative frontier with the French. Instead, it was decided to maintain Hon on as economic a scale as possible. The British PO was withdrawn in May 1944 and the administration was carried out by an Arab *mudir* or *qaim maqam*. A British PO paid regular visits.[93]

De Gaulle had ensured that 'Le Fezzan doit etre la part de la France dans la bataille d'Afrique.' Well might he write in later years that 'Ainsi était enfin cueilli, à force d' audace et de méthode, ce fruit savoureux du désert.'[94]

LIBYA UNDER BRITISH AND FRENCH MILITARY ADMINISTRATION

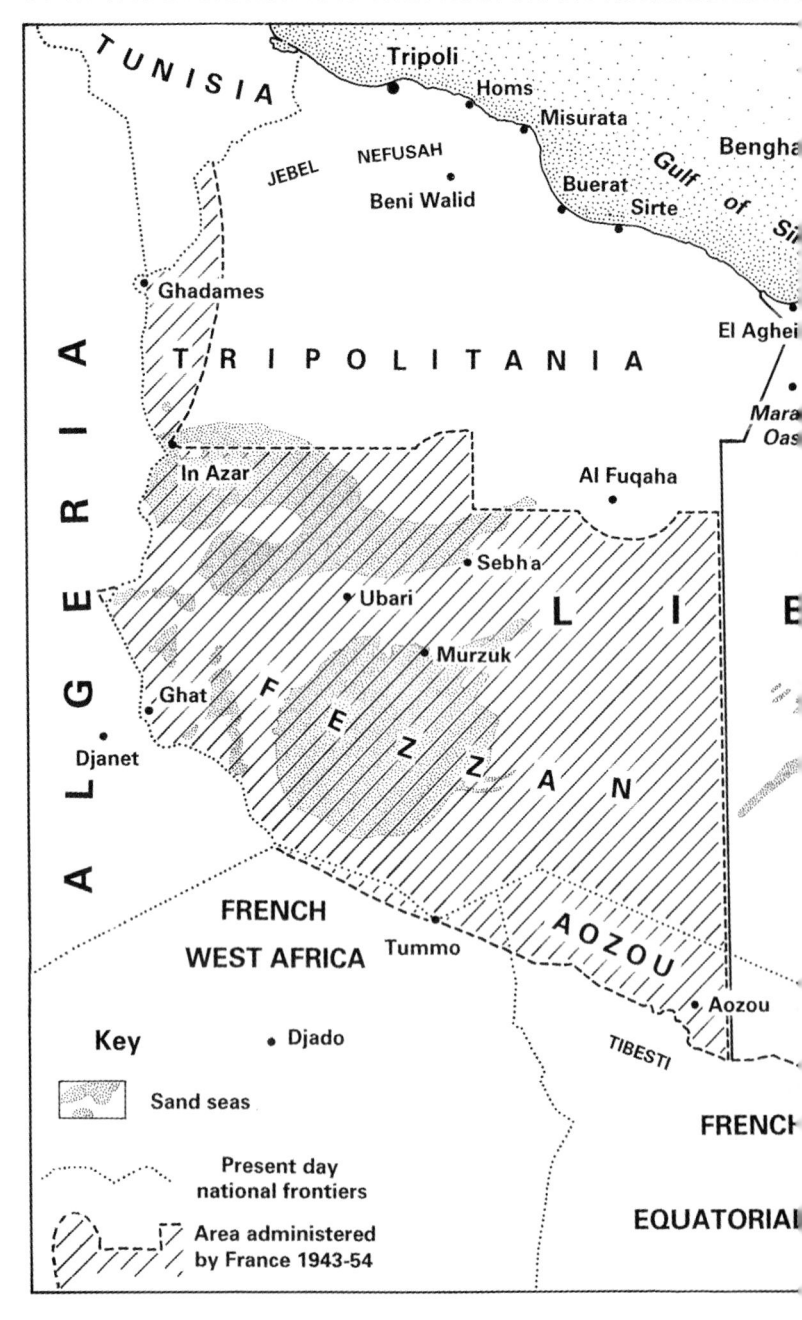

Map showing Libya with labelled locations: Tripoli, Homs, Misurata, Benghazi, Buerat, Sirte, Jebel Nefusah, Beni Walid, Ghadames, El Aghei, Mara Oas, In Azar, Al Fuqaha, Sebha, Ubari, Murzuk, Ghat, Djanet, Tummo, Djado, Aozou, Tibesti. Regions: Tunisia, Algeria, Tripolitania, Fezzan, Aozou, French West Africa, French Equatorial. Gulf of Sirte.

Key
- Sand seas
- Present day national frontiers
- Area administered by France 1943-54

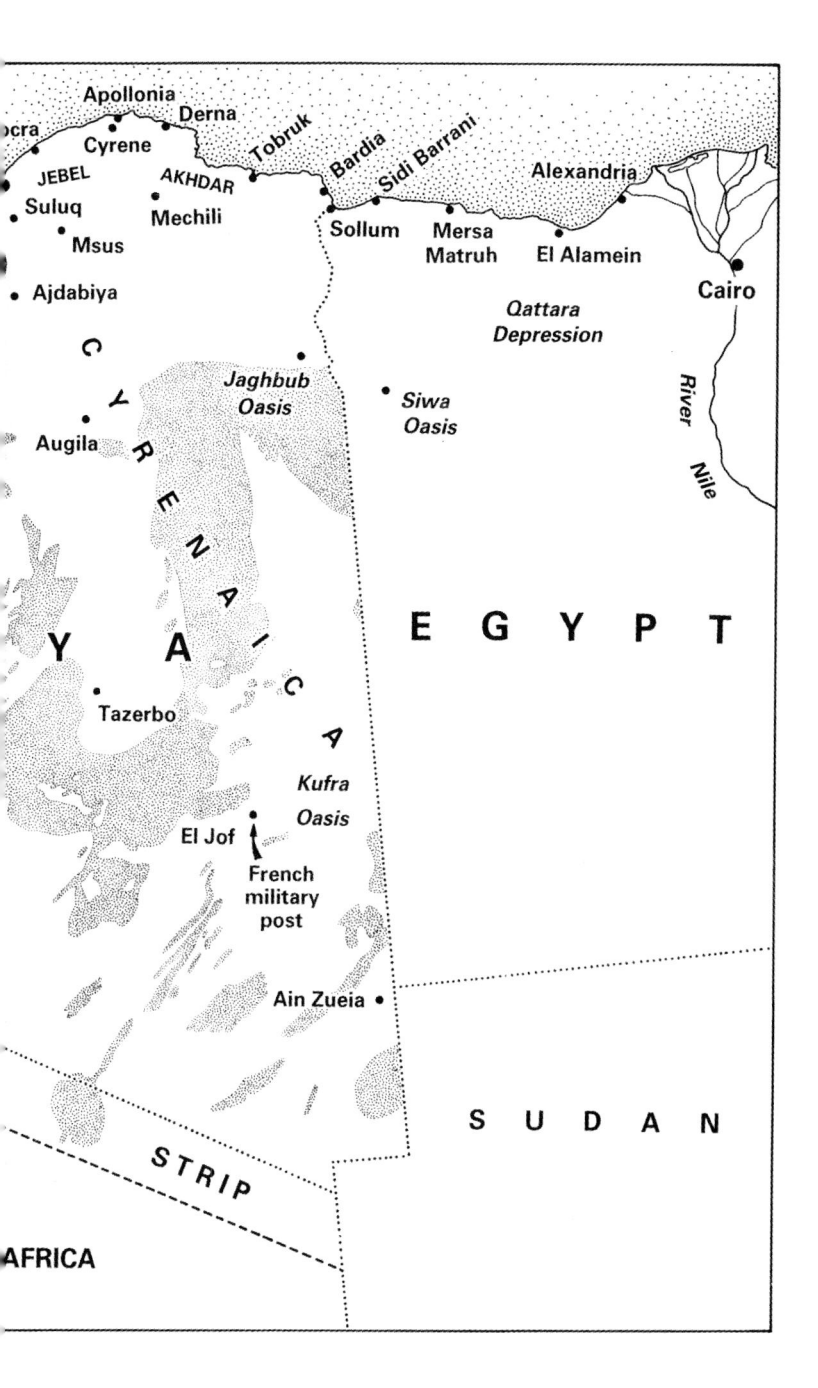

Apollonia
cra Cyrene • Derna
JEBEL   Tobruk Bardia
• Suluq AKHDAR   Sidi Barrani Alexandria
      • Mechili   Sollum Mersa
   • Msus   Matruh   El Alamein
                                              Cairo
• Ajdabiya
                              Qattara
          C   Depression
          Y
          R   • Jaghbub • Siwa
          E   Oasis   Oasis
      • Augila
          N
          A
          I   EGYPT
   Y   C
          A
       • Tazerbo

          • Kufra
            Oasis
        El Jof
          ↖ French
            military
            post

          Ain Zueia •

                         SUDAN

   ── ── STRIP
AFRICA

summary

THE WINTER of 1942–43 saw the final conquest of Libya. Following the Eighth Army's crossing of Tunisia's eastern frontier on 4 February 1943, Alexander informed Churchill, who was in Algiers, 'Sir, the orders you gave me on August 15th 1942 have been fulfilled. His Majesty's enemies together with their impedimenta have been completely eliminated from Egypt, Cyrenaica, Libya, and Tripolitania. I now await your further instructions.'[95] The Desert War was over.

The Sanusis of Cyrenaica had been liberated at last from Italian rule. Sayyid Idris continued to be unsuccessful, however, in his attempts to extract a pledge from Britain on the future independence of Cyrenaica or Libya as a whole. But now he had the added incentive of apparent Tripolitanian acquiescence in a Sanusi amirate of Libya. The Tripolitanians had again demonstrated their proclivity for seeking benefits from the Anglo-Sanusi relationship when it suited their political purposes.

The immediate task confronting the British in Libya was the setting up of military administrations in Cyrenaica and Tripolitania and they refused to engage in any public discussion of the future of these territories. It may be asked, however, whether the nature of the British military administrations prejudged the political future of Cyrenaica and Tripolitania to a certain extent. The decision to maintain Cyrenaica as a purely Arab country during the war allowed the Sanusis to re-establish their way of life without fear of Italian retribution. British administrators started to develop rural and municipal government on native lines in Cyrenaica with the co-operation of Sayyid Idris.

It was a natural progression from this policy to consider some form of British or Egyptian protection for an autonomous Sanusi amirate in Cyrenaica after the war, which would meet both the local economic and political needs of a new native state and at the same time satisfy British strategic requirements. The decision to govern Tripolitania in accordance with a rigid interpretation of international law relating to occupied enemy territories meant that the British administrators maintained a strict impartiality between the often competing interests of the native majority and the Italian minority. Tripolitanian Arab, Jew and Italian alike were represented on the advisory bodies set up to aid the British military administration. It was possible to envisage a future mixed form of government in Tripolitania, under British protection or perhaps even retaining a link with a reformed Italy.

Certainly the French seizure of the Fezzan and the establishment of a military administration along Algerian lines gave a strong indication of the likely future of that territory, as part of French Africa, if the French were allowed to realise their aims. The varying nature of the military administrations in Libya was to influence British thinking on the future of Libya. This developed rapidly following the fall of Italy's last colony in Africa and the signs of an impending collapse in Italy. Another stimulus was the growing evidence of American planning on the future of ex-enemy colonial territories.

The Foreign Office was to find it very difficult to ascertain the official American position on the future of Libya, as on other colonial questions. This was due, in part, to the divided state of opinion within the Roosevelt Administration about the future of colonial territories in general. It was the result also of the reluctance of American leaders to refer publicly to specific colonies in order to avoid any controversy which might prejudice the Allied war effort. It is not clear why Roosevelt initially opposed the setting up of a British military administration in Tripolitania. It is possible, as the Foreign Office seemed to believe, that the President thought that as both Tunisia and Tripolitania had large Italian communities they should come under the same American administration. There may, however, be another explanation.

Sumner Welles was under the impression in December 1942 that Britain had designs on French territory in Africa, in particular Bizerta and Djibouti, a belief which was also certainly prevalent among the French. It is feasible to suggest that, as a close advisor to the President on foreign affairs, Welles was behind Roosevelt's opposition to Britain's administering Tripolitania and his preference for an American administration which would effectively thwart what Welles perceived to be Britain's territorial ambitions in Tunisia. Certainly Roosevelt was receptive to such a view. As he made clear on 7 January, he did not trust the Foreign Office on French issues.[96]

It took the combined weight of Hull and the Joint Chiefs of Staff to convince Roosevelt that Tripolitania fell more naturally under the jurisdiction of British Middle East Command. After all, the French position in Tunisia could be adequately safeguarded by a temporary American civil administration. Roosevelt and Hull were to prove more flexible than Welles in their thinking on the future of strategically important colonies. But Welles was to have a marked influence on the evolution of official policy on the future of Libya, and he continued to demonstrate his suspicion of British motives in North Africa.

Welles would have done better to have concentrated his attention on Free French ambitions in the Fezzan and the British reaction to them. De Gaulle managed to accomplish his aim of controlling the Fezzan because of the success of Leclerc's exploits and the refusal of the Foreign Office to force de Gaulle to agree to the French military administration in the Fezzan coming under the overall command of the C-in-C Middle East. De Gaulle turned the situation in North Africa in the winter of 1942–43, which initially seemed so unfavourable to the Free French, to his advantage.

The Free French had not been allowed to participate in the Allied invasion of North Africa so as to avoid provoking the Vichy authorities and encouraging them to resist the Allies, as had happened at Dakar in 1940 and in Syria in 1941. For reasons of security, it was decided that de Gaulle should not even be informed of the landings in Morocco and Algeria until after they had taken place. In order to defuse the expected crisis with De Gaulle, Churchill and Eden decided to 'sweeten the pill' by handing over the administration of Madagascar, which had been taken by the British in August 1942, to the Free French as a 'consolation prize'.[97]

It is probable also that, by way of compensation for their exclusion from Operation 'Torch', the Free French were allowed to take part in the conquest of Libya. A small Free French force was to conduct operations against the Italians in the Fezzan and then link up with the Eighth Army. However, Leclerc's epic 2,250-km trek from Chad to Tripoli was unnecessary from a military point of view. The Eighth Army's advance along the Libyan coast meant that the Italian garrisons in the Fezzan would inevitably have fled north to escape into Tunisia or they would have surrendered. If they had tried to defend the Fezzan then the Long Range Desert Group or the Sudan Defence Force would have had little trouble in mopping-up any resistance. The importance of Leclerc's operation lies in the propaganda and political spheres. 'La colonne Leclerc' caught the imagination of the French public and helped to inspire the growing resistance to the German occupation regime in France. In addition, it ensured that France would have a say in determining the future of Libya.[98]

De Gaulle had strengthened his political position by remaining aloof from the events in Algiers in late 1942. Following the Darlan episode, both the British and American governments became aware of the need to reconcile Giraud and de Gaulle in order to form a single authority in French North Africa. The Foreign Office was unlikely to have pressed de Gaulle to accept local British administrative requirements in the Fezzan at a time when the British government was trying to persuade him to reach an agreement with Giraud. De Gaulle had acquired Madagascar, Djibouti and the Fezzan with British assistance during the winter of 1942–43.

It is not surprising, therefore, that the Foreign Office should brush aside the considered objections of the C-in-C Middle East and the Minister of State in the Middle East to a French military administration in the Fezzan. In order to justify this attitude, the Foreign Secretary, on the advice of the Egyptian Department, even went so far as to make dubious assertions about the tribal and economic situation in the Fezzan, designed to show that it belonged more naturally to French rather than Italian North Africa. Although Grigg and the War Office were prepared initially to contradict this argument, in the end they deferred to the political judgement of Eden and the Foreign Office. In the short term, Foreign Office policy may be said to have been a success, in that a single authority representing liberated France was established in French North Africa. In the long term, however, the French retention of the Fezzan served only to complicate the process of finding a solution to the problem of Libya's future.

NOTES

1 Martin Gilbert, *Road to Victory. Winston S. Churchill. 1941–45,* London 1986, p. 170.
2 *ibid.*, p. 330.
3 Hone to Director of Military Operations (M.0.11) War Office, 27 December 1942, enclosing Cumming, 'Summary of Factors Relating to the Administration of Cyrenaica', 10 December 1942, FO 1015/71.
4 Hirszowicz, *op. cit.*, pp. 239–43.
5 Barnett, *op. cit.*, p. 251.
6 Lampson to FO, tel. 1543, 11 June 1942, FO to Lampson, tel. 1628, 17 June 1942, J 2141/38/161 FO 371/31573.
7 Eran Lerman, 'The Egyptian Question, 1942–47. The Deterioration of Britain's position in Egypt, Al-Alamain to the UN Debate of 1947,' PhD. Thesis, University of London 1982, pp. 155–7.
8 Scrivener, 'The Sudan', 1 September 1942, J 3736/1528/16, FO 371/31587.
9 Coulson minute, 3 September 1942, J 3736/1528/16, FO 371/31587.
10 Peterson minute, 7 September 1942, Scrivener to Shone, 10 September 1942, J 3736/1528/16, FO 371/31587.
11 Lampson to Cadogan, 1 December 1942, enclosing Huddleston to Lampson, no. 73, 18 November 1942, J 5145/1528/16, FO 371/31587.
12 *ibid.*
13 Minutes by Chapman-Andrews, 17 December, Scrivener, 18 December, Peterson, 23 December 1942, J 5145/1528/16, FO 371/31587.
14 Rennell, *op. cit.*, pp. 250–1.
15 *ibid.*, pp. 248–9.
16 The majority of the Italian agricultural colonists from the Jabal Akhdar were resettled in Tripolitania, finding work in the cities or on the farms of the two colonisation companies. Approximately one hundred families returned to Italy. As a result of the war the Italian population of Cyrenaica had declined from 30,000 to 100 by early 1943. The latter were mostly nuns and priests who remained behind to tend the sick. Segre, *op. cit.*, pp. 167–8.
17 Rennell, *op. cit.*, p. 249.
18 C-in-C Middle East to WO. For M 0 11 from Chief Pol., tel. OET/83679 13 December 1942, FO 1015/71.
19 During the winter of 1942–43 it was decided to adopt a uniform nomenclature for the military government of occupied territories which could be used by both the British Eighth Army and General Eisenhower's armies in French North Africa. The term 'Civil Affairs' was adopted and as a result the 'Political Branches' (e.g. in Cairo) became 'Civil Affairs Branches', the 'Chief Political Officer' became 'Chief Civil Affairs Officer', etc. The old terms continued to be used, however, until the spring of 1943, in correspondence between Cairo and London, and will be used in this chapter. Rennell, *op. cit.*, pp. 250–1, 317–8.
20 Rennell (*op. cit.*, p. 258) does not give any statistical information on the population of Cyrenaica in 1943. The anthropologist Evans-Pritchard estimated that the beduin of Cyrenaica, who constituted the overwhelming majority of the population, were reduced probably by about a half or two-thirds by death and emigration between 1911 and 1932. Losses of livestock were enormous (*The Sanusis of Cyrenaica,* Oxford 1949, p. 171). The BMA Cyrenaica estimated

that the population of Cyrenaica was about 250,000 in 1945 (Pitt to Ronald, 19 June 1945, enclosing draft 'Appendix I – Cyrenaica' by CCAO, Middle East, U 4860/51/70, FO 371/50790).
21 Rennell, *op. cit.*, pp. 263–4.
22 Hone to DMO (M.0.11) WO, 27 December 1942, enclosing Cumming, 'Summary of Factors Relating to the Administration of Cyrenaica', 10 December 1942, FO 1015/71.
23 *ibid.*
24 *ibid.*
25 *ibid.* The Sudan and Palestine governments refused to release suitably qualified political officers to serve in Cyrenaica. Hone managed, however, to obtain the Assistant Resident in Transjordan, Hugh Foot, for six months on secondment from the end of 1942. This would seem to indicate that Hone had in mind the British experience in Transjordan when it came to setting up the Military Government in Cyrenaica (C-in-C Middle East to WO, tel. OET/83679, 13 December 1942, FO 1015/71; Sir Hugh Foot, *A Start in Freedom,* London 1964, p. 78). Hone had also sent W B Tripe (seconded from the Tanganyika government) to Transjordan in the first half of 1942 to investigate and report on the working of the desert administration in that territory. Tripe's Transjordan Report is undated but it was probably drawn up by the summer of 1942. He returned to Tanganyika before Second Alamein. Tripe became Secretary for Arab Affairs in Tripolitania in 1944 and organised the administration of the desert areas in Tripolitania. His memory may be at fault in the covering note to his report, written in 1982, in which he says that the latter was intended as a guide to the administration of Tripolitania. The report itself discusses the applicability of the Transjordan administration as a model for Cyrenaica (Tripe's Transjordan Report, with covering note, St Antony's College, Oxford, MEC Archives).
26 WO to C-in-C Middle East. For Political, tel. (M.0.11) 92861, 9 January 1943, FO 1015/71.
27 C-in-C Middle East to WO. For M.0.11 from CPO, tel. OET/96240, 13 January 1943; WO to C-in-C Middle East. For Political, tel. 50418, 13 January 1943. C-in-C Middle East to WO, For M.0.11 from Civaffairs, tel. OET/22145, 15 March 1943, C-in-C Middle East to WO. For M.0.11 from Chief, Civaffairs, tel; OET/33895, 11 April 1943, FO 1015/71; French to Mackereth, 17 January 1943, with enclosure; Mackereth minute of 20 January, Mackereth to French, 25 January 1943, J 343/73/66, FO 371/35660.
28 Rennell, *op. cit.*, pp. 254–6.
29 It is interesting to note that Lord Rennell felt it necessary to omit all reference to Eden's instruction to Casey of 25 June 1942 on the administrative policy to be followed in Cyrenaica during the third British occupation. Rennell was anxious to convey the impression that Britain was strictly adhering to international law on the administration of occupied enemy territories, even to the rather absurd extent of maintaining the Italian legal system in Cyrenaica. This was intended, no doubt, to impress international opinion at the time he wrote his official history (1948) when the question of the future of the Italian colonies was under active consideration by the Great Powers. Rennell, *op. cit.*, pp. 251–3.
30 *ibid.*, pp. 253, 256–7, 260–3; Khadduri, *op. cit.*, p. 45; Hone to DCPO Cyrenaica, 1 December 1942, Cumming to CPO, 10 December 1942, WO
31 Segre, *op. cit.*, p. 168; Foot, *op. cit.*, p. 83–4; Rennel1, *op. cit.*, pp. 258–60.

32 WP (43)84, 'British Military Administration of Occupied Territories', memorandum by the Secretary of State for War, 24 February 1943, CAB 66/34; WM (43)36, 1 March 1943, CAB 65/33.
33 Minute for VCIGS, 28 November 1942, FO 1015/74; J S M Washington to WCO London, tel. 549, 10 December 1942 enclosing Freedom Algiers (Eisenhower) to AGWAR (CCS Washington) undated tel. 1526, AGWAR to US FOR London, For Eisenhower from US COS Z 10201/8325/17, FO 371/32146; Leahy (for JCS) to Hu11, 10 December 1942, enclosing paraphrase of Eisenhower tel. to CCS 865C.01/13 Hull Memorandum of Conversation with Halifax on North African situation, 15 December 1942, 865C.01/16, RG 59/Box 5059.
34 Churchill minute, 12 December 1942, Strang to Hollis, 16 December 194 1942, Z 10201/8325/17, Halifax to FO, tel. 6095, 15 December 1942, FO to Halifax, tel. 8079, 20 December 1942, Z 10217/8325/17, FO 371/32146.
35 Hollis to Strang, 16 December 1942, enclosing JP(42)1009, 'Civil Administration in North Africa', 13 December 1942, Z 10285/8325/17, FO 371/32147.
36 Halifax to Hull, 21 December 1942, 865C.01/14, Hull to Leahy, 23 December 1942, 865C.01/B, Leahy to Hull, 8 January 1943, 865C.01/15, Hull to Halifax, 23 January 1943, 865C.01/15, RG 59/Box 5059.
37 Alexander to Grigg, 8 January 1943, enclosing 'Memorandum by the Chief Political Officer, Middle East, on Administrative Policy in Tripolitania', 4 December 1942, WO 258/34.
38 Hone to Kennedy, 9 January 1943, WO 258/34.
39 Alexander to Grigg, 8 January 1943, *op. cit.*
40 WO to C-in-C Middle East. For Political, tel. (M.0.11) 92861, 9 January 1943, FO 1015/71.
41 WP (43)84, 'British Military Administration of Occupied Territories', *op. cit.*
42 Lampson to Eden, despatch 34, 11 January 1943 enclosing Anderson to CPO, 2 January 1943, FO 371/35666; Harris to FO, 23 August 1945 enclosing undated Civil Affairs Branch, Middle East memorandum 'The Senussi and Tripolitania', U 6517/51/70, FO 371/50792.
43 Minutes by Mackereth, 28 January, Scrivener and Peterson, 29 January 1943, J 440/440/66, FO 371/35666.
44 Bovenschen to Cadogan, 10 March 1943 enclosing Rucker to Under Secretary of State, War Office, 10 February 1943, which enclosed translations of 'Mohamed Idris el Mahdi el Senussi to HE The Representative of the British War Cabinet in Egypt, Mr Casey', 25 January 1943, and 'Mohamed Idris el Mahdi el-Senussi to the British Prime Minister, Mr Winston Churchill', 25 January 1943, and 'R G Casey to Mohamed Idris Mahdi el Senussi', J 1169/73/66, FO 371/35660.
45 *ibid.*
46 Minutes by Mackereth, 16 March 1943, Cadogan for PM 'Senussi leader's claim to sovereignty over Libya', 22 March 1943, Churchill, 23 March 1943, Scrivener to Rucker, Office of Minister of State, Cairo, J 1169/73/66, FO 371/35660. The American Minister to Egypt, Alexander Kirk, kept a close watch on the British occupation of Libya and British policy towards Sayyid Idris. Kirk also took note of Egyptian reaction to Britain's activities in Libya. A prominent Egyptian, Fuad Abaza, who had visited Algeria, Tunisia and Libya in 1939, had called for closer ties between Egypt and the peoples of North Africa. State Department to American Legation, Cairo, tel. 200, 4 February 1943, 8650.00/102, Minister, Egypt to S of S, despatch 839, 10 February 1943, enclosing Kirk to Sayyid Idris, 6 February

1943, 8650.00/104, Minister, Egypt to S of S, despatch 850, 10 February 1943, with enclosures 8650.00/105, Minister, Egypt to S of S, despatch 1013, 30 April 1943, enclosing Casey to Idris, 19 April 1943, 8650.00/107, RG 59/Box 5059.

47 Following the second British occupation of Cyrenaica in the winter of 1941–42, Mussolini had ordered the 'clearing out' of the Jews of Cyrenaica in retaliation for their collaboration with the Eighth Army. The foreign Jews were deported to Italy and Tunisia, while the Libyan and Italian Jews were interned in camps, first at Giado and then at Garian in Tripolitania. Living conditions at Giado were difficult but not terrible and in December 1942 the local Italian commander, General Ettore Bastico, fearing the outbreak of a typhus epidemic in the camp, freed many of the internees. However, the bulk of Cyrenaican Jewry, numbering over two thousand, had been interned at Garian (Renzo de Felice, *Jews in an Arab Land. Libya. 1835–1970*. Austin 1985, pp. 179–180). They had been abandoned to their fate by the retreating Axis forces. They were discovered by the Eighth Army in early 1943. They were in a 'state of despair and bewilderment and utter destitution'. The British troops 'had given them what they could spare from their rations, but the Jews had no news of the war and no hope of ever getting home again'. On Hugh Foot's initiative they were repatriated to Cyrenaica. As the 'extraordinary convoy' approached Benghazi, the local Arab leaders 'came out several miles along the road to welcome them home again' (Foot, *op. cit.*, pp. 81–2). The Jews of Tripolitania did not suffer such a tortuous experience, although their position was made difficult by the economic effects of war, the forcible conscription of Jewish labour and Fascist racial legislation (de Felice, *op. cit.*, pp. 180–3). In 1987 the Mayor of Jerusalem, Mr Teddy Kollek, informed the Mayor of Stuttgart, Herr Manfred Rommel (the son of Field Marshal Rommel) that a group of Israeli Jews, who were originally from North Africa, 'had told him that they believed they escaped death because of Rommel's opposition to the Nazi extermination programme' (*The Times*, 15.6.87). As has been indicated above, the Italian authorities rather than Rommel were responsible for the treatment of the Jews in Libya. Moreover, it is extremely doubtful whether during the retreat of the Panzerarmee Afrika into Tunisia Rommel would have been concerned with the fate of Libyan Jews.

It should be noted that just before they left Tripoli German soldiers sacked the Jewish shops in Suq al-Turq (Renzo de Felice, *op. cit.*, p. 184). The Mayor of Stuttgart was made an 'Honorary Guardian of Jerusalem' in honour of his city's financial contributions to social welfare programmes in Jerusalem. It is a pity that during this celebration of Germano-Israeli amity, a thought was not spared for the men of the Eighth Army who liberated Libya and its inhabitants from the Axis and for the British military administrators, like Foot, who ensured that the Jews of Benghazi, Derna and Barce did not die of starvation and disease in Garian camp.

48 Gilbert, *Road to Victory, op. cit.*, p. 332; Rennell, *op. cit.*, pp. 270–84; Segre, *op. cit.*, p. 168–9.

49 In the past, Italian rule in Libya had afforded protection for the Jewish community *vis-à-vis* the Arabs. It seems that the Jews of Tripoli recalled this when 'once the fear was over and they had to deal with the realities of occupation, the women of the *hara*, whenever some group of drunken British soldiers tried to break into their houses, would shout "Long Live Italy", as they fled to the roof tops' (de Felice, *op. cit.*, p. 184).

50 Rennell, *op. cit.*, pp. 284–9.
51 WP (43) 84, 'British Military Administration of Occupied Territories', *op. cit.*
52 Charles de Gaulle, *Mémoires de Guerre. L'Unité, 1942–44,* Paris 1956, p. 63.
53 De Gaulle recognised that Britain had a better claim to Kufra, as it had come within the British sphere of influence under the Anglo-French Agreement of 21 March 1899. But, as he made clear to General Larminat (the Free French High Commissioner in Brazzaville) on 10 March 1941, 'je persiste à croire qu'il n'est pas opportun de prendre dès maintenant des engagements au sujet de Koufra alors que, par exemple, nous ignorons quelle sera l'attitude britannique si nous avions un jour à poser la question du Fezzan' (Charles de Gaulle, *Mémoires de Guerre, L'Appel, 1940–42,* Paris 1954, p. 359). (I still think now is not the right moment to make commitments about Kufra when we don't know how the British will react if we later have to raise the question of the Fezzan.) The Free French were unable, however, to maintain a full garrison at Kufra. The LRDG used Kufra from April 1941 as an advanced base for operations in Libya (Kennedy-Shaw, *passim*). Consequently it was agreed on 26 June 1941 that the British would administer Kufra but that the French would maintain a nominal presence there of one platoon and an officer who would act as deputy to the British Political Officer. The permanent British garrison consisted of one company of the Sudan Defence Force and other small detachments including the Libyan Arab Force Gendarmerie. Following the end of the Desert War the C-in-C Middle East wanted to withdraw the British garrison from Kufra on grounds of cost, but was prevented from doing so by the insistence of the French on maintaining their political presence in Kufra. The British for their part felt obliged to keep a small garrison in Kufra, in case the Sanusis tried to eject the French observer post from the oasis of al-Taj, which contained the shrine of Sayyid al-Mahdi al-Sanusi (information on FO 1015/71 and FO 371/36039). De Gaulle rather unconvincingly denied that French behaviour was dictated by political considerations. Mackereth thought that 'It looks like an attempt to re-assert the French claim to Kufra based on a previous occupation – a third Fashoda (?)!' (minute of 17 December 1943, Z 12406/95/17, FO 371/36039). As will be seen, it did not occur to Mackereth that the obstinacy displayed by the French over Kufra and the Fezzan were related.
54 De Gaulle, *L'Appel, op. cit.*, pp. 119–120, 134–5, 249–51; Chef de Bataillon Jean-Noel Vincent, *Les Forces-Françaises Libre en Afrique. 1940–43. Les Forces Françaises Dans La Lutte Contre l'Axe en Afrique,* Ministre de la Defense Etat Major de l'Armée de Terre Service Historique, Chateau de Vincennes, Chapters XII and XIII, *passim.*
55 De Gaulle, *L'Unité, op. cit.*, pp. 29–30; Charles de Gaulle, *Lettres, Notes et Carnets. Juillet 1941–Mai 1943,* Paris 1982, pp. 401, 403.
56 De Gaulle, *L'Appel, op. cit.*, pp. 249–51.
57 Thuker to Strang, 6 February 1943, enclosing McGreery to Rucker, 31 January 1943, Z 2102/95/17, FO 371/36039.
58 Hone to Director of Military Operations, GHQMEF, 25 November 1942, C-in-C Middle East to Fanion (no. 20 Mission, Brazzaville) For General Leclerc, tel. 0/77183, 27 November 1942, rpt'd. to WO, Alexander to Leclerc, 29 November 1942, Fanion, Brazzaville to C-in-C Middle East, tel. G/3815, 29 November 1942, rpt'd. to WO, Lush to Acland, 29 November 1942, FO 1015/72.
59 C-in-C Middle East to WO, For M.0.11, tel. OET/78164, 30 November 1942; Minister of State, Cairo to FO, tel. 2059, 30 November 1942, FO 1015/72.

60 Minutes by Nye and Bovenschen, 1 December 1942; 'Record of Conversation with General de Gaulle at 16:30 Hours on 2 December 1942', Peake to de Gaulle, 1 December 1942, FO 1015/74; minutes by Stirling, Peake and Strang, 2 December 1942, Z 10932/221/17, FO 371/31987.
61 De Gaulle, *L'Unité, op. cit.*, p. 423.
62 Minutes by Nye, 4 December, and Bovenschen, 5 December 1942, Minister of State, Cairo to FO, Personal and Most Secret for Foreign Secretary from Minister of State, tel. 2091, 4 December 1942; Rooker to Stirling, 5 December 1942, FO 1015/74. Minutes by Stirling, 5 December, Strang, 7 December, Cadogan, 8 December 1942, FO to Minister of State, Cairo, tel. 3026, 5 December 1942, Z 10934/221/17, FO 371/31987; Francois Kersaudy, *Churchill and de Gaulle,* London 1981, pp. 223–30.
63 Chari, Ft. Lamy to C-in-C Middle East. For Political from Acland, tel. M194, 7 December 1942; C-in-C Middle East to Chari, Ft. Lamy, tel. 0/81181, 7 December 1942, Alexander to Leclerc, 7 December 1942, FO 1015/72.
64 Hone to Deputy Minister of State, Cairo, 13 December 1942, Minister of State, Cairo to FO. For Minister of State from Deputy (Moyne) tel. 2162, 12 December 1942; C-in-C Middle East to WO. For M.0.11 from Political, tel. OET/85206, 17 December 1942, Hone to McGreery, 17 December 1942, FO 1015/72.
65 Minutes by Stirling, 15 December, Strang, 18 December, Eden, 19 December, Armstrong to Strang, 19 December, Strang to Armstrong, 24 December 1942, Z 10170/221/17, FO 371/31987.
66 As Casey did not return to Cairo until the latter half of January 1943 it was not until 26 January that Moyne and Hone learnt of the negative response of the Foreign Office to the Deputy Minister of State's proposal. In the meantime the situation had changed drastically. When the Foreign Office (FO) was informed by Sir Arthur Rucker (Secretary to the Minister of State) on 30 December about the origins of Leclerc's operation, the FO's French Department thought that de Gaulle's 'narrow-minded and unco-operative behaviour' was consistent with his general policy of doing everything possible to strengthen the position of France at the peace conference. It was likely that he suspected the British of trying to rob him of valuable territory. Eden commented on 6 January 1943 that 'The French are tenacious, even grasping as ever.' Armstrong to Strang, 30 December 1942, enclosing 'Note on French Operations in the Fezzan by GHQ Middle East', Z 95/95/17, FO 371/36039; Note by WO on 'Defence C'tte (DC(42)84) Para 50 Operations in the Fezzan'. Issued on 21 December 1942 by Army Council Secretariat; Most Secret 0143/41380 'Visit of Minister of State to United Kingdom, December 1942. Middle East Command.' WO 32/10151.
67 Hone to DMO (M.0.11) WO, 30 December 1942, enclosing undated memorandum on 'The Southern Frontiers of Italian Libya', FO 1015/72.
68 *Les Forces Françaises, op. cit.*, Chapter XIV *passim;* Jacques Massu, *7 Ans Avec Leclerc,* Paris 1974, pp. 72–6; Bernard Lanne, *Tchad-Libye. La Querelle des Frontières,* Paris 1982, p. 179.
69 Charles de Gaulle, *Discours et Messages Pendant La Guerre. Juin 1940–Janvier 1946,* Paris 1970, pp. 256–7.
70 De Gaulle, *Lettres, Notes et Carnets, op. cit.*, pp. 499–500.
71 On 13 January 1943 Leclerc's men had entered Hon in the Giofra, which was not part of the Fezzan proper but acted as the administrative capital of the Italian *Territorio del Sud,* which included the Fezzan. They discovered that a LRDG

patrol, with a British political officer, had arrived the night before after having advanced from Kufra via Zella and Waddan. It is ironic to note, however, that it was the LRDG which both forestalled a French occupation of Hon and guided 'la colonne Leclerc' on its epic march. A Rhodesian half-patrol, S2, under the command of Lt. Henry, navigated through the southern Fezzan from Zouar to Sebha. Then a half-patrol of the Indian Long-Range Squadron under Lt. Canthoy took Leclerc's force across the waterless desert north of Murzuk towards Tripoli. *Les Forces Françaises. op cit.*, p. 295; Henry Maule, *Out of the Sand. The Epic Story of General Leclerc and the Fighting Free French*, London 1966, pp. 134–141.

72 Lush to Chief Political Officer, Cairo, 12 January 1943, C-in-C Middle East to WO. For M.0.11 from Chief Pol., tel. OET/96800, 14 January 1943, FO 1015/72; Minister of State's Office, Cairo to FO. For Foreign Secretary and Secretary of State for War from Deputy Minister of State, tel. 94, 14 January 1943, Z 1313/95/17, FO 371/36039.

73 Minutes by Speaight and Mackereth, 18 January 1943, Grigg to Eden, 20 January 1943; Eden to Grigg, 22 January 1943, Z 1313/95/17, FO 371/36039.

74 Eden revealed a less than perfect knowledge of the Fezzan in justifying its retention by the Free French. He seems to have relied on Gilbert Mackereth for information (minute by Mackereth, 18 January 1943, Z 1313/95/17, FO 371/36039). Both Eden and Mackereth were apparently under the mistaken impression that the Laval-Mussolini Agreement of 7 January 1935 covered the western as well as the southern frontier of Libya (explanatory note by Miss Carlyle for D Scott-Fox, 14 February 1948, J 1052/277/68, FO 371/69406). In fact this agreement referred only to the alignment of the Libya-Chad frontier which was to be moved southward at the expense of France. However, this agreement did not come into force as the instruments of ratification were never exchanged. It was nullified on 17 December 1938 (Ian Brownlie, *African Boundaries. A Legal and Diplomatic Encyclopedia*, London 1979, pp. 21–123. Lanne, *op. cit.*, Chapters 8–10, *passim.*) Later, the French claimed that their territory extended up to the pre-1935 frontier. The British government recognised the French right to this desert strip on 2 December 1946. The western frontier of Libya had been agreed just after the First World War. Under the Franco-Italian Exchange of Notes of 12 September 1919, approved by the French Parliament in 1923, the three salients of Italian territory which terminated in the oases of Ghadames, Ghat and Tummo were straightened out by removing the two salients of French territory interposed between them. The frontier followed the crest of the mountains between Ghat and Tummo, but no provision was made for the allocation of Tummo, with the result that both the Italians and the French continued to claim it. By virtue of this agreement the chain of wells between Ghadames, Ghat and Tummo, and consequently this section of the caravan route between Lake Chad and the Mediterranean, fell under Italian control (FORD memorandum, 'The Western and Southern Frontiers of Libya', 12 January 1948, J 1053/277/66, FO 371/69406). Eden laboured under the further illusion that the Fezzan was predominantly Tuareg. Mackereth thought this might be a good argument for uniting the territory with the Tuareg areas of Algeria and Tunisia, thus including the Tuareg capitals of Ghadames and Murzuk. This would form 'a long Tuareg country running from Fezzan to Southern Morocco and fairly pure ethnographically and socially'. Mackereth concluded, therefore, that the separation of the Fezzan from Tripolitania might be 'the right policy' (minute by Mackereth, 18 January 1943, *op. cit.*).

But the Tuareg, belonging to the extensive Ajjera confederation of Berber race and language, and superficially islamicised, were not numerous (about 2,000). The Fezzanese, the settled population of mixed race with the black Hamitic strain predominating, constituted the majority of the population – approximately 30,000 (United Nations General Assembly. General A/1387, 22 September 1950. 5th Session, Former Italian Colonies. Reports of the Powers Administering Libya. Letter dated 13 September 1950, from Minister of Foreign Affairs of the French Republic to the Secretary-General, transmitting the annual report of the French Government concerning the administration of the Fezzan, pp. 9–16.) Moreover, any attempt to link up the Fezzan with French Equatorial Africa, Southern Algeria or Tunisia was economically and geographically unsound. The Fezzan was, with the exception of the Sebha-Ghat corridor, cut off from the east, south and west by great sand seas. The Fezzan had been an integral part of Tripolitania for centuries. Reid to FO, 11 September 1945, enclosing CCAO, Cairo to DCA, War Office, 15 June 1945, which included undated memorandum by CCAO on 'The Fezzan', U 7102/51/70, FO 371/50792.
75 WO to C-in-C Middle East. From VCIGS to Alexander. Personal. tel. 96432, 23 January 1943, FO 1015/72; WO to C-in-C Middle East. From VCIGS to Alexander. Personal, tel. 200, 23 January 1943, and minutes on FO 1015/74.
76 Hone to DCPO Tripolitania, 29 January 1943, FO 1015/72.
77 C-in-C Middle East to DCPO Tripolitania. For Political, tel. OET/03328, 30 January 1943, DCPO Tripolitania to C-in-C Middle East. For Political, tel. OET/T/16, 31 January 1943, FO 1015/72; *Les Forces Françaises, op. cit.*, p. 301–3. De Gaulle, *Lettres, Notes et Carnets. op. cit.*, p. 510.
78 C-in C Middle East to WO. For M.0.11 from: Political. tel. OET/03185, 30 January 1943, Z 1460/95/17, Minister of State, Cairo to FO. For Secretary of State for Foreign Affairs and Secretary of State for War, tel. 214, 1 February 1943, and minutes on Z 1516/95/17, FO 371/36039.
79 Ghadames, Derg and Sinauen were part of the same oasis group which had strong racial and tribal ties with southern Tunisia. However, these oases had never belonged to France. The Turks had been in occupation of these oases since about 1840. Under the Franco-Turkish Convention of 19 May 1910 delimiting the frontier between the French protectorate of Tunisia and the Turkish vilayet of Tripoli, Ghadames, Derg and Sinauen were included in Turkish territory. The frontier was demarcated in 1910–11. Italy recognised the frontier alignment during her period of sovereignty in Libya although she made some general territorial demands on Tunisia in 1938. Brownlie, *op. cit.*, pp. 141–6.
80 Minutes by Speaight, 2 and 3 February 1943, Z 1516/95/17, FO 371/36039.
81 Minister of State, Cairo to FO. From DCPO Tripolitania, tel. 321, 13 February 1943, Z 2094/95/17; C-in-C Middle East to WO. For M.0.11 from Political. tel. OET/12555, 21 February 1943, French to Mackereth, 17 March 1943, enclosing Hone to DMO (M.0.11) WO, with enclosure, Lush memorandum, 11 February, Z 2622/95/17, FO 371/36039.
82 Minutes by Kennedy, 16 February, Bovenschen, 17 February, Nye, 19 February 1943, FO 1015/74; Grigg to Eden, 22 February 1943, Z 2623/95/17, FO 371/36039. The VCIGS, Nye, had earlier suggested that the British government should refuse to allow Larminat's Free French division, which was re-forming in Cyrenaica, to fight in Tunisia unless de Gaulle agreed to unequivocal British control of Tripolitania. Minutes by VCIGS, 4 and 5 February 1943, FO 1015/74.

83 C-in-C Middle East to WO. From Minister of State, tel. 13350, 24 February 1943, Copy to FO. Z 2682/95/17, FO 371/36039.
84 Minutes by Rumbold, 2 March, Mackereth, 3 and 6 March 1943, Z 2682/95/17, FO 371/36039; minutes by Nye, 7 March, Bovenschen, 19 March 1943, FO 1015/74.
85 Bovenschen to Sargent, 16 March 1943, Sargent to Bovenschen, 22 March 1943, WO to C-in-C Middle East, M.0.11 for Minister of State, tel. 63176, 23 March 1943, Z 3462/95/17, FO 371/36039.
86 C-in-C Middle East to WO. For Political from M.0.11, tel. OET/24519, 21 March 1943, minutes by Mackereth and Rumbold, 25 March 1943, Z 3782/95/17, FO 371/36039; French to Hone, 28 March, FO 1015/74; C-in-C Middle East to WO, tel. OET/30621, 4 April 1943, and minutes on Z 4380/95/17, FO 371/36039.
87 For the record, whilst Ghadames (pop. approx 2,000) was all Berber, Derg (pop. approx. 1,000) and Sinauen (pop. approx. 900) were Arabic-speaking but of Berber stock. These oases were linked with the Ifoghas and Imanghassaten Tuareg, who owed allegiance to the French, and were tied to certain tribes in southern Tunisia. Undated note, 'Adjustment to the Frontier between Libya and the adjacent territories coming under French administration.' JT 10317/8, FO 371/97285.
88 Minute by Nye, 11 April 1943; WO to C-in-C Middle East, tel. 73972, 26 April 1943, FO 1015/74; Bovenschen to Sargent, 13 April 1943, Strang to Bovenschen, 20 April 1943, FO to Minister of State, Cairo, tel. 1393, 1 May 1943, Z 4697/95/17, FO 371/36039; CCAO memorandum, 17 May 1943, FO 1015/72.
89 Kersaudy, *op. cit.*, pp. 283–4.
90 Lord Rennell was obliged to excise these criticisms of French policy in the Fezzan from the final text of his book on British military administration in Africa. The official who censored the book was Sir Andrew Cohen, then head of the East African Department in the Colonial Office. Rennell to Robinson, 26 November 1955, MS Rennell 1; unexpurgated typescript of *British Military Administration of Occupied Territories in Africa During the Years 1941–47* by Lord Rennell of Rodd, Chapter XII, pp. 30–1, MS Rennell 4, Rennell Papers, Nuffield College, Oxford; CCAO memorandum, 17 May 1943, FO 1015/72; Reid to FO, 11 September 1945, enclosing CCAO GHQ/MEF to DCA War Office, 15 June 1945, which included undated memorandum 'The Fezzan', U 7102/51/70, FO 371/50792j FORD memorandum, 'The Fezzan', 12 February 1948, J 1052/277/66, FO 371/69406.
91 Adjutant to DCCAO, Tripolitania (Sillery) to CCAO, GHQ/MEF, 13 June 1943, enclosing SCAO Eastern (Schofield) to DCCAO, 9 June 1943, **Sillery** to CCAO, 9 September 1943, FO 1015/72.
92 Reid to FO, 11 September 1945, enclosing CCAO, GHQ/MEF, to DCA War Office, 15 June 1945, which enclosed undated memorandum 'The Fezzan', U 7102/51/70, FO 371/50792.
93 Thuker to Strang, 6 February 1943, enclosing McGreery to Rucker, 31 January 1943, Z2102/94/17, FO 371/36039; Lush to CCAO, GHQ/MEF (Parsons) 11 September 1943; Anderson memorandum, 20 September 1943; Parsons to CGS, GHQ/MEF (Scobie) 23 September 1943, enclosing Lush to Parsons, 11 September 1943; Scobie to Parsons, 26 September 1943, Anderson to Lush, 28 September 1943; Blackley to Parsons, 3 December 1943; Anderson to Blackley, 11 December 1943, FO 1015/72.

94 De Gaulle, *L'Unité, op. cit.*, p. 63.
95 Gilbert, *Road to Victory, op. cit.*, p. 333.
96 Thorne, *op. cit.*, p. 147.
97 Kersaudy, *op. cit.*, pp. 216–7; R T Thomas, *Britain and Vichy. The Dilemma of Anglo-French Relations. 1940–42*. New York 1979, pp. 140–1.
98 Maule, *op. cit.*, p. 147.

epilogue
BRITAIN, LIBYA AND THE START OF THE COLD WAR[1]
1943 to 1954

POSTWAR PLANNING

As we have seen, the constituent parts of Libya were in 1943 put under military administration, in accordance with the Hague Convention on the laws of war. While Cyrenaica and Tripolitania were put under separate British Military Administrations, the Fezzan in the south-west, which had been conquered by the Free French, was put under their administration. The British and the Free French were required to administer these territories on a 'care and maintenance' basis until their fate was decided in the postwar peace settlement.[2]

The postwar planners in the Foreign Office engaged during the war in desultory conversations on the future of Libya with their counterparts in the US State Department, as part of that general attempt by the Foreign Office to influence the direction of US policy on the postwar world at the planning stage, before it crystallised. But the Foreign Office failed to win American support for the break-up of Libya into its constituent parts, in accordance with British imperial security interests in the Mediterranean and the Middle East. These demanded that Italy should not again be in a position to threaten British communications, oil supplies and client regimes in the region. Thus, the Foreign Office favoured the Fezzan being incorporated into the French Saharan empire and Tripolitania being returned in some secure form to Italy. Cyrenaica was to become an autonomous Sanusi amirate, in accordance with Eden's 1942 pledge that the Sanusis would not be returned to Italian rule.

Cyrenaica was to be under some form of Egyptian or British protection, with base facilities to guard the western flank of the British position in Egypt and the Middle East. Initially, in 1943, the Foreign Office calculated that offering Egypt control of Cyrenaica might provide a useful card in extracting facilities for Britain's postwar defence requirements in Egypt. The Foreign Office hoped that the defence of the Suez Canal could be arranged without stationing troops in the Nile Delta, and instead depending on a ring of satellite bases around Egypt, including Cyrenaica, in which the Strategic Reserve could be located.

It was thought that the Soviet Union would not object; in the summer of 1943 it was assumed by the Foreign Office to be a co-operative and friendly power (although not by the Strategic Planners of the Joint Planning Staff). In fact it was at this time that the Soviets first indicated that they favoured depriving Italy of Libya and that, as a great power with legitimate security requirements equal to those of Britain and the USA, they expected to be consulted on its future. It was this factor which effectively stymied the British government's attempts to refashion territorial affairs in Italian North Africa in accordance with British imperial needs in the eastern Mediterranean.[3]

The Foreign Office found itself thwarted by the US Joint Chiefs of Staff (JCS) who in May 1944, in what appears to be the earliest American assessment of the Soviets as a possible enemy, were anxious that the United States should not be drawn into a possible area of conflict with the Soviet Union. The JCS thought that the Soviets 'might well have a political interest' in the future of Libya and the other Italian colonies and might react violently, with serious consequences for the Grand Alliance, if they were confronted with an Anglo-American agreement upon which they had not been consulted beforehand.[4] The JCS, under the influence of the Joint Strategic Survey Committee, would not support British security requirements in Libya in case it endangered their main aim, which was a quid pro quo understanding between the Soviet Union and the USA on the Balkans and the Pacific, where the JCS wanted exclusive US control of the Japanese mandated islands.

Before and during the Yalta Conference in February 1945 there were distinct signs that the USA was no longer interested in joint planning with Britain on the future of Libya and that it might be prepared to co-operate with the USSR in determining the future of this territory without giving due weight to British interests, with consequent damage to Britain's standing as a great power. On New Year's Day 1945, the Soviet Ambassador to the USA, Andrei Gromyko, had informed Leo Pasvolsky, Special Adviser to the Secretary of State, that since the Soviet Union had fought Italy it should assume responsibility concerning Libya and the other Italian colonies.

At Yalta, President Roosevelt and the State Department (in particular the pro-Soviet Deputy Director of the Office of Special Political Affairs, Alger Hiss) acted with Stalin's support to force a poorly briefed Churchill to agree in principle to the American idea of placing any dependent territories taken from the enemy (such as Libya) under international trusteeship, and to the setting up of the necessary machinery by the new United Nations. Since the JCS objected to territorial negotiations that might prolong the war, no discussion was envisaged at the forthcoming UN conference at San Francisco or in preliminary talks as to which territories were to be put under international trusteeship.

However, Roosevelt had talked to Stalin at Yalta about trusteeships in the Far East (Korea and Indochina) in which the Soviets could share. It would have been natural, therefore, for the Soviets to have expected to participate in the new trusteeship system to be elaborated by the UN and for their agent of influence, Alger Hiss, to help them achieve it.[5] And Hiss did, indeed, play a prominent behind-the-scenes role at San Francisco in convincing US Secretary of State Stettinius, in order to encourage the USSR to co-operate in the new UN, to issue a statement to the effect that the US would support in principle the USSR's eligibility for a trusteeship.[6]

It is not surprising, therefore, that the Soviets should have raised this issue at the Potsdam Conference in July 1945. Just before the conference opened, the Soviet delegation notified the British and American delegations that they wanted to add certain topics for discussion to the agenda, namely Tangiers, Spain, Syria and Lebanon and 'Territorial Trusteeship and the role of the USSR'.[7] The Soviet delegation seems to have been drawing on the recommendations of the Litvinov Commission the month before that the USSR should attempt to acquire trusteeships over the Italian colonies of the Dodecanese islands, Somalia, Eritrea and Tripolitania (western Libya) and even Palestine, as well as some control over the Turkish Straits. In admitting the 'great strategic importance' of Libya and the other Italian colonies to Britain, and anticipating strong British resistance to Soviet claims to them, Litvinov banked on American help: 'To knock Britain down from her position we would undoubtedly need strong support from the USA.'[8]

POTSDAM

The Soviet initiative evoked different responses from the members of the British delegation at Potsdam. This helped to set the parameters of the early postwar debate within the British government on how to deal with Soviet pressure on Britain's position in the Mediterranean and the Middle East. At Potsdam, the British Foreign Secretary, Anthony Eden, expressed his disgust and disquiet to his Prime Minister, Winston Churchill, about further evidence of Soviet 'aggrandisement', following Soviet demands on Turkey, and its potential threat to the British position in the Mediterranean. Although aware of the Soviet interest in discussing trusteeship at Potsdam, at the time Eden was ignorant of the private proposal on 17 July by the Soviet leader, Joseph Stalin, to the new US President, Harry S Truman, that the Soviets should be given the trusteeship of an Italian colony. Reflecting the opinion of many of his senior officials, Eden denied that the Soviet Union had any direct interest in the countries to be placed under trusteeship and it was, in any case, a matter for the UN and not for the Big Three Powers at Potsdam.

Eden's intention was to warn his Prime Minister not to succumb to the blandishments of Stalin, which Churchill was inclined to do, and engage in discussion at Potsdam of facilitating 'Russian access to the seas'. Churchill's deputy, the leader of the Labour Party, Clement Attlee, agreed with Eden on the necessity of countering 'the increasing pressure' from the Soviet Union but believed that this was best done by confronting 'the Russians with the requirements of a world organisation for peace, not with the needs of the British Empire'.

Attlee favoured international control of such strategic parts of the world as the Turkish Straits, the Suez Canal and Gibraltar. Reinforcing Attlee's internationalism was his belief that the advent of air power rendered these positions untenable and his conviction that Britain could not, in any case, in its much-straitened circumstances, afford to defend them. These views were to determine his attitude to the future of Libya and the other Italian colonies when, as Prime Minister of the new Labour government, he came to deal with this question. They were also to set him at odds with his Foreign Secretary, Ernest Bevin, who embraced the Foreign Office approach.[9]

Although Churchill was forced by President Truman to agree to the question being considered by the Foreign Ministers at Potsdam, the new US Secretary of State, James Byrnes, reflecting US concern to avoid an Anglo-Soviet clash in the Mediterranean, sided with Eden to block the attempt by the Soviet Foreign Minister, V M Molotov, to proceed with the discussion of the future of Libya and the other Italian colonies at Potsdam. This was deferred to the London Council of Foreign Ministers in September, which was to begin work on the peace treaty with Italy. Molotov intimated that he knew that Britain and the United States had been considering this question during the war, although Eden and Byrnes denied that their governments had come to any conclusions on the matter.

Unknown to Eden and Byrnes, Molotov would have learnt of these Anglo-American exchanges on Libya and the other Italian colonies from 'secret sources'. Firstly from the State Department official Alger Hiss, who had worked assiduously for a Soviet trusteeship in 1945 and who seems, from evidence in the Soviet archives, to have passed US briefing papers to Moscow.

Then there was the British diplomat Donald Maclean (first secretary and acting head of chancery at the British Embassy in Washington). The latter had had access since 1944 to all the Embassy's classified cable traffic and had been working with the State Department on the peace terms with Italy. He was to reveal his interest in this question in early September when he reported State Department thinking on Libya and the other Italian colonies to the Foreign Office. Soviet espionage would have confirmed the British government's failure to secure joint planning on the Italian colonies with the US government, and the latter's refusal to support British imperial interests in the Mediterranean and the Middle East. The Soviets had clearly attempted at Potsdam to exploit the lack of Anglo-American co-operation on this issue.[10]

By the end of the Potsdam Conference, as John Kent has pointed out, the Soviet claim to the trusteeship of an Italian colony, combined with a call for the revision of the Montreux Convention of 1936 and bases in the Turkish Straits, represented a major threat to vital British interests in the Eastern Mediterranean and the Middle East.[11] It was regarded by the Foreign Office and the Chiefs of Staff as a far greater threat to the British Empire than that posed by American anti-colonialism and economic nationalism.

The response of the Foreign Office, the Colonial Office, the service ministries and the South African Prime Minister, Jan Smuts, was to advocate a policy of no concessions to the Soviets on Libya and the other Italian colonies and to try and secure American support for bolstering the British position in the Mediterranean and the Middle East through the creation of a British strategic base in Cyrenaica in eastern Libya. In the summer of 1945 there was no sign that US support would be forthcoming, and it was doubted whether this would allow Britain to reduce its military requirements in Egypt. Moreover, the Chief of the Imperial General Staff, Sir Alan Brooke, kept it from the politicians that it would be two years before Britain could use the base facilities in Cyrenaica because of the extensive wartime damage to Tobruk and Benghazi and the shortage of labour. Even then it would only be possible to accommodate one division of the Imperial (rather than purely Middle East) Strategic Reserve.[12]

LONDON COUNCIL OF FOREIGN MINISTERS

At this time, US Secretary of State Byrnes was anxious to avoid an Anglo-Soviet clash in the Mediterranean which would put the United States in the seemingly untenable position of having to defend the British Empire against the Soviet Union. In an attempt to play the 'honest broker', and to expedite the peace settlement. Byrnes tried in September 1945 to persuade the London Council of Foreign Ministers, that first test of great-power co-operation, that his proposal for a UN collective trusteeship for Libya and the other Italian colonies represented the best way of reconciling the conflicting interests of all concerned. It was also intended to promote collective security in the Middle East as an alternative to British control, a position which was also favoured by Attlee.[13]

Immediately realising the popular appeal of Byrnes's initiative, Bevin, who was as determined as Churchill and Eden to defend Britain's position in the Mediterranean and Middle East, realised that the time was not right to put forward the combined Foreign Office/Colonial Office proposals for a British strategic trusteeship of Cyrenaica. It was for this reason, rather than the lack of a policy, as Raymond Smith and John Zametica have asserted, that Bevin could not take the initiative at the London conference.[14] The British Cabinet had, indeed, approved on 11 September the joint FO/CO proposals as the basis of the British negotiating position at the conference, despite the serious doubts of Attlee as to Britain's ability any longer to defend the imperial lines of communication through the Mediterranean and the Middle East.

Since Bevin believed a French proposal for Italian trusteeship of Libya to be unacceptable from the moral and strategic points of view, he was faced with a stark choice. He could either support collective trusteeship or agree to Molotov's hinted Anglo-Soviet deal over Libya, whereby the Soviets would receive the trusteeship of Tripolitania (in accordance with the decision taken by the Central Committee of the Communist Party of the Soviet Union on 6 September) in exchange for the British securing their strategic trusteeship in Cyrenaica. But Bevin, the Chiefs of Staff and the Cabinet were worried about the potential strategic threat which a Soviet base in Tripolitania would pose to the British position in the region.[15]

In the event Bevin, with Cabinet approval, gave his qualified support on 15 September to collective trusteeship mainly in an attempt to involve the United States in the defence of British interests in the Middle East as soon as possible. Bevin told the French Foreign Minister, Bidault, that in six months it would be too late.[16] Bevin's determination to exclude the Soviets from the Mediterranean, Molotov's insistence that with the decline of Italian and French power Britain should not have a monopoly over the Inner Sea, and Byrnes's concern to avoid an Anglo-Soviet clash in the region, played a vital part, along with Balkan and Far Eastern differences, in the breakdown of the London Council of Foreign Ministers.

The British and the Americans, as well as the French, had perceived the Soviets as being difficult in insisting on their claim to the trusteeship of Tripolitania. Consequently they had refused to accede to it, which the Soviets interpreted as a refusal to acknowledge their great-power status. On the basis of a purloined French Intelligence document, the Soviets drew the conclusion that their strategy of playing on perceived Anglo-American differences over the Mediterranean and the Middle East had failed since both Britain and the United States seemed to be united in their determination to exclude the Soviet Union from the region.[17] This clearly falls within, and contributed to, the first stage of that deterioration of great-power relations which led to the Cold War.

However, the extent of the East-West divide or western co-operation at this point should not be exaggerated. In fact the limits of Anglo-American co-operation on Libya and the other Italian colonies were made clear at the Moscow Conference in December 1945. Byrnes showed no desire to back a British trusteeship of Cyrenaica or to alleviate Bevin's fear that the Soviet Union was trying to undermine the British position in the Middle East where, to some in the Foreign Office, Britain was trying to build up 'a kind of Monroe System'. (This was an allusion to the equally toothless Monroe Doctrine, named after US President Monroe who in the 1820s, during the revolutions in Spanish America, declared the Americas to be out of bounds to European powers. It relied upon the power of Britain and her navy to enforce it.)

As Kent has pointed out, the question of the future of Libya lay at the heart of the British Monroe system and was a vitally important strategic area for the British. But Byrnes showed little interest in Bevin's worries and continued to complain about spheres of influence. He was more concerned with reconciling Soviet and American interests in the Far East, the Balkans and over atomic energy in order to revive the peace process.[18]

PARIS COUNCIL OF FOREIGN MINISTERS

As John Kent has commented, it is both appropriate and significant that the Paris Council of Foreign Ministers from April to July 1946 should have been dominated by Mediterranean problems and procedural disputes arising from the peace treaty with Italy, given the growing Anglo-Soviet rivalry in the Mediterranean. It should also be noted that in the first meeting the Soviets showed themselves to be 'more conciliatory and helpful' on procedural questions than they had been at the London Conference.[19]

Byrnes rejected Bevin's renewed bid for American support for British base rights in Cyrenaica. In line with US policy, he continued to oppose the sole trusteeship of an Italian colony by the Soviet Union or any other power and to favour collective trusteeship. Bevin, anxious to make no concessions to the Soviets in the Mediterranean, frustrated by the lack of American support and fully aware of the debate between Attlee and the Chiefs of Staff over whether Britain should withdraw from the Middle East and take up a strategic defence line in Africa, proposed to the Dominion Prime Ministers on 28 April that the peace treaty with Italy should only provide for the renunciation of Italian rights. The disposal of Libya and the other colonies would be left over for later settlement by the UN.[20]

Attlee had again questioned the assumption held by the Chiefs of Staff that the route through the Mediterranean was vital to the British Empire and that it could, in the age of air power, be defended. He thought that Britain simply could not afford the cost of maintaining large air forces in North Africa, large military forces in Egypt and Palestine, and of occupying 'deficit areas' such as Libya in order to retain the chance of keeping this route open in time of war. It would also be risky to rely on the strength and friendship of Spain, Italy, Turkey or the Levant states. Moreover, British insistence on controlling the Mediterranean route might lead the Soviets to make similar claims to control of the Baltic and the Dardanelles and passage through the Suez Canal in order to keep open the sea routes between their Baltic, Black Sea and Far Eastern ports.

Warning that 'we must not for sentimental reasons based on the past, give hostages to fortune', Attlee with great prescience suggested that Britain might have to redefine its position, and consider itself 'as an easterly extension of a strategic [area], the centre of which is the American Continent, rather than as a power looking through the Mediterranean to India and the East.' Attlee and his Chancellor of the Exchequer, Hugh Dalton (supported by the strategic musings of the military historian Basil Liddell-Hart) favoured Britain's withdrawal from the Mediterranean and the Middle East, to avoid clashing with the Soviets. They also wanted to move the strategic reserve from Egypt to Kenya, link it by road to Lagos in Nigeria and build up defence facilities in Australia.[21]

Attlee's radical reappraisal of Britain's place in the world caused consternation in the Foreign Office and among the Chiefs of Staff. Gladwyn Jebb predicted that if Britain withdrew from the Mediterranean, the Soviet Union would replace it, forcing France to join the Soviet bloc.

This would render the British Isles indefensible, even with American support. And if the United States did not think Britain worth defending, then it would become a Soviet client state and British social democracy 'would be snuffed out between the rival forces of Capitalism and Communism.' Oliver Harvey thought there were 'far weightier reasons than the route to India argument for our making heavy sacrifices to hold on in the Mediterranean'. These were to exert influence on the 'soft underbelly' of Europe, thus preventing it from falling under Soviet control, to protect the British position in the Middle East and to prevent the Soviets from gaining access to Africa with incalculable results. If, in fact, Britain could not hold on in the Mediterranean, then Harvey thought the British should try to turn it into a UN 'Regional Security Area'.

Sir Orme Sargent agreed with Harvey that the crucial issue was that 'Our position as a World Power and therefore as a Great Power depends surely on our maintaining our position in the Mediterranean, and this not for strategic reasons but on political grounds.' He doubted whether Britain would be able to create a 'Western group' if it abandoned its control of the 'Mediterranean zone'. Sargent predicted that the retreat from the Mediterranean would mean the end of Britain as a world power and a fatal loss of prestige.[22]

Bevin employed the arguments of his officials to impress upon the Cabinet's Defence Committee the political and economic, rather than the purely strategic, importance of a continued British presence in the Mediterranean.

He went on to develop his ideas about modernising the defence of the Mediterranean, the Middle East and the Indian Ocean. He called for the investigation of Attlee's idea of locating Britain's defence centre in Kenya, rather than Egypt, which would strengthen the British position in defence negotiations with Egypt and the other Middle Eastern countries. He also wanted consideration given to building an alternative strategic route across Africa should the Mediterranean be closed.

The Chiefs of Staff argued that Kenya was too far from Egypt and lacked the necessary communications, facilities and labour to be a large base, although it might be used in reserve. They were, in fact, opposed to any plan which might undermine their case for the retention of Egypt as the main wartime base in the Middle East. Thus, they also stressed the limitations of developing Cyrenaica as an alternative base, although the First Lord of the Admiralty, A V Alexander, and the Chief of the Air Staff, Lord Tedder, wanted to establish air bases in Cyrenaica despite Attlee's warning about cost, since it was 'the air key to the Mediterranean sea route.'

The Chiefs were even more strongly opposed, as was Bevin, to Attlee's idea of a complete British withdrawal from the Mediterranean and the Middle East. They argued that it was vital to deny the Soviet Union the use of these areas in war to protect Africa and to be able to launch air attacks from bases in the Middle East, upon the 'important industrial and oil producing area of southern Russia and the Caucasus.' The Chiefs argued that the best place to defend Britain and its communications was as far east as possible in Europe and the Mediterranean. This may have been true, but the limited range of the existing British Lincoln bomber in 1946 meant the Egyptian base was of limited use in a strategic air offensive (though the RAF were developing the longer-range Canberra bomber). The bomber bases would have to be much further forward, in Iraq. The insistence by the Chiefs and Bevin on the need for Britain to stay in the Mediterranean and the Middle East had far more to do with political than military objectives, i.e. the maintenance of Britain's imperial system and continued role as a world power. Although unconvinced by their arguments, Attlee was forced to agree to it being debated by the Dominion Prime Ministers in London, on the eve of the Four Power discussion on the future of Libya at the Paris CFM.[23]

The ensuing discussion revealed Commonwealth divisions over the best way to proceed. Although the Dominion Prime Ministers all agreed that any Soviet claim to a single trusteeship should be firmly resisted, both the Australian and New Zealand Prime Ministers, Ben Chifley and Walter Nash respectively, were prepared, in contrast to Smuts, to support the 'experimental' US proposal of collective trusteeship if it proved impossible to secure British Commonwealth trusteeship of Cyrenaica. Detecting ominous signs of Soviet expansion from the Adriatic to the Persian Gulf since the London Conference, Smuts advocated the outright rejection of the US proposal since he feared that it might lead the Soviet Union to assume a dominant role in the Mediterranean. He counselled delay until the international situation became clearer. Unlike Smuts, Chifley and Nash were opposed to delaying a settlement.

The Australian Foreign Minister, Evatt, proposed that if the Council of Foreign Ministers failed to solve this question, it should be referred to the 21 powers who were to sign the peace treaty with Italy, rather than to the UN, for settlement. In line with his internationalist approach Attlee thought that the best way to keep the Soviets at bay was to advocate self-determination for Libya and the other Italian colonies. Concerned to cut the British commitment, he stressed that these were 'deficit areas' which needed money spent on them.

According to the senior Foreign Office official Oliver Harvey, Attlee's 'wobbly' behaviour and the attempt by Smuts and Evatt 'to impose a veto on British foreign policy', proved too much for Bevin. Warning Smuts that 'if the British Empire is liquidated, it will be liquidated by you', he complained that the Dominions expected Britain to oppose the United States and the Soviet Union but were not prepared to offer any material support.

Shaken by this 'dressing down' both Nash and Smuts proposed that all the Dominions should, in view of the importance of securing Commonwealth communications, contribute to the cost of any British Commonwealth trusteeship of Cyrenaica. But since this would lead to a Soviet counter-claim, as the Colonial Secretary, George Hall, was quick to point out, the only possible solutions were either collective trusteeship or independence. Bevin returned to Paris 'full of fight' with instructions 'to oppose both the Soviet and US proposals' and determined to put forward the British case for strategic facilities in Cyrenaica.[24]

During the first session of the Paris Council of Foreign Ministers, Bevin tried to wrest the initiative from the Americans and the Soviets. The latter were now prepared to share the trusteeship of Tripolitania with Italy in what seems to have been a triple bid: first, to secure de facto control of the territory by partnership with a weak Italy and to boost the fortunes of the Italian Communist Party in the forthcoming constitutional elections in Italy; second, to gain the French, who favoured Italian trusteeship, as allies and to encourage their formation of a Latin bloc to offset Britain's Western bloc idea; third, to wring concessions from the Western powers on the Italian peace treaty.

Bevin championed a solution for Libya (namely independence) which not only corresponded to the perceived wishes of the inhabitants but met British political and strategic requirements in the Mediterranean and Middle East.

Coming as it did on the eve of the publication of the Anglo-American Committee's report on Palestine and the Anglo-Egyptian treaty negotiations, Bevin aimed, at the very least, to improve the atmosphere in the Middle East and demonstrate to the Arab League that Britain was its closest ally on some issues. Indeed, the British proposal of Libyan independence made an excellent impression in Cyrenaica and Cairo. Bevin and the Foreign Office were even prepared to revise their attitude towards Egyptian claims to Cyrenaica depending on how well the Anglo-Egyptian treaty negotiations went.[25]

In an interesting reflection of the still fluid state of great-power relations in the first part of 1946, the US, French and Soviet foreign ministers rejected this attempt to bolster the British position in the Mediterranean and the Middle East. Instead they sought agreement on the basis of a new Soviet decision to back the French proposal for Italian trusteeship as part of a deal on the other main aspects of the Italian peace treaty, namely the Dodecanese, Trieste and reparations. But Bevin successfully thwarted this move by springing a British claim to the trusteeship of Cyrenaica, where the British government had promised the predominantly Sanusi Arab population in 1942 that they would not be returned to Italian rule. Molotov now objected to the British claim since the Soviets had abandoned their own claim to the trusteeship of Tripolitania.

It was clear to Bevin that Byrnes was only interested in finding a solution which would prevent the spread of Communist influence. Once collective trusteeship had been rejected, Byrnes was prepared to follow the advice of the Europeanists in the State Department and support Italian trusteeship. It was a mark of Byrnes's frustration at the failure of the Foreign Ministers to agree on this that he proposed postponing a solution to this question.[26]

The inability of the Four Powers to agree on the future of Libya and the other Italian colonies, except that they should be taken away from Italy, led them in July 1946 to postpone further consideration of this question in order not to hold up the conclusion of a peace treaty with Italy. The terms of the draft article and declaration embodying this decision on Libya and the other Italian colonies for insertion in the peace treaty represented a success for Bevin and the Foreign Office.[27] They had effectively prevented the Soviet Union from securing a foothold in Africa from which they would be able to challenge the British position not only in the continent but in the Mediterranean and the Middle East. In the latter part of the Paris conference they had also enlisted French and more importantly American support in resisting

Soviet encroachments in Britain's sphere of influence, thus offering the prospect of similar co-operation in the future.

Byrnes and Bidault had joined with Bevin in opposing Molotov's suggestion of a Four Power supervisory body to assist the administration of Libya and the other Italian colonies for an interim period of one year before a decision was reached on their future. Byrnes had rather reluctantly backed Bevin after his military adviser, Brigadier Lincoln, supported by the US War Department, pointed out that granting the Soviets a 25% partnership over Libya for a year might lead them to make annexationist claims, and at the very least might strengthen their bargaining position during the final settlement. The US military had also given 'cogent reasons affecting US world strategy' why the British should be granted their military requirements in Cyrenaica in the wake of their decision to withdraw from Egypt.[28] This represented a hardening of the American attitude to the Soviet Union on this question, in line with the general thrust of US policy.

Byrnes's support for Bevin was decisive in persuading Bidault to accept the British draft article and declaration on Libya and the other Italian colonies. Molotov, who had already made concessions on Trieste and the Dodecanese, followed suit in order to secure western agreement to $100 million reparations from Italy. This 'western front' had effectively bought Soviet concessions not only on Libya and the other colonies but on the other Mediterranean issues at stake in the Italian peace treaty.[29] They had done so in order to keep the Soviet Union out of what they increasingly saw as a western lake.

The alignment of attitudes on this question can be seen to mark a significant step in the growing sense of confrontation with the USSR in the Mediterranean. This can be said to fall within the second stage of the deterioration of great-power relations leading to the Cold War. However, the western powers had still to engineer a decision on the future of the colonies. This was to prove more elusive.

Nonetheless, there were some grounds for optimism over Libya where, in a significant shifting of the US stance, the Joint Chiefs and the State-War-Navy Co-ordinating Committee had identified the defence of British imperial interests against Soviet pressure as a US interest. The military members of the US delegation at Paris had hinted, as we have seen, that the United States might be prepared to support Britain's acquisition of strategic rights in Cyrenaica, in view of its intended withdrawal from Egypt. But it was clear that the French and particularly the Soviets would not accept this without a quid pro quo. This raised the question of what would be acceptable to the British without prejudicing their strategic interests. The answer to this question depended on the outcome of the debate between the Chiefs of Staff and Attlee over Britain's position in the Mediterranean and the Middle East.

The Chiefs of Staff had failed to convince Attlee of the crucial importance of the Middle East in the war. At a staff conference on 12 July he reiterated his scepticism and a week later in the Defence Committee he attacked the premise that the region could provide bases (including Cyrenaica) from which an effective counter-offensive could be launched against strategic targets in the south-eastern Soviet Union in order to reduce the force of a Soviet attack against the British Isles. He did not think that any Middle Eastern country would be prepared to grant facilities for such purposes. He feared also that planning and preparing bases for offensive action would only excite Soviet suspicions and increase the likelihood of war. He thought that access to Persian Gulf oil could be secured by agreement with the Soviets.[30]

Attlee successfully persuaded the Defence Committee to defer a decision on this question until the situation in Europe and the Middle East became clearer, the Peace Conference was over, and there had been a reassessment of the overall strategic position of the British Commonwealth in the light of the conditions of modern warfare.[31] The enforced delay effectively prevented Bevin and the Foreign Office from seeking American, French and Soviet acquiescence in British control of Cyrenaica. British strategic requirements would first have to be agreed by the British government before Bevin and the Foreign Office could take any further initiative on the future of Cyrenaica and the other Italian colonies at an international level.

FAILURE OF THE FOUR POWERS

The American historian William Roger Louis has said that 'In 1947 the crisis in Greece drew the British and Americans into general agreement on problems of the eastern Mediterranean. In roughly the first half of 1948, Palestine and the uncertainty of the outcome of the Italian elections caused a hiatus in the planning of the general settlement' on Libya and the other ex-Italian colonies.[32] But if looked at from the British perspective this process of convergence can be seen to have started in June–July 1946 at the Paris CFM and the Peace Conference and contributed to the breakdown of Four Power co-operation on this issue at the second Paris Council of Foreign Ministers in September 1948. Bevin pursued a delaying strategy, endorsed by the Dominions, at the Paris

Peace Conference in the latter half of 1946, until the Americans were prepared to support British policy on the ex-Italian colonies.

Bevin pointed out to the British Commonwealth delegations the advantages of a year's delay, as proposed by the Council of Foreign Ministers, with regard to Egypt, Indonesia, the Turkish Straits, Cyrenaica and the political situation in the United States: 'Given time, when the Treaties with the European satellites were out of the way, the Egyptian problem might also be settled, and we might hope that some arrangements would be come to in Indonesia ....'

If a settlement of the Straits could be made at a conference in the next year, 'much of the mist of uncertainty in regard to Cyrenaica would lift'. He feared that if he discussed the Italian colonies with Molotov, the latter would in turn raise the subject of the Straits. Bevin's talks with Stalin during the Moscow Conference had revealed to the Foreign Office that the Soviets accorded the issue a high priority. Bevin and the Foreign Office had considered a possible deal whereby the Soviets would agree to a British trusteeship of Cyrenaica in exchange for a revision of the Montreux Convention. This would allow the Soviets to close the Straits in wartime. But the Foreign Office rejected this when it learnt that the Soviets sought joint defence arrangements with Turkey, which it held would undermine Turkish independence.

The 'Dardanelles scare' of August 1946 had led the Truman Administration to dispatch a naval carrier force to the eastern Mediterranean to reinforce the battleship USS *Missouri* at Istanbul. The Foreign Office was impressed by this unilateral demonstration of American resolve in repelling possible Soviet aggression. It showed that the US government connected the defence of Turkey with that of the Middle East. Since Bevin was clearly anxious to encourage such thinking, it is understandable that he should want to align the British government with the US action. He also wanted to avoid any initiative, such as discussion with Molotov of a deal over the Straits, which might prejudice the chances of Anglo-American co-operation in the eastern Mediterranean and the Middle East, and the exclusion of the Soviets from the British sphere. In the meantime he consolidated the British position in Cyrenaica.[33]

But by the winter of 1946–47 the failure to acquire base facilities in Cyrenaica, combined with the deterioration of the British position in Greece, Turkey, Palestine and Egypt, was now threatening to undermine the strategy of Bevin, the Foreign Office and the Chiefs of Staff for preserving Britain's sphere of influence in the eastern Mediterranean and the Middle East. Furthermore, Attlee remained opposed to this strategy. He was extremely reluctant to bow to the combined pressure of the

Chiefs of Staff and the Foreign Office to sanction continued support for Greece, and by implication Turkey. He was sceptical about the chances of securing stronger American support and remained unconvinced about the strategic value of the Mediterranean and the Middle East. Concerned about the high level of defence expenditure, he argued that Britain did not command the resources to make Greece, Turkey, Iraq and Iran into an effective barrier against the Soviet Union. He proposed an Anglo-Soviet agreement to turn these countries into a 'neutral zone' (as suggested by Liddell-Hart).[34]

Attlee continued to believe that a new line of defence should be formed across Africa, from Lagos and Mombasa, and on to the Indian Ocean and the Persian Gulf. Bevin was interested in a trans-African trunk road or rail link but, in contrast to Attlee, he regarded it as a useful support to Britain's position in the Middle East. With increasing attention being given in late 1946 to the economic and strategic importance of Africa to Britain's recovery *vis-à-vis* the USA and the USSR, the Russophobes and the imperialists in the Foreign Office were able to argue that Britain's position in the Middle East was necessary for the defence of Africa. Thus, Bevin's Private Secretary, Dixon, pointed out that a neutral zone would not stop the Soviets from penetrating into the Mediterranean and Africa.

Bevin was prepared to suggest to Attlee on 27 December that it might be possible to strike a bargain with the Soviets for the withdrawal of their troops from Bulgaria in exchange for a British withdrawal from Greece. He also wanted to delay any decision to pull out of Palestine until he was able to see whether Stalin would be interested in a deal which would give Britain the trusteeship of Cyrenaica. He did not specify what the Soviets would receive in return. This indicates that Bevin did not completely rule out bargaining with the Soviets, although he was against conducting it on a piecemeal basis. He intended to keep to this view until the full scale of Soviet ambitions became clear.

In a significant development, Attlee agreed in Cabinet on 2 January 1947 that if the British could secure bases in Cyrenaica, then there would be no need to remain in either Palestine or Egypt. It would also be possible to conclude an agreement with the Egyptian government. Bevin voiced his regret to the Cabinet that the British government had not asserted its 'right' to Cyrenaica during the war, for 'we could have spared ourselves our present difficulty in retaining a foothold elsewhere in the Mediterranean'.[35]

Although Attlee seemed to be prepared to sanction a British presence in North Africa, he attacked the determination of the Chiefs of

Staff to stay in the Middle East as 'a strategy of despair', which threatened to provoke the war it was designed to prevent. Before being forced to accept this, he wanted to investigate the possibilities of reaching an Anglo-Soviet agreement. The chilling prospect of a full-scale British withdrawal from the Middle East, and the consequent loss of great-power status, led Bevin and the Foreign Office to denigrate the chances of an agreement. They also used emotive language to stress the disastrous political consequences for Britain in the region, in Africa, in Europe and the world. 'It would be Munich over again.'

In line with their policy of making no concessions to the Soviets in the British sphere, they argued that they were only prepared to negotiate with the Soviets after Britain had rebuilt its strength. In the meantime they favoured the retention of 'essential positions' in the region, if necessary with American help, and the use of the UN. The Chiefs of Staff seemed to have relied on the threat of resignation rather than the power of argument to force Attlee to accept their strategic concept that the Middle East should be one of the three main pillars of British defence policy, although the case for British bases in the Middle East must have been strengthened by the decision at this time to proceed with the production of the British atom bomb. This raised the prospect of launching nuclear strikes against the Soviet Union in wartime.[36]

The decision to stay in the Mediterranean and the Middle East, and to protect Africa, was undoubtedly a great triumph for Bevin, the Foreign Office and the Chiefs of Staff and their policy of defending Britain's global status. They continued to remain alive, however, to any possible threats to it. Thus, in March the Chiefs of Staff were quick to denounce the following as international setbacks: the referral of the Palestine question to the UN, the decision to give no further aid to Greece and Turkey, the announcement that the British would quit India, the lack of progress over Cyrenaica and Egypt's breaking off negotiations and placing its dispute with Britain before the UN. They demanded that the closest possible links be forged with the Americans, that agreements be reached giving the British facilities in Egypt, Palestine, India, rights in Cyrenaica and sovereignty over Cyprus. They wanted nothing to prejudice Anglo-Arab relations and they insisted that the Soviets should be excluded from Libya and the Northern Tier.

When Bevin suggested in May 1947 that the USSR might be prepared to support a British trusteeship of Cyrenaica if they were allowed to participate in a collective (that is Four Power) trusteeship of the Tripolitanian coast, his officials, led by Robin Hankey of the Northern Department, were to quick to squash the idea, alarmed as they were by the prospect of letting the Soviets into the Mediterranean, and advanced the idea of an American trusteeship, hoping that 'large quantities of the invaluable dollar' would have a convincing effect upon the Tripolitanians.

After this last attempt to consider bargaining with the Soviets over Libya, Bevin lent his weight to A V Alexander (Minister of Defence) and the Chiefs of Staff to persuade Attlee, who still had lingering doubts in June 1947, to accept their recommendations and, therefore, to endorse an anti-Soviet Middle East-based defence strategy. Despite the constraints imposed by the economic crisis of 1947, it was to remain the basis of British imperial strategy until 1950.[37]

In the wake of the deterioration of East-West relations and fears of the collapse of the British position in the Eastern Mediterranean, the new US Secretary of State, George Marshall, and his State Department advisers formally abandoned Byrnes's policy of collective trusteeship for Libya and the other ex-Italian colonies and supported a British trusteeship of Cyrenaica at the Anglo-American defence talks at the Pentagon in October–November 1947.

The determination of the British and American representatives at the Pentagon Talks, which were subsequently endorsed by Attlee and Truman, to prevent the Soviets from obtaining a foothold in ex-Italian North Africa, and therefore in the British sphere in the Eastern Mediterranean and the Middle East, made it probable that the Soviets would not agree to a British trusteeship of Cyrenaica. They effectively ensured then that the question would have to be referred by the Council of Foreign Ministers to the UN General Assembly in September 1948 (as provided for under the Italian peace treaty). There they hoped at best to secure a British trusteeship of Cyrenaica. At worst they hoped to be able to block any unacceptable solution, and remain in occupation until an independent Cyrenaica granted the British government the strategic facilities it desired.[38]

The British and the Americans also co-operated in the autumn of 1947 in defeating Soviet plans to use the Four Power Commission of Investigation as a weapon against the West in the Italian elections of 1948 (the Commission was sent to Libya and the other ex-colonies to find out the views of the inhabitants as to their future).[39] It is clear that Anglo-American diplomatic and strategic co-operation over Libya demonstrates an active partnership, working to stabilise the British position in the Eastern Mediterranean, following the Attlee government's decisions to pull out of Greece, Turkey and Palestine and the collapse of the Anglo-Egyptian treaty negotiations. It also shows that both the British and the Americans were prepared to see the breakdown of Four Power co-operation rather than make concessions to the Soviets over Cyrenaica. This falls within, and helped to contribute to, the last stage of the deterioration of great-power relations leading towards the Cold War.

There was certainly a hiatus, as Louis has pointed out, in the planning of the general settlement on Libya and the ex-Italian colonies between the second London Council of Foreign Ministers in December 1947 (which marks the formal breakdown of tripartite Allied cooperation) and the Italian elections in April 1948 in the early stages of the Cold War.[40] The Foreign Office's attempt to secure the return of Italy to East Africa in order to further British policy on Libya and Western Europe was thwarted by the State Department's reluctance to see it become an Italian election issue and the Colonial Office's opposition to a Euro-African approach.[41] By the summer of 1948, however, the British and US governments could agree concessions to Italy in east Africa in order to retain Italy on the right side of the Iron Curtain. But Britain and the United States remained divided over the future of Tripolitania, where the US desired strategic facilities.[42] In an interesting indication of the difficulties of the new Anglo-American Cold War partnership, the US government baulked at British attempts to persuade it to assume some responsibility for Tripolitania. This casts doubt on William Roger Louis's conclusion that the summer of 1948 saw the interlocking of British and US aims with regard to the future of Libya.[43]

Louis has said that both Britain and the United States were now working for the development of a major American base at Mellaha in Tripolitania (later renamed Wheelus Field) and the securing of 'British strategic rights in Cyrenaica'.[44] While it is true that the State Department backed a British trusteeship of Cyrenaica, it refused, largely for US domestic reasons, to countenance the British proposal for an American trusteeship of Tripolitania, preferring a British trusteeship. Bevin had no desire to see Britain continuing to shoulder the burden of administering Tripolitania on behalf of the United States.[45] He also refused to allow the US Air Force to turn Mellaha airfield into a major base in the summer of 1948 in case it offended Arab sentiments and further antagonised the Soviets, thus prejudicing the chances of obtaining a British trusteeship of Cyrenaica.[46]

This was Bevin's main aim, for which he was prepared in 1948 even to stall American military and political involvement in the Middle East. Agreement on Libya was limited to the future of Cyrenaica and the Fezzan (which was to be under a French trusteeship). The State Department and the Foreign Office wanted to postpone a decision on the future of Tripolitania until they had had more time to reconcile their differences of opinion, not only between themselves but with the French (who were anxious for an Italian trusteeship which would act as a buffer against what they regarded as the British-backed Arab 'contagion' in Cyrenaica).[47] Until this Anglo-American reconciliation occurred British and American aims in Libya would not fully interlock.

Another noticeable feature of this period was the growing conviction of both the British and US governments that they stood a better chance of securing their strategic aims from the UN than from the Council of Foreign Ministers, where the Soviets could exercise an effective veto.[48] This proved to be an over-confident assessment but it, along with Soviet intransigence, ensured the failure of the Council of Foreign Ministers by September 1948 to find a solution to the problem of Libya and the other ex-Italian colonies.

The Soviet spymaster Yuri Modin has revealed that the Soviets were fully appraised, through their spy Guy Burgess in the Foreign Office, of the role which Cyrenaica and Tripolitania played in British and American strategic planning.[49] They realised as well, as the Soviet Ambassador to the UN Andrei Gromyko later revealed, that in a western-dominated UN General Assembly they would not ultimately be able to prevent the British and US governments from obtaining their strategic aims in Libya. They could only hope to delay them in the short term.[50]

THE UN DECISION AND THE REALISATION OF BRITISH AND US STRATEGIC AIMS

William Roger Louis has further argued that in the early stages of the Cold War 'from the summer of 1948 until the birth of the state of Libya in the winter of 1951–2, the British and the Americans worked together in bringing about the consensus of the United Nations'.[51] This, however, ignores the fact that the British and the Americans had to resolve their own policy differences on this question before they could try and bring about a consensus in the UN. Even then it was not a foregone conclusion. Thus, American reluctance to see this issue raised in the US elections meant that it was not considered until December 1948 at the end of the first part of the third session of the UN General Assembly. Then the American conviction that only an inconclusive discussion was possible effectively ensured postponement until the second part of the third session in April 1949, much to the chagrin of the Foreign Office, which wanted to embark upon a positive administrative policy in Cyrenaica in order to bolster the British position.[52]

In the spring of 1949, the Foreign Office attempted to reconcile British, European and African aims by proposing, in the Bevin-Sforza Plan, a British trusteeship of Cyrenaica, a French trusteeship of the Fezzan and a continued British administration of Tripolitania until 1951, when the Italians would take responsibility until the projected independence of Libya in 1959. Italy was also to have the trusteeship of Somalia; most of Eritrea was to be ceded to Ethiopia, with the exception of the western province, which was to be incorporated into the Sudan; Asmara and Massawa were to be given a special status. Following the rejection of the plan by the UN General Assembly in May, however, the British and US governments finally reached agreement in principle in favour of Libyan independence.

This was not in itself enough for them to realise their strategic aims in Libya. This was due to their inability to influence the behaviour of the rival Latin American and Arab voting blocs in the UN General Assembly. It meant that in implementing the November 1949 UN resolution on the independence of Libya, much work remained to be done before Britain and the United States could secure their strategic goals.[53] The struggle over the structure of the new Libyan state was of vital importance to Britain and the United States. The fulfilment of their strategic requirements depended upon a satisfactory outcome, namely the creation of a federal state which would safeguard British and American influence in Cyrenaica and Tripolitania.

The creation of a client state was intended to bolster Britain's predominant position in the Mediterranean and the Middle East, its status as a world power and its influence within the American-dominated North Atlantic Alliance.[54] With the decline of the strategic importance of Libya to Britain and the United States after the Suez Crisis, the base agreements under the Anglo-Libyan Treaty of 1953, the US-Libyan Agreement of 1954 and the preservation of the federal structure became less important.[55] The latter was abandoned in favour of a united Kingdom of Libya in 1963, and the British and US bases were progressively run down until they were abandoned altogether in 1969–70.

American support for the creation by Britain of an independent Libya proved to be a beneficial achievement for both the Libyans and the western powers as long as their interests coincided. When these interests began to diverge and then conflict, following the advent to power of Colonel Gaddafi in 1969, it is noticeable that the Soviets tried to recoup their losses during the First Cold War.

The apparent continuity of Soviet aims towards Libya lies beyond the scope of this book. After the Second World War, British and American estimates of Soviet policy on this question led them, to paraphrase Cameron Watt, from considering the Soviets to be 'difficult' to considering them to be 'impossible' and then finally to a deep belief in their fundamental hostility to British and American strategic aims.[56] These were finally achieved, after much struggle, during the early stages of the Cold War. In this way, great-power discord over Libya contributed to the start of the Cold War.

NOTES

1 This epilogue is a slightly shortened version of my article, 'Britain, Libya, and the Start of the Cold War', which was published in *The Maghreb Review*, vol. 31, nos. 1–2, 2006, pp. 42–61. For a more detailed study, also see my *Cold War in the Desert*, London 2000.
2 Lord Rennell of Rodd, *British Military Administration of Occupied Territories in Africa during the years 1941–1947*, London 1948, pp. 20–4.
3 FO 371/35414/U3575/682/70, Hood minute, 11 August 1943, Mackereth minute, 16 August 1943; FO 371/35407/U516/516/70, MSC/53 (Revise), 22 June 1943 and FO note, 29 June 1943; CAB 119/65, JP (42) 1025, 20 December 1942.
4 RG 59/SDDF 1940–44, Box 5042, 865.014/5-1644, Leahy to Hull, 16 May 1944; Marc A Stoler, 'From Continentalism to Globalism', *Diplomatic History*, 6, 1991, pp. 312–3.
5 *FRUS, The Conferences at Malta and Yalta 1945*, Washington, DC, USGPO, 1955, p. 74–5; W R Louis, *Imperialism at Bay, 1941–45*, Oxford 1977, pp. 456–7; C Andrew and O Gordievsky, *KGB*, London 1980, pp. 273–7.
6 *FRUS 1945*, vol. 1, Washington, DC 1967, pp. 1398–9, 1428–9.
7 *FRUS 1945, The Conference of Berlin (Potsdam)*, vol. 2, Washington, DC 1960, pp. 43–7.
8 V O Pechatnov, 'Working Paper #13', CWHP – Woodrow Wilson Centre, Washington, DC, p. 18; S Mazov, 'The USSR and the former Italian Colonies, 1945–50', *Cold War History*, vol. 3, no. 3, April 2003, pp. 51–5.
9 R Butler and M E Pelly, eds, *Documents on British Policy Overseas (DBPO)*, ser. 1, vol. 1, London 1984, pp. 352–4, 363–4.
10 *ibid.*, pp. 454, 539–42, 566–7; Andrew, *op. cit.* pp. 260–1, 322–3; FO 371/50792/U7012/51/70, Maclean to Western Department, 5 September 1945; Mazov, *op. cit.*, p. 54.
11 J Kent, *British Imperial Strategy and the Origins of the Cold War, 1944–49*, Leicester 1993, pp. 61–2.
12 R Bullen and M E Pelly, eds, *DBPO*, ser. 1, vol. 2, London, HMSO 1985, p. 81–3; WO 193/280, GS 'Comments on ORC(45)21', undated.
13 *FRUS 1945*, vol. 2, Washington, DC 1985, pp.179–81; D C Watt, *Succeeding John Bull*, Cambridge 1984, p. 244.
14 *DBPO*, ser. 1, vol. 2, p.168–71; R Smith and J Zametica, 'The Cold Warrior. Clement Attlee Reconsidered', *International Affairs*, vol. 61, no. 2, 1985, p. 244.
15 *DBPO*, ser. 1, vol. 2, pp. 81–3, 158–67; Mazov, *op. cit.*, p. 56.
16 *ibid.*, pp. 158–67, 190–92.
17 *DBPO*, ser. 1, vol. 2, pp. 349–50, 449–55, 473–6, 482–4; *FRUS 1945*, vol. 2, p. 629–32; A Berard, *Un Ambassadeur Se Souvient*, Paris 1978, p. 41; Mazov, *op. cit.*, pp. 61–2.
18 Kent, *op. cit.*, pp. 90–1; *DBPO*, ser. 1, vol. 2, pp. 733–6; *FRUS 1945*, vol. 2, pp. 629–32.
19 Kent, *op. cit.*, p. 102.
20 FO 371/57176/U4539/106/70, Bevin to FO, 27 April 1946; CAB 133/86, PMM (46) 6th mtg, 28 April 1946; *FRUS 1946*, vol. 7, Washington, DC 1969, pp. 71–2.
21 CAB 131/2, DO(46)27, 21 February 1946; CAB 80/100, COS(46)54(0), 22 February 1946; J Tomlinson, 'The Attlee Government and the Balance of Payments,

1945–51', *Twentieth Century British History*, 2, 1, 1991, p. 54; R Hyam, 'Africa and the Labour Government, 1945–1951', *Journal of Imperial and Commonwealth History (JICH)*, 16, 1988, p. 159.

22 FO 371/57173/U2749/106/70, minutes by Jebb, 8 March, Harvey, 11 March 1946 and Sargent, 12 March 1946; J Kent, 'The British Empire and the Origins of the Cold War, 1944–49', in A Deighton, ed., *Britain and the First Cold War*, London 1990, pp. 165–83.

23 CAB 131/2, DO(46)40, 13 March 1946, DO(46)47 & 48, 2 April 1946; CAB 131/1, DO(46)8th mtg, 8 March 1946, DO(46)10th mtg, 5 April 1946; J Kent, 'The Egyptian Base and the Defence of the Middle East, 1945–54', *JICH*, 16, 1988, pp. 46–7.

24 CAB 133/86, PMM(46)6th mtg, 28 April 1946; Harvey Diaries, 29 April 1946.

25 FO 371/57177/U4652/106/70, Ward minute, 30 April 1946; Mazov, *op. cit.*, pp. 61–3.

26 FO 371/57129/U5196/106/70, Bevin to Attlee, 11 May 1946; *FRUS 1946*, vol. 2, Washington, DC 1970, pp. 334–8, 384–7, 392, 423–4.

27 *FRUS 1946*, vol. 2, pp. 738–42, 899–900, 907–8.

28 RG 165/092.3 Paris, 16 April 1946, Box 101, Lincoln to Byrnes, 29 June 1946, Lincoln to JCS, 9 July 1946.

29 *FRUS 1946*, vol. 2, pp. 738–42, 899–900, 907–8; P D Ward, *The Threat of Peace*, Kent State University Press, 1979, pp. 113–5.

30 CAB 21/2086, COS(46)108th mtg, 12 July 1946.

31 CAB 131/1, DO(46)22nd mtg, 19 July 1946; CAB 131/3, DO (46)80, 18 July 1946.

32 W R Louis, *The British Empire in the Middle East, 1945–51*, Oxford 1984, p. 295.

33 DO 35/1833, Cockram to Stevenson, 21 August 1946; FO 371/53518/J4025/640/66, UK Del. Circular tel. 25, 22 September 1946.

34 Kent, *Imperial Strategy*, p. 109; *British Documents on the End of Empire (BDEEP)*, A2; R Hyam, ed., *The Labour Government and the End of Empire, Pt 3*, London 1992, doc. 279; Smith, *IA*, pp. 247–8.

35 Kent, *Imperial Strategy*, p. 109, 129–30; Kent, 'Origins of Cold War', pp. 176–7; *BDEEP*, A2, 3, doc. 280.

36 Kent, *Imperial Strategy*, pp. 109–10; *BDEEP*, A2, 3, docs 281, 282; Smith, IA, pp. 249–51; C J Bartlett, *The Special Relationship*, London, Macmillan 1992, p. 27.

37 J Lewis, *Changing Direction*, London 1978, pp. 315–34; Bartlett, *op. cit.*, p. 27.

38 *FRUS 1947*, vol. 5, Washington, DC 1972, p. 54; *FRUS 1947*, vol. 3, Washington, DC 1972, pp. 601–5; P L Hahn, *The United States, Great Britain and Egypt, 1945–1956*, Chapel Hill 1991, pp. 49–51.

39 *FRUS 1947*, vol. 3, Washington, DC 1974, pp. 609–10, 615–6; Y Modin, *My Five Cambridge Friends*, London 1994, p. 138; Mazov, *op. cit*, pp. 66–9.

40 Louis, *op. cit.*, p. 295.

41 CAB 129/24, CP(48)43, 4 February 1948; CAB 128/12, CM(48)12, 5 February 1948; CAB 131/6, DO (48)31, 27 April 1948; FO 371/69330/J2350/6/66, Bevin to Alexander, 15 April 1948; *FRUS 1948*, vol. 3, Washington, DC 1974, pp. 906–7.

42 *BDEEP*, A2, 3, doc. 305: FO 371/69341/J5286/6/66, Scott-Fox minute,

5 August 1948; *FRUS. 1948*, vol. 3, pp. 933–9.
43 Louis, *op. cit.*, p. 302.
44 *ibid.*
45 *FRUS 1948*, vol. 3, pp. 912–4, 922–7, CAB 131/6, DO(48)48, 27 July 1948; FO 371/69340/J5204/6/66, Clutton minute.
46 FO 371/69430/J3724/216/66, Bevin to Franks, 4 June 1948, J6259/216/66, Henderson to Bevin, 30 August 1948, Sargent minute, 9 September 1948.
47 *FRUS 1948*, vol. 3, pp. 933–9.
48 RG 59/SDDF 1945–49, Box 6684, 865.014/9-1548, Caffery to Marshall, 15 September 1948; FO 371/69440/J6630/6071/66, Scott-Fox minute, 21 September 1948.
49 Modin, *op. cit.*, p. 138.
50 R E Patman, *The Soviet Union in the Horn of Africa*, Cambridge 1990, p. 39.
51 Louis, *op. cit.*, p. 295.
52 FO 371/69941/J7999/6283/6283/66, Scott-Fox to Clutton, 12 December 1948; FO 371/69350/J7925/6/66, Clutton minute; *FRUS 1948*, vol. 3, p. 953.
53 FO 371/73904/J9099/15113/122, Clutton to Stewart, 15 October 1948.
54 W R Louis, 'Libyan Independence, 1951: The Creation of a Client State' in P Gifford and W R Louis, *Decolonization and African Independence*, New Haven 1988, pp. 176–9.
55 D Devereux, *The Formulation of British Defence Policy towards the Middle East, 1948–1956*, London 1990, pp. 149–50; Wright, *op. cit.*, p. 83.
56 D Cameron Watt, 'Britain, the United States and the Opening of the Cold War' in R Ovendale, ed., *The Foreign Policy of the British Labour Governments, 1945–51*, Leicester 1984, p. 59.

bibliography

1 MANUSCRIPT SOURCES

A GREAT BRITAIN

British Government (The National Archives, Kew)

AIR 23 Air Ministry and Ministry of Defence: Royal Air Force Overseas Commands: Reports and Correspondence.
CAB 21 Cabinet Office: Registered Files.
CAB 65 War Cabinet and Cabinet: Minutes (WM and CM Series), 1939–45.
CAB 66 War Cabinet and Cabinet: Memoranda (WP and CP Series), 1939–45.
CAB 69 War Cabinet and Cabinet: Defence Committee (Operations) Minutes and Papers (DO series).
CAB 80 Cabinet Office: Registered Files: Chiefs of Staff Committee, Memoranda.
CAB 95 War Cabinet and Cabinet: Committees on the Middle East and Africa: Minutes and Papers (ME, A and other series).
CAB 129 Cabinet: Memoranda, 1945–51.
CAB 131 Cabinet: Defence Committee: Minutes and Papers (DO, D and DC series).
CAB 133 Cabinet: Commonwealth and International Conferences.
DO 35 Dominions Office and Commonwealth Relations Office: Original Correspondence.
FO 371 Foreign Office: General Correspondence: Political.
FO 1015 Foreign Office: Administration of African Territories.
WO 32 War Office: Registered Files (General Series) 1945–85.
WO 193 War Office: Directorate of Military Operations and Plans, later Directorate of Military Operations: Files concerning Military Planning, Intelligence and Statistics (Collation Files).

WO 201 War Office: Middle East Forces. Military Headquarters Papers, Second World War, 1939–46.
WO 230 War Office: British Military Administration of the African Territories, Papers, 1939–51.
WO 258 War Office: Department of the Permanent Under-Secretary of State: Private Office Papers, 1939–62.

Killearn Diaries, Middle East Centre, St Antony's College, Oxford.
Longrigg Papers, Middle East Centre, St Antony's College, Oxford.
Mitchell Diaries, Rhodes House Library, Oxford.
Rennell Papers, Nuffield College, Oxford.

B UNITED STATES

United States Government (The National Archives, Washington, DC)

State Department: Record Group 59/State Department Decimal Files, 1940–44.

War Department: Record Group 165/General and Special Staffs: Plans and Operations Division.

2 PRINTED SOURCES

A OFFICIAL
Britain

Butler, R and Pelly, M E , eds, Documents on British Policy Overseas, series 1, vols 1 and 2 (London 1984 and 1985).
Foreign Office Weekly Political Intelligence Summaries, vol. 4, July–December 1941, London 1983.
Hinsley, F H, British Intelligence in the Second World War, vols I–II, London 1979 and 1984.
Hyam, R, ed., The Labour Government and the End of Empire, pt 3, London 1992, in the British documents on the End of Empire Series (BDEEP).

Parliamentary Debates, 5th Series, House of Commons.
Playfair, I S O, The Mediterranean and the Middle East, vols I–IV, London 1954–66.
Rodd, Lord Rennell of, British Military Administration of Occupied Territories in Africa During the Years 1941–47, London 1948.
Woodward, Sir C, British Foreign Policy in the Second World War, vol.1, London 1970.

France

Vincent, J-N, Les Forces Françaises Libre en Afrique, 1940–43. Les Forces Françaises Dans La Lutte Contre l'Axe en Afrique, Ministère de la Défense Etat major de l'Armée de Terre Service Historique, Château de Vincennes 1983.

United States

Department of State, Foreign Relations of the United States, Washington, DC, 1941–51, multi-vols, 1955–82.
V O Pechatnov, 'Working Paper #13', Cold War History Project, Woodrow Wilson Centre, Washington, DC.

B NEWSPAPERS AND PERIODICALS

Oriente Moderno.
Review of the Foreign Press, 1939–45, series A and B, RIIA, Chatham House 1980.
The Times.

C MEMOIRS, DIARIES, LETTERS AND PAPERS

Avon, The Earl of, *The Eden Memoirs: The Reckoning*, London 1965.
Bérard, A, *Un Ambassadeur Se Souvient*, Paris 1978.
Casey, R, *Personal Experience, 1939–46*, London 1962.
Chandos, The Lord, *Memoirs*, London 1964.
Churchill, Winston S, *The Second World War*, vol. 3 *The Grand Alliance*, London 1950.
Cunningham, The Lord, *A Sailor's Odyssey*, London 1951.

De Gaulle, C, *Mémoires de Guerre. L'Appel. 1940–42*, Paris 1944.
— *L'Unité 1942–44*, Paris 1956.
— *Lettres, Notes et Carnets, Juillet 1941–Mai 1943*, Paris 1982.
— *Discours et Messages Pendant La Guerre, Juin 1940–Janvier 1946*, Paris 1970.
De Guingand, F, *Operation Victory*, London 1947.
Dilks, D, ed., *The Diaries of Sir Alexander Cadogan, 1938–45*, London 1971.
Evans, T E, ed., *The Killearn Diaries, 1934–46*, London 1972.
Foot, Sir H, *A Start in Freedom*, London 1964.
Gilbert, M, *Finest Hour. Winston S Churchill 1939–41*, London 1983.
— *Road to Victory. Winston S Churchill, 1941–45*, London 1986.
Harvey, J, ed., *The War Diaries of Oliver Harvey*, London 1978.
Holmboe, K, tr. Holbek, H, *Desert Encounter. An Adventurous Journey through Italian Africa*, London 1936.
Ismay, Lord, *The Memoirs of General Lord Ismay*, London 1960.
Lawrence, T, *Seven Pillars of Wisdom*, second edn, eighth reprint, London 1949.
Liddell Hart, B, *The Rommel Papers*, London 1953.
Massu, J, *7 Ans Avec Leclerc*, Paris 1974.
Montgomery, B, *El Alamein to the River Sangro*, London 1948.
— *Memoirs*, London 1958.
Wilson, The Lord, *Eight Years Overseas, 1939–47*, London 1950.

3 PRINTED SECONDARY WORKS: BOOKS

Andrew, C and Gordievsky, O, *KGB*, London 1980.
Baram, P J, *The Department of State in the Middle East, 1919–45*, Pittsburgh 1978.
Barnett, C, *The Desert Generals*, third edn, London 1983.
Barr, N, *Pendulum of War*, London 2004.
Bartlett, C J, *The Special Relationship*, London 1992.
Bennett, R, *Ultra and the Mediterranean Strategy*, London 1989.
Birkenhead, The Lord, *The Life of Lord Monckton of Brenchley*, London 1969.
Bosworth, R J B, *Italy, the Least of the Great Powers. Italian Foreign Policy before the First World War*, Cambridge 1979.
Brownlie, I, *African Boundaries*, London 1979.
Bungay, S, *Alamein*, London 2003.
Carver, M, *Tobruk*, London 1962.

— *El Alamein*, London 1962.
— *Dilemmas of the Desert War*, London 1986.
Childs, T W, *Italo-Turkish Diplomacy over the war in Libya, 1911–12*, Leiden 1990.
Cohen, M, *Palestine; Retreat from the Mandate. The Making of British Policy, 1936–45*, London 1978.
De Candole, *The Life and Times of King Idris of Lybya*, London 1988.
De Felice, R, *Jews in an Arab Land. Libya, 1835–1970*, Austin 1985.
Deighton, A, *Britain and the First Cold War*, London 1990.
Devereux, D, *The Formulation of British Defence Policy towards the Middle East, 1948–56*, London 1990.
Evans-Pritchard, E E, *The Sanusis of Cyrenaica*, Oxford 1948.
Gifford, P and Louis, W R, *Decolonization and African Independence*, New Haven 1988.
Hahn, P L, *The United States, Great Britain and Egypt, 1945–56*, Chapel Hill 1991.
Hirszowicz, L, *The Third Reich and the Arab East*, London 1966.
Holland, J, *Together We Stand*, London 2005.
Kennedy-Shaw, W B, *The Long Range Desert Group. The Story of its Work in Libya. 1940–43*, London 1945.
Joffe, E G H and McLachlan, K, eds, *Social and Economic Development of Libya*, Wisbech 1982.
Kelly, S, *Cold War in the Desert*, London 2000.
Kent, J, *British Imperial Strategy and the Origins of the Cold War, 1944–49*, Leicester 1993.
Kersaudy, F, *Churchill and de Gaulle*, London 1981.
Khadduri, M, *Modern Libya. A Study in Political Development*, Baltimore 1963.
Kirk, G, *The Middle East in the War. Survey of International Affairs, 1939–46*, RIIA, London 1952.
Knox, M, *Mussolini Unleashed 1939–41. Politics and Strategy in Fascist Italy's Last War*, Cambridge 1982.
Lamb, R, *The Ghosts of Peace, 1939–45*, Salisbury 1987.
Lanne, B, *Tchad-Libye. La Querelle des Frontières*, Paris 1982.
Latimer, J, *Alamein*, London 2002.
Leonard, R A, *A Short Guide to Clausewitz on War*, New York 1967.
Lewin, R, *Rommel as Military Commander*, London 1968.
— *Montgomery as Military Commander*, London 1971.
— *The Life and Death of the Afrika Korps*, London 1977.
Lewis, I M, *A Modern History of Somalia*, Harlow 1980.
Lewis, J, *Changing Direction*, London 1978.

Louis, W R, *Imperialism at Bay, 1941–45*, Oxford 1977.
— *The British Empire in the Middle East, 1945–51*, Oxford 1984.
Lucas Phillips, C E, *Alamein*, London 1962.
Macartney, H H and Cremona, P, *Italy's Foreign and Colonial Policy, 1914–37*, London 1938.
Marcus, H G, *Ethiopia, Great Britain and the United States, 1941–74*, London 1983.
Markakis, J, *National and Class Conflict in the Horn of Africa*, Cambridge 1987.
Maule, H, *Out of the Sand. The Epic Story of General Leclerc and the Fighting Free French*, London 1966.
Miège, J L, *L'Impérialisme Colonial Italien de 1870 à nos Jours*, Paris 1968.
Modin, Y, *My Five Cambridge Friends*, London 1994.
Moore, M, *The Fourth Shore: Italy's Mass Colonisation of Libya*, London 1940.
Ovendale, R, ed., *The Foreign Policy of the British Labour Governments, 1945–51*, Leicester 1984.
Pitt, B, *The Crucible of War*, 3 vols, London 1986.
Porath, Y, *In Search of Arab Unity, 1930–45*, London 1986.
Reynolds, D, *The Creation of the Anglo-American Alliance, 1937–41. A Study in Competitive Co-operation*, London 1981.
Rubin, B, *The Great Powers in the Middle East, 1941–47*, London 1980.
Segre, C G, *Fourth Shore. The Italian Colonization of Libya*, Chicago 1974.
Silverfarb, D, *Britain's Informal Empire in the Middle East. A Case Study of Iraq, 1929–41*, New York 1986.
Thorne, C, *Allies of a Kind*, London 1978.
Thomas, R T, *Britain and Vichy. The Dilemma of Anglo-French Relations, 1940–42*, New York 1979.
Trevaskis, G K N, *Eritrea. A Colony in Transition, 1941–52*, London 1960.
Vatikiotis, P J, *The History of Egypt*, third edn, London 1985.
Ward, P D, *The Threat of Peace*, Kent State 1979.
Watt, D C, *Succeeding John Bull*, Cambridge 1984.
Winstone, H V F, *The Illicit Adventure*, London 1982.
Wright, J, *Libya. A Modern History*, London 1981.

4 PRINTED SECONDARY WORKS: ARTICLES

Bowring, W, 'Great Britain, the United States and the Disposition of Italian East Africa', *The Journal of Imperial and Commonwealth History*, vol. 20, 1992, pp. 88–107.

Cole, S M, 'Secret Diplomacy and the Cyrenaican Settlement of 1917', *Journal of Italian History*, vol. 2, 1979, no. 2, pp. 258–280.

Hyam, R, 'Africa and the Labour Government, 1945–51', *The Journal of Imperial and Commonwealth History*, vol. 16, 1988, no. 3, pp. 148–172.

Kelly, S, '"Ce Fruit Savoureux du Désert": Britain, France and the Fezzan, 1941–56', *The Maghreb Review*, vol. 26, 2001, no. 1, pp. 2–21.

— 'Britain, Libya and the Start of the Cold War', *The Maghreb Review*, vol. 31, 2006, nos. 1–2, pp. 48–61.

Kent, J, 'The Egyptian Base and the Defence of the Middle East, 1945–54', *The Journal of Imperial and Commonwealth History*, vol. 21, 1993, no. 3, pp. 45–65.

Kraiem, M, 'La Question de l'annexation italienne de la Libye', *Revue d'histoire Maghrebine*, July 1976, no. 6, pp. 157–79.

Mazov, S, 'The USSR and the Former Italian Colonies, 1945–50', *Cold War History*, April 2003, 3, 3, pp. 49–78.

Rainero, R, 'La Capture. L'Exécution d'Omar El Mukhtar et la fin de la guerrilla libyenne', *Cahiers de Tunisie*, vol. 38, 1980, nos. 111–2, pp. 59–73.

Smith, C D, '4 February 1942: Its Causes and its influence on Egyptian politics and on the future of Anglo-Egyptian Relations, 1937–45', *International Journal of Middle East Studies*, vol. 10, 1979, no. 4, pp. 435–451.

Smith, R, and Zametica, J, 'The Cold Warrior. Clement Attlee Reconsidered', *International Affairs*, vol. 61, 1985, no. 2, pp. 237–251.

Stoler, 'From Continentalism to Globalism', *Diplomatic History*, 6, vol. 16, 1982, no. 2, pp. 303–320.

Tomlinson, J, 'The Attlee Government and the Balance of Payments, 1945–51', *Twentieth Century British History*, vol. 2, 1991, no. 1, pp. 47–66.

Varsori, Antonio, 'Italy, Britain and the Problem of a Separate Peace During the Second World War: 1940–43', *Journal of Italian History*, vol. 1, winter 1978, no. 3, pp. 455–491.

5 UNPUBLISHED MANUSCRIPTS

Lerman, E, 'The Egyptian Question, 1942–47. The Deterioration of Britain's position in Egypt, al-Alamain to the UN Debate of 1947', London PhD, 1982.

Tripp, C, 'Ali Mahir and the Palace in Egyptian Politics, 1936–42. Seeking Mass Enthusiasm for Democracy', London PhD, 1984.

index

Page numbers in *italics* refer to photograph captions.

Abd al-Aziz al-Saud *see* Ibn Saud, King of Saudi Arabia
Abd al-Illah, Crown Prince of Iraq 60
Abdallah, Amir, Arab leader 106
adwar 21
Agreement of al-Rajma (1920) 21
al-Baruni, Sulaiman 19
al-Basil, Abdul Sattar Bey 174
al-Din al-Sanusi, Safi 21, 22
al-Shutaywi, Ahmad *see* al-Suwayhili, Ahmad
Alexander, A V 224, 232
Alexander, General 186–8, 192–3
al-Gaylani, Rashid Ali 60, 105
al-Hud, Khalil 41
al-Mukhtar, Umar 22, 23
al-Murayyid, Ahmad 47, 48
al-Nahhas, Mustafa 156–7
al-Nasir, Ahmad Saif 189
al-Sadawi, Bashir 22, 41
al-Said, Nuri 38, 39, 56, 60
al-Sanusi, Sayyid Abu al-Qasim 167
al-Sharif, Ahmad 18–21
al-Suwayhili, Ahmad 47, 48
Anglo-Egyptian Treaty (1936) 68, 156, 158
Archdale, Lt Colonel O A 187
Atlantic Charter (1941) 109, 114

Attlee, Clement 63, 218, 222–4, 230
Auchinleck, Sir Claude 109, 115, 117, 120, 129, 156
Azzam, Abd al-Rahman 116, 174

Badawi Pasha 68
Badoglio, Marshal 23, 75
Baggallay, Lacy 38
Balbo, Marshal Italo 23
Bardia 68, *69*
Bateman 111, 112
Bateman, C H 65, 66, 69, 76, 78
Baxter, C W 60
Benghazi 73
  capture of 161
Bevin, Ernest 218, 220–1, 222–3, 225–7, 228–34
Bevin-Sforza Plan 235
Bey, Azzam 21, 22
Bey, Hassanein 66
Bidault Georges 221, 227
Bovenschen, Sir Frederick 188
British Military Administration (BMA) (Cyrenaica) 63
Bromilow, Lt Colonel 44, 45
Brooke, General Sir Alan 186, 219
Bu Maryam Agreement (1921) 21
Burgess, Guy 233
Butler, Neville 115
Butler, R A 70
Byrnes, James 218–19, 220, 221, 222, 226, 227

249

Cadogan, Sir Alexander 55, 56, 62, 70, 115, 188
Calosso, Professor 80
Casey, R G 133, 134, 177, 178, 189, 193
Chapman-Andrews, E A 159
Chifley, Ben 224
Churchill, Sir Winston 35, 57, 72, 73–83, 106, 128–9, 156, 178, *179*, *181*, *182*, 218
Cold War 233–6
Committee of Union and Progress (the Young Turks) 18
Coulson, J 157
Council of Foreign Ministers, London (1945) 220–1
Council of Foreign Ministers, Paris (1946) 222–8
Council of Foreign Ministers, Paris (1948) 228
Coverley-Price, A V 56
Cumming, Lt. Colonel D C 152, 160–8
Cunningham, General 117
Cyrenaica 18–23, 107, 108, 215
   British Military Administration (BMA) 63
   British trusteeship of 231
   Egyptian claims to 64–73
   First British occupation of 59–64
   Free Italian colony in 73–83
   Sanusi claims to 64–73
   Second British occupation of 123–31
   Third British occupation of 160–8
Cyrenaica-Sudan Barter Plan 155–9

Dalton, Hugh 223
'Dardanelles scare' 229
Darlan. Admiral 188
de Gaulle, General Charles 153, 185–97, *191*

Delange, Lt Colonel 189, 194–5
Di Martino, Giacomo 21, 22
Dill, Sir John 115
Dixon, Pierson 112, 113

Eden, Anthony 35, 56–8, 60, 67, 78, 112–17, 120, *120*, 123, 134, 172, 192, 218–19
   Mansion House statement (1941) 106, 108, 111
Egypt 20, 112, 114, 125, 155–9
   Egyptian Plans for Libya 37–42
Eisenhower, General Dwight D 169
El Agheila 101, 120
El Alamein 134, 151, 156, 160
en Nasr, Shaikh *44*
Eritrea 77, 80–1
exiles, Libyan 23–7

Faruk, King of Egypt 41, 68, 71, 105, 114, 125, 155, 156
Fellers, Colonel Bonner 125
Fezzan, Free French conquest of the 185–97, *186*,
Foot, Sir Hugh 168
Free French force 151–3
   military administration of the Fezzan 185–97
Free Italian Colony 112
Free Italian Force 75
Fundamental Law for Cyrenaica (October 1919) 21
Fundamental Law for Tripolitania (June 1919) 21, 22

'G Expansion Scheme' 25, 43
Gaddafi, Colonel 235
Gazala, Battle of 130
Giraud, General Henri 153, 193
Graziani, Marshal Rodolfo 22, 43, 51, *51*
Grigg, Sir James 174, 183, 191
Gromyko, Andrei 216, 233

250

INDEX

Haile Selassie 80, 177
Halifax, Lord 41, 55–6, 58
Hankey, Robin 231
Hare, Raymond A 116
Hill Farms Scheme 168
Hitler, Adolf 61, 74, 155
Hone, Brigadier H R 131, 132, 152, 164–7, 172, 173, 174, 188, 190
Hopkinson, Henry L d'Hard Alys 110
Huddleston, H J 158, 159
Hussein, Shari 42

Ibn Saud, King of Saudi Arabia 37, 41, 42, 66, 105
Idris, Muhammad 20, 21
Idris, Sayyid *see* Sayyid Idris, Emir of Cyrenaica
ikhwan 19
Italy 123
  colonists 23, 25, 126, *126*, *127*, 132, 133, 173, 180, 181
  conquest of Libya 17-23

Jabal Akhdar 22, 126–7
Jaghbub 19, 20, 68, 70
Jewish Territorial Organisation 164

Kenya 223–4
Kirk, Alexander 124
Kitchener Line A 68

Lampson, Sir Miles 34, 40, 49–58, 67, 69–70, 78, 79, *110*, 111, 114, 152, 159
Lausanne, Treaty of (1923) 18, 19
Leahy, Admiral William B 171
Leclerc de Hauteclocque, General 151, 185–90
Libyan Arab Force (LAF) 64, 107
Lincoln, Brigadier 227
Litoranea, The 23
Lloyd, Lord 35, 39, 40, 41, 106

Longrigg, Brigadier Stephen H 63, 67, 117, 126
Lost Oases (1923) 66
Lush, Brigadier Maurice Stanley 190, 194
Lyttelton, Oliver 107–11, *110*, 112–19, 128

Mackereth, Gilbert 166, 176, 178, 193, 194
Maclean, Donald 219
Maher, Aly *see* Mahir, Ali
Mahir, Ali 37, 39, 40, 68, 71, 155
Malta 129, 155
marabouts 19
'Marble Arch' *171*, *172*
Marshall, George 232
McMahon, Sir Henry 42
McMahon pledges 42
Milner-Scialoja Agreement (1920) 68
Mitchell, Sir Philip 62–3, 67
Modin, Yuri 233
Molotov, V M 218–19, 227
Montgomery, Lt General Bernard Law 160, *176*, *182*, 194
Moyne, Lord 106, 188
Muhammad Ali, Crown Prince of Egypt 25
Murray, Wallace 116, 125
Muslim population 24, 25
Mussolini, Benito *24*, 25, 60, 61, 75, 81, 155, 156

Napier, Sir Robert 77
Nash, Walter 224, 225
Newton, Sir Basil 38
North African Campaign 82, 101
Norton, C J 50
Nye, General Sir Archibald 192

O'Connor, General Sir Richard 57, 62, 74
Occupied Territories Administrations (OTA) 131

251

Operation 'Acrobat' 120
Operation 'Battleaxe' 107
Operation 'Crusader' 116, 117, *118*
Operation 'Exporter' 107
Operation 'Hercules' 155
Operation 'Torch' 151, 156, 169

Palestine, 1939 White Paper on 38, 39
Paris Peace Conference (1946) 229
Pentagon Talks (1947) 232
Peterson, Sir Maurice 158, 176
Potsdam Conference (1945) 217–20

Ritchie, General 117, 120, 130, *130*, 134
Robertson, Major General Sir Brian 179
Rommel, Generalfeldmarshschall Erwin 74, 81–2, 101, 120, *125*, 129, 134, 151, 155, 156, 160, 161
Roosevelt, President Franklin D 115, 156, 170, 217

Sanusis 18, 19
  arab force 42–9
  declaration on the 111–21
Sargent, Sir Orme 62
Sargent Committee 76
Saudi plans for Libya 37–42
Sayyid Idris, Emir of Cyrenaica 25, 26, 42–9, *44*, *46*, *47*, 50, 52, 53, 57, 64, 65, *65*, 66, *66*, 67, *70*, 70, 71, 102, 106–9, 111–21, 124, 127–8, 135, 152–3, 162, *165*, 166, *166*, 174, 176–7, 196
Sayyid Muhammad Ali al-Sanusi, founder of the Senussi order 18
Scott, Sir David 115, 116
Scrivener, P J 157, 176
Selassie, Haile *see* Haile Selassie
Seymour, Sir Horace 51, 55, 70, 71, 112, 115, 119
Shuckburgh, Sir John 42

Sidi Barani 59, 61
Sidi Rezegh 116
Sirri, Husain 67, 71
Smuts, Jan 219, 224, 225
Soviet Union 216, 218, 220, 232–4
Speaight, R L 193
Sperrverband 74
Stalin, Joseph 217, 218
Strang, Sir William 170, 189
Sudan 157–9

Taranto, Battle of 59
Tedder, Lord 224
Thompson, Geoffrey 72
Tobruk 82
  fall of 130, 134, 155, 160
Treaty of Lausanne (1923) 18, 19
Tripoli, occupation of *175*
Tripolitania 18–23, 109, 128
  British occupation of 178–83
  planning occupation of 169–78
  trusteeship of 221
Tripolitanian Committee 48
Truman, Harry S 218
Turkey 18, 19

UN Decision on Libya 234

Wahba, Hafiz 38, 39, 41, 42, 55, 71
Wavell, General Archibald 27, 34, 42, 57, 62–3, 64, 69, 74, 80
Welles, Sumner 115, 116
White Paper on Palestine (1939) 38, 39, 106, 115
Wilson, General Henry Maitland 25, 26, 34, *34*, 42–9, 63, 65, *72*, 78
Woolley, Sir Leonard 35, 39, 40, 54–5, 58, 71–3, 76

Yalta Conference (1945) 216–7
Young Turks *see* Committee of Union and Progress

SILPHIUM PRESS: ARCHAEOLOGY, HISTORY AND TRAVEL IN LIBYA

Silphium Press is the popular imprint of The Society for Libyan Studies. Silphium was a plant renowned in antiquity as a contraceptive, a medicinal herb and a spice. Found only in Cyrenaican Libya, it was appreciated throughout the Mediterranean world from the seventh century BC to the first century AD when it became extinct, probably through overexploitation. Our logo is based on a classical coin minted in Cyrene.

The Society for Libyan Studies promotes and co-ordinates the activities of scholars working on the archaeology, history, linguistics and natural history of Libya. It publishes a journal, detailed reports on its field projects and Silphium Press popular titles. Regular lectures are held in London on a wide range of topics relating to Libya's rich culture and heritage, which are open to the public.

PUBLICATIONS AVAILABLE FROM THE SOCIETY FOR LIBYAN STUDIES

Titles published under the Silphium Press imprint are identified by an asterisk (*)

Libyan Studies: Select Papers of the late R. G. Goodchild: collected articles from 1949–1967. Edited by J. M. Reynolds. 1976. xxii + 345 pp, 96 pls, index. Published by Elek Books Ltd.

Excavations at Sidi Khrebish Benghazi (Berenice). Volume I, Buildings, Coins, Inscriptions, Architectural Decoration. (Supplement to *Libya Antiqua V*, vol. I). Edited by J. A. Lloyd with contributions by J. M. Reynolds, R. M. Reece, F. Sear, P. Kenrick. 1977. xxx + 311 pp, 71 figs, 32 pls. Arabic summary: 120 pp.

— **Volume II, Economic Life at Berenice, Sculptures and Terracottas, Amphoras and Plain Wares.** (Supplement to *Libya Antiqua V*, vol. II).

Edited by J. A. Lloyd with contributions from G. W. W. Barker, A. Wheeler, D. Webley, A. Bonanno and J. A. Riley. 1979. vi + 467 pp, 153 figs, 43 pls. Arabic summary: 19 pp. *Out of print.*

— **Volume III, part 1: The Fine Pottery.** (Supplement to *Libya Antiqua V*, vol. III.1). By P. M. Kenrick. 1985. xviii + 515 pp, 78 figs, 24 pls, foldout plan, appendices. Arabic summary: 12 pp.

— **Volume III, part 2: The Lamps.** (Supplement to *Libya Antiqua V*, vol. III.2). By D. M. Bailey. 1985. ix + 194 pp, 19 figs, 39 pls (incl. foldout). Arabic summary: 3 pp.

— **Volume IV, part 1: The Mosaics and Marble Floors.** (Supplement to *Libya Antiqua V*, vol. IV.1). By Demetrios Michaelides. 1998. xiv +160 pp, 16 pls, 110 black and white ills.

Ghirza: A Libyan Settlement in the Roman Period. By O. Brogan and D. J. Smith. 1984. 330 pp, 115 figs, 172 pls, 15 appendices, index.

Cyrenaica in Antiquity. Edited by G. Barker, J. Lloyd and J. M. Reynolds. 1985. xiv + 403 pp, 58 figs, 77 pls, 9 tables. Society for Libyan Studies Occasional Papers I, Publisher: BAR International Series 236. *Out of print.*

Town and Country in Roman Tripolitania, Papers in honour of Olwen Hackett. Edited by D. J. Buck and D. J. Mattingly. 1985. xvi + 311 pp, 111 figs. Society for Libyan Studies Occasional Papers II. Publisher: BAR International Series 274. *Out of print.*

Libya: Research in Archaeology, Environment, History and Society, 1969–1989. (*Libyan Studies* 20). Edited by D. J. Mattingly and J. A. Lloyd. 1989. xi + 262 pp, 45 figs, 3 pls. Arabic summary: 4 pp.

Excavations at Sabratha, 1948–1951, Volume II. part 1. The Finds. The Amphorae, Coarse Pottery and Building Materials. By John Dore and Nina Keay with contributions by H. Dodge, D. P. S.Peacock and R. H. Seager-Smith. Edited by M. G. Fulford and M. Hall. 1989. xiii + 298 pp, 72 figs, 5 tables. Arabic summary. Society for Libyan Studies Monograph no. 1.

The Severan Buildings of Lepcis Magna, an architectural survey. By J. B. Ward-Perkins. General Editor: G. D. B. Jones. Edited by

P. M. Kenrick with drawings by R. Kronenburg. 1993. xvii + 140 pp, 42 figs (some foldout), 45 pls, maps (some foldout), Arabic summary. Society for Libyan Studies Monograph no. 2.

Excavations at Sabratha, Volume II, Part 2. The Fine Wares. Edited by M. G. Fulford and R. Tomber with contributions by N. Keay, J. R. Timby, J. W. Hayes and D. M. Bailey. 1994. xiii + 210 pp, 48 figs. Arabic summary. Society for Libyan Studies Monograph no. 3.

Cyrenaican Archaeology: An International Colloquium (*Libyan Studies* 25). Edited by J. M. Reynolds. iv + 298 pp, 38 figs, 172 pls. Arabic summary: 14 pp.

Farming the Desert, The UNESCO Libyan Valleys Archaeological Survey. Vol. I: Synthesis. By G. W. W. Barker, D. Gilbertson, B. Jones, D. J. Mattingly. 1996. xx + 404 pp, 193 figs, 29 tables, index.

Farming the Desert, The UNESCO Libyan Valleys Archaeological Survey. Vol. II: Gazetteer 1979–1989 and Pottery. By G. W. W. Barker, D. Gilbertson, B. Jones, D. J. Mattingly. 1996. xxiv + 393 pp, 291 figs, 9 tables, index.

Excavations at Surt (Medinet al-Sultan) Between 1977 and 1981. By Geza Fehervari with contributions from 'Abbas Hamdani, Masoud Shaglouf, Hal Bishop, John Riley, Muhammed Hamid and Ted Hughes. Edited by Elizabeth Savage. 2002. viii + 120 pp, 11 figs, 45 pls (some colour), foldout plan. Arabic summary: 7 pp.

Christian Monuments of Cyrenaica. By J. B. Ward-Perkins and R. G. Goodchild. Edited Joyce Reynolds with contributions by R. M. Harrison, H. M. Dodge, Sheila Gibson, John Lloyd, Joyce Reynolds and Susan Walker. 2002. 387 pp. figs and plans, map (foldout), index. Society for Libyan Studies Monograph no. 4.

The Archaeology of Fazzan. Vol. 1: Synthesis. Edited by David Mattingly. 2003. xxvi + 428 pp, 460 figs (many in colour), 31 tables. Arabic summary. Society for Libyan Studies Monograph no. 5.

* Travellers in Libya. Selected and edited by John Wright. 2005. 255 pp, 2 maps.

The Libyan Desert: Natural Resources and Cultural Heritage. Edited by David Mattingly, Sue McLaren, Elizabeth Savage, Yahya al-Fasatwi, Khaled Gadgood. 2006. 349 pp. Society for Libyan Studies Monograph no. 6.

The Archaeology of Fazzan. Vol. 2: Site Gazetteer, Pottery and Other Survey Finds. Edited by David J. Mattingly. 2007. xxix + 552 pp. Arabic summary. Society for Libyan Studies Monograph no. 7.

* **Wheels Across the Desert: Exploration of the Libyan Desert by Motorcar 1916–1942.** By Andrew Goudie. 2008. 205 pp, 55 photographs, 12 maps.

* **The Emergence of Libya.** By John Wright. 2008. 368 pp, 1 map.

* **Libya Archaeological Guides: Tripolitania.** By Philip Kenrick. 2009. ix +220 pp, 113 maps, drawings and photographs.

Book and journal orders and membership enquiries should be sent to:

The General Secretary,
The Society for Libyan Studies,
c/o The Institute of Archaeology,
31-34, Gordon Square,
London, WC1H OPY.
http://www.britac.ac.uk/institutes/libya/